HIROSHIMA DIARY

HIROSHIMA DIARY

The Journal of a Japanese Physician
August 6–September 30, 1945

by
Michihiko Hachiya, M.D.

Translated and Edited by
WARNER WELLS, M.D.

Chapel Hill
THE UNIVERSITY OF NORTH CAROLINA PRESS

Foreword

THE BOMBING of Hiroshima marked a new era in man's growing skill in the art of self-destruction. During the saturation bombing of Germany and Japan in World War II, cities were destroyed, but the destruction was segmental, requiring days or weeks, so that city dwellers had some chance to flee or find shelter. Moreover, those who were killed or injured had the comfort of knowing they were being killed by more or less familiar and acceptable weapons. But at Hiroshima, on the bright clear morning of August 6, 1945, thousands were killed, more thousands were fatally injured, and the homes of a quarter million people were destroyed, within seconds of the falling of a single bomb. Since that day, terrifying progress in the technology of nuclear warfare and the appalling knowledge that indulgence in atomic weapons may permanently impair the biological future of the human race have combined to emphasize the fact that Hiroshima presented mankind with a fateful choice.

Perhaps it was some sense of this that led me in 1950 to accept an offer to become a surgical consultant to the Atomic Bomb Casualty Commission. It was a position that I held for two and a half years. The Commission, operating in Hiroshima and Nagasaki, had been formed to discover if there were delayed effects of the atom bombs dropped on these cities in 1945. Since most of my work was outside the Commission's headquarters, in Japanese hospitals and clinics, I came to know and admire the Japanese medical profession and became acquainted with their patients. It was only natural, therefore, to want to know what the people, as people and not as medical case histories, experienced after the atom bombs were dropped.

By a stroke of good fortune I learned that Dr. Hachiya, Director of the Hiroshima Communications Hospital, had written a diary of his experiences as a patient and bed-ridden hospital director. I also learned that, with some misgivings as to the likelihood of renewing painful memories, he had been persuaded by friends who saw its value as a historical document to publish the diary. It appeared serially in the *Teishin Igaku*, a small medical journal circulated among the medical employees of the Japanese Communications Ministry.

On an overcast, bone-chilling afternoon in the early spring of 1951 I met Dr. Hachiya in his hospital reception room and over warming cups of hot green tea asked his permission to examine his diary with the view of having it translated and published in English. Dr. Hachiya graciously consented and placed at my disposal his manuscript copy and reprints of the medical journal.

I do not know at what point I decided to supervise the translation and do the editing myself. I know I felt it as a very personal responsibility. I cannot read Japanese except in tedious and laborious fashion with complete dependence on dictionaries and grammars. This almost insurmountable handicap I was able to overcome by the assistance of Dr. Neal Tsukifuji, a brilliant young Japanese doctor born in Los Angeles and educated in America and Japan, who worked with me as assistant and interpreter. During our spare time for the next year, on week-ends, holidays, and evenings, we rendered the diary into crude English. When there was any question regarding the meaning of a word, phrase, or sentence, we consulted Dr. Hachiya, so the translation could be as accurate as possible and preserve the Japanese idiom. We met and talked with many of the people mentioned in the diary, and with Dr. Hachiya visited all of the places he describes. Trying to relive Dr. Hachiya's experience, I succeeded to the extent that I came to dream of the bombing and on occasion awakened in terror.

Japanese, like other oriental languages, has a dignity, a subtlety, and a beauty that make it extremely difficult to render into English. It can be done, however, as evidenced by the magnificent prose of Lafcadio Hearn. Perhaps because I chose him as a model, I have spent the last three years revising and editing the original rough translation, in the hope I could preserve the balance, simplicity, and quality of values Dr. Hachiya achieved in his own tongue.

I have tried to limit the apparatus of the translation to the essential. I have used footnotes to explain some of the technical medical terms, to provide background information needed by the reader for an understanding of the text, and occasionally to provide an approximate meaning for an untranslatable Japanese term. It seemed helpful to prepare a Cast of Characters, preceding the text, and a Glossary, following the text. I have retained the metric system used in Japan for all measurement, except that I have changed longer distances into miles and centigrade temperature readings into Fahrenheit.

Among those I wish to thank for helping me, besides Dr. Tsukifuji, are my friends in Hiroshima, and I take occasion to wish them health, peace of mind, and a long life. I owe a great deal to Dr. Robert B. Hall, Professor of Geography in The University of Michigan and Director of the Center for Japanese Studies. He introduced me to Japan and by his wise counsel and farsighted way of thinking about people and their place in the world helped me immeasurably. I can say the same about Dr. Robert Ward, Dr. John Hall, Dr. Richard Beardsley, Dr. Mischa Titiev, Dr. Joseph Yamagiwa, and Dr. Dougal Eyre, members of the University of Michigan faculty in sociology, history, anthropology, Japanese language, and geography and also part of the Center for Japanese Studies. If all of the world's ambassadors were of their quality, there would never be any more wars.

I acknowledge with gratitude the help I was given by many

people in the Atomic Bomb Casualty Commission and the National Research Council of the American Academy of Science, calling to mind particularly Dr. Grant Taylor and Col. Carl Tessmer, past directors of the Commission.

Mr. Henry Schuman, publisher and authority in medical and scientific history, has helped, advised, and encouraged me from the start. And I am grateful to Frances Gray Patton for her sympathetic reading of an early draft of the translation and for her thoughtfulness in introducing me to the director of the University of North Carolina Press. To the staff of the Press I am indebted for help and suggestions that seem to me to go well beyond the call of publishing duty and to give it the status of true collaborator in this enterprise.

I wish to express thanks to my secretary, Mrs. Elizabeth Dickson, for her expert stenographic assistance.

While working on the manuscript, I was fortunate to be able to turn for help to a remarkably versatile person. She would spell a word, construct a sentence, or retype a corrected manuscript. She was never too busy to give me the benefit of her insight and judgement, or too tired from looking after the house and five children to encourage me or see that I had a pot of hot tea at one o'clock in the morning. To her, words of thanks are inadequate.

All of us will be repaid beyond measure if this diary helps to refresh our memories, stimulate our imaginations, and temper our thinking about war, and especially the horror of atomic war. For if we cannot enliven our humanity, we are doomed.

WARNER WELLS

March 15, 1955

The Place and the People

SINCE DR. HACHIYA began his diary with no thought that it might be published, he saw no need to describe either the hospital that was its setting or the members of the staff who were the principal characters. The Hiroshima Communications Hospital served the employees in the Hiroshima area of the Ministry of Communications, which in Japan controls postal, telegraph, and telephone service. Since Hiroshima was a city of half a million population, and the capital of the Prefecture of Hiroshima, with over two million population, the hospital was an institution of considerable importance. It had approximately 20 on its staff and 125 beds, this latter figure does not give a proper sense of the scale of its operations since out-patient service in Japan, as in America, is frequently greater than in-patient service.

The hospital adjoined the main office of the Communications Bureau, and both were of strong, reinforced concrete construction. After the bombing, the Bureau became an annex to the hospital. Both were located about 1,500 meters from the hypocenter of the bomb, on the northeast border of a large military area, the Hiroshima Military Barracks, which was totally destroyed. Dr. Hachiya's home was a few hundred meters from the hospital.

Hiroshima had not been bombed during the current war, but in anticipation of a raid the military authorities, a few months before, had demolished thousands of houses to make fire lanes and had evacuated much of its personnel. Following this, on his own authority, Dr. Hachiya had evacuated his in-patients to the interior, so that at the time of the bombing the hospital was practically empty.

Following are the members of the staff and others who figure most prominently in the diary:

Dr. Akiyama—Head of the Obstetrics and Gynecology Department.

Dr. Chodo—A member of the Dental Department.

Dr. Fujii—Head of the Dental Department.

Dr. Hachiya—Director of the hospital and author of this diary.

Dr. Hanaoka—Head of the Internal Medicine Department.

Dr. Harada—A pharmacist.

Miss Hinada—A nurse in the hospital.

Dr. Hinoi—Chief pharmacist.

Mr. Iguchi—Communications Bureau chauffeur.

Mr. Imachi—A member of the administrative staff; he doubled as chief cook.

Mr. Isono—He became Chief of the Hiroshima Division of the Communications Bureau when Mr. Yoshida was killed.

Miss Kado—Dr. Hachiya's private nurse.

Dr. Katsube—Chief of the Surgery Department.

Dr. Kitajima—Chief of the Hiroshima Sanitary Department.

Mr. Kitao—A member of the administrative staff.

Dr. Koyama—Deputy Director and head of the Ophthalmology Department.

Mr. Mizoguchi—Formerly an office clerk, he acted as quartermaster, ration supervisor, hospital administrator, public relations officer, and general trouble shooter.

Dr. Morisugi—An internist.

Mr. Okamoto—Head of the Western District of the Communications Bureau.

Dr. Okura—A dentist.

Mrs. Saeki—Classified as a janitress, but this appellation hardly does justice to Mrs. Saeki. Bereaved of three sons and her husband, all lost in the war, this woman of sturdy build and sturdier character, acquainted with sorrow, hardship, and poverty, was friend, councillor, sounding board, and mother to staff, patients, and visitors to the hospital. She is generally referred to as *baba-san* which, translated freely, means "dear old grandmother."

Mr. Sasaki—A near neighbor and friend of Dr. Hachiya.

Dr. Sasada—Head of the Pediatrics Department.

Mr. Sera—Head of the hospital business office.

Mr. Shiota—A business officer.

Miss Susukida—A nursing supervisor.

Miss Takao—Dr. Katsube's surgical nurse.

Dr. Tamagawa—Professor of Pathology, Hiroshima Medical School.

Mr. Ushio—Head of General Affairs.

Yaeko-san—Dr. Hachiya's wife.

Miss Yama—Head nurse in surgery.

Mr. Yamazaki—A business officer who looked after the crematory.

Mrs. Yoshida—Wife of the former Chief of the Communications Bureau.

HIROSHIMA DIARY

6 August 1945

THE HOUR was early; the morning still, warm, and beautiful. Shimmering leaves, reflecting sunlight from a cloudless sky, made a pleasant contrast with shadows in my garden as I gazed absently through wide-flung doors opening to the south.

Clad in drawers and undershirt, I was sprawled on the living room floor exhausted because I had just spent a sleepless night on duty as an air warden in my hospital.

Suddenly, a strong flash of light startled me—and then another. So well does one recall little things that I remember vividly how a stone lantern in the garden became brilliantly lit and I debated whether this light was caused by a magnesium flare or sparks from a passing trolley.

Garden shadows disappeared. The view where a moment before all had been so bright and sunny was now dark and hazy. Through swirling dust I could barely discern a wooden column that had supported one corner of my house. It was leaning crazily and the roof sagged dangerously.

Moving instinctively, I tried to escape, but rubble and fallen timbers barred the way. By picking my way cautiously I managed to reach the *rōka* and stepped down into my garden. A profound weakness overcame me, so I stopped to regain my strength. To my surprise I discovered that I was completely naked. How odd! Where were my drawers and undershirt?

What had happened?

All over the right side of my body I was cut and bleeding. A large splinter was protruding from a mangled wound in my thigh, and something warm trickled into my mouth. My cheek was torn, I discovered as I felt it gingerly, with the lower lip laid wide open. Embedded in my neck was a sizable fragment of glass which I matter-of-factly dislodged, and with the detachment of one stunned and shocked I studied it and my blood-stained hand.

Where was my wife?

Suddenly thoroughly alarmed, I began to yell for her: "Yaeko-san! Yaeko-san! Where are you?"

Blood began to spurt. Had my carotid artery been cut? Would I bleed to death? Frightened and irrational, I called out again: "It's a five-hundred-ton bomb! Yaeko-san, where are you? A five-hundred-ton bomb has fallen!"

Yaeko-san, pale and frightened, her clothes torn and blood-stained, emerged from the ruins of our house holding her elbow. Seeing her, I was reassured. My own panic assuaged, I tried to reassure her.

"We'll be all right," I exclaimed. "Only let's get out of here as fast as we can."

She nodded, and I motioned for her to follow me.

The shortest path to the street lay through the house next door so through the house we went—running, stumbling, falling, and then running again until in headlong flight we tripped over something and fell sprawling into the street. Getting to my feet, I discovered that I had tripped over a man's head.

"Excuse me! Excuse me, please!" I cried hysterically.

There was no answer. The man was dead. The head had belonged to a young officer whose body was crushed beneath a massive gate.

We stood in the street, uncertain and afraid, until a house across from us began to sway and then with a rending motion fell almost at our feet. Our own house began to sway, and in a minute it, too, collapsed in a cloud of dust. Other buildings caved in or toppled. Fires sprang up and whipped by a vicious wind began to spread.

It finally dawned on us that we could not stay there in the street, so we turned our steps towards the hospital.* Our home was gone; we were wounded and needed treatment; and after all, it was my duty to be with my staff. This latter was an irrational thought—what good could I be to anyone, hurt as I was.

We started out, but after twenty or thirty steps I had to stop. My breath became short, my heart pounded, and my legs gave way under me. An overpowering thirst seized me and I begged Yaeko-san to find me some water. But there was no water to be found. After a little my strength somewhat returned and we were able to go on.

I was still naked, and although I did not feel the least bit of shame, I was disturbed to realize that modesty had deserted me. On rounding a corner we came upon a soldier standing idly in the street. He had a towel draped across his shoulder, and I asked if he would give it to me to cover my nakedness. The soldier surrendered the towel quite willingly but said not a word. A little later I lost the towel, and Yaeko-san took off her apron and tied it around my loins.

Our progress towards the hospital was interminably slow, until finally, my legs, stiff from drying blood, refused to carry me farther. The strength, even the will, to go on deserted me, so I told my wife, who was almost as badly hurt as I, to go on alone. This she objected to, but there was no choice. She had to go ahead and try to find someone to come back for me.

Yaeko-san looked into my face for a moment, and then, without saying a word, turned away and began running towards the hospital. Once, she looked back and waved and in a moment she was swallowed up in the gloom. It was quite dark now, and with my wife gone, a feeling of dreadful loneliness overcame me.

I must have gone out of my head lying there in the road because the next thing I recall was discovering that the clot on my thigh had been dislodged and blood was again spurting from the wound.

* Dr. Hachiya's home was only a few hundred meters from the hospital.

I pressed my hand to the bleeding area and after a while the bleeding stopped and I felt better.

Could I go on?

I tried. It was all a nightmare—my wounds, the darkness, the road ahead. My movements were ever so slow; only my mind was running at top speed.

In time I came to an open space where the houses had been removed to make a fire lane. Through the dim light I could make out ahead of me the hazy outlines of the Communications Bureau's big concrete building, and beyond it the hospital. My spirits rose because I knew that now someone would find me; and if I should die, at least my body would be found.

I paused to rest. Gradually things around me came into focus. There were the shadowy forms of people, some of whom looked like walking ghosts. Others moved as though in pain, like scarecrows, their arms held out from their bodies with forearms and hands dangling. These people puzzled me until I suddenly realized that they had been burned and were holding their arms out to prevent the painful friction of raw surfaces rubbing together. A naked woman carrying a naked baby came into view. I averted my gaze. Perhaps they had been in the bath. But then I saw a naked man, and it occurred to me that, like myself, some strange thing had deprived them of their clothes. An old woman lay near me with an expression of suffering on her face; but she made no sound. Indeed, one thing was common to everyone I saw—complete silence.

All who could were moving in the direction of the hospital. I joined in the dismal parade when my strength was somewhat recovered, and at last reached the gates of the Communications Bureau.

Familiar surroundings, familiar faces. There was Mr. Iguchi and Mr. Yoshihiro and my old friend, Mr. Sera, the head of the business office. They hastened to give me a hand, their expressions of pleasure changing to alarm when they saw that I was hurt. I was too happy to see them to share their concern.

No time was lost over greetings. They eased me onto a stretcher and carried me into the Communications Building, ignoring my protests that I could walk. Later, I learned that the hospital was so overrun that the Communications Bureau had to be used as an emergency hospital. The rooms and corridors were crowded with people, many of whom I recognized as neighbors. To me it seemed that the whole community was there.

My friends passed me through an open window into a janitor's room recently converted to an emergency first-aid station. The room was a shambles; fallen plaster, broken furniture, and debris littered the floor; the walls were cracked; and a heavy steel window casement was twisted and almost wrenched from its seating. What a place to dress the wounds of the injured.

To my great surprise who should appear but my private nurse, Miss Kado, and Mr. Mizoguchi, and old Mrs. Saeki. Miss Kado set about examining my wounds without speaking a word. No one spoke. I asked for a shirt and pajamas. They got them for me, but still no one spoke. Why was everyone so quiet?

Miss Kado finished the examination, and in a moment it felt as if my chest was on fire. She had begun to paint my wounds with iodine and no amount of entreaty would make her stop. With no alternative but to endure the iodine, I tried to divert myself by looking out the window.

The hospital lay directly opposite with part of the roof and the third floor sunroom in plain view, and as I looked up, I witnessed a sight which made me forget my smarting wounds. Smoke was pouring out of the sunroom windows. The hospital was afire!

"Fire!" I shouted. "Fire! Fire! The hospital is on fire!"

My friends looked up. It was true. The hospital *was* on fire.

The alarm was given and from all sides people took up the cry. The high-pitched voice of Mr. Sera, the business officer, rose above the others, and it seemed as if his was the first voice I had heard that day. The uncanny stillness was broken. Our little world was now in pandemonium.

I remember that Dr. Sasada, chief of the Pediatric Service, came in and tried to reassure me, but I could scarcely hear him above the din. I heard Dr. Hinoi's voice and then Dr. Koyama's.

Both were shouting orders to evacuate the hospital and with such vigor that it sounded as though the sheer strength of their voices could hasten those who were slow to obey.

The sky became bright as flames from the hospital mounted. Soon the Bureau was threatened and Mr. Sera gave the order to evacuate. My stretcher was moved into a rear garden and placed beneath an old cherry tree. Other patients limped into the garden or were carried until soon the entire area became so crowded that only the very ill had room to lie down. No one talked, and the ominous silence was relieved only by a subdued rustle among so many people, restless, in pain, anxious, and afraid, waiting for something else to happen.

The sky filled with black smoke and glowing sparks. Flames rose and the heat set currents of air in motion. Updrafts became so violent that sheets of zinc roofing were hurled aloft and released, humming and twirling, in erratic flight. Pieces of flaming wood soared and fell like fiery swallows. While I was trying to beat out the flames, a hot ember seared my ankle. It was all I could do to keep from being burned alive.

The Bureau started to burn, and window after window became a square of flame until the whole structure was converted into a crackling, hissing inferno.

Scorching winds howled around us, whipping dust and ashes into our eyes and up our noses. Our mouths became dry, our throats raw and sore from the biting smoke pulled into our lungs. Coughing was uncontrollable. We would have moved back, but a group of wooden barracks behind us caught fire and began to burn like tinder.

The heat finally became too intense to endure, and we were left no choice but to abandon the garden. Those who could fled; those who could not perished. Had it not been for my devoted friends, I would have died, but again, they came to the rescue and carried my stretcher to the main gate on the other side of the Bureau.

Here, a small group of people were already clustered, and here I found my wife. Dr. Sasada and Miss Kado joined us.

Fires sprang up on every side as violent winds fanned flames from one building to another. Soon, we were surrounded. The ground we held in front of the Communications Bureau became an oasis in a desert of fire. As the flames came closer the heat became more intense, and if someone in our group had not had the presence of mind to drench us with water * from a fire hose, I doubt if anyone could have survived.

Hot as it was, I began to shiver. The drenching was too much. My heart pounded; things began to whirl until all before me blurred.

"*Kurushii,*" I murmured weakly. "I am done."

The sound of voices reached my ears as though from a great distance and finally became louder as if close at hand. I opened my eyes; Dr. Sasada was feeling my pulse. What had happened? Miss Kado gave me an injection. My strength gradually returned. I must have fainted.

Huge raindrops began to fall. Some thought a thunderstorm was beginning and would extinguish the fires. But these drops were capricious. A few fell and then a few more and that was all the rain we saw.†

The first floor of the Bureau was now ablaze and flames were spreading rapidly towards our little oasis by the gate. Right then, I could hardly understand the situation, much less do anything about it.

An iron window frame, loosened by fire, crashed to the ground behind us. A ball of fire whizzed by me, setting my clothes ablaze. They drenched me with water again. From then on I am confused as to what happened.

I do remember Dr. Hinoi because of the pain, the pain I felt when he jerked me to my feet. I remember being moved or rather

---

* The water mains entered the city from the north and since the Communications Bureau was in the northern edge of the city, its water supply was not destroyed.

† There were many reports of a scanty rainfall over the city after the bombing. The drops were described as large and dirty, and some claimed that they were laden with radioactive dust.

dragged, and my whole spirit rebelling against the torment I was made to endure.

My next memory is of an open area. The fires must have receded. I was alive. My friends had somehow managed to rescue me again.

A head popped out of an air-raid dugout, and I heard the unmistakable voice of old Mrs. Saeki: "Cheer up, doctor! Everything will be all right. The north side is burnt out. We have nothing further to fear from the fire."

I might have been her son, the way the old lady calmed and reassured me. And indeed, she was right. The entire northern side of the city was completely burned. The sky was still dark, but whether it was evening or midday I could not tell. It might even have been the next day. Time had no meaning. What I had experienced might have been crowded into a moment or been endured through the monotony of eternity.

Smoke was still rising from the second floor of the hospital, but the fire had stopped. There was nothing left to burn, I thought; but later I learned that the first floor of the hospital had escaped destruction largely through the courageous efforts of Dr. Koyama and Dr. Hinoi.

The streets were deserted except for the dead. Some looked as if they had been frozen by death while in the full action of flight; others lay sprawled as though some giant had flung them to their death from a great height.

Hiroshima was no longer a city, but a burnt-over prairie. To the east and to the west everything was flattened. The distant mountains seemed nearer than I could ever remember. The hills of Ushita and the woods of Nigitsu loomed out of the haze and smoke like the nose and eyes on a face. How small Hiroshima was with its houses gone.

The wind changed and the sky again darkened with smoke.

Suddenly, I heard someone shout: "Planes! Enemy planes!"

Could that be possible after what had already happened? What was there left to bomb? My thoughts were interrupted by the sound of a familiar name.

A nurse calling Dr. Katsube.

"It is Dr. Katsube! It's him!" shouted old Mrs. Saeki, a happy ring to her voice. "Dr. Katsube has come!"

It was Dr. Katsube, our head surgeon, but he seemed completely unaware of us as he hurried past, making a straight line for the hospital. Enemy planes were forgotten, so great was our happiness that Dr. Katsube had been spared to return to us.

Before I could protest, my friends were carrying me into the hospital. The distance was only a hundred meters, but it was enough to cause my heart to pound and make me sick and faint.

I recall the hard table and the pain when my face and lip were sutured, but I have no recollection of the forty or more other wounds Dr. Katsube closed before night.

They removed me to an adjoining room, and I remember feeling relaxed and sleepy. The sun had gone down, leaving a dark red sky. The red flames of the burning city had scorched the heavens. I gazed at the sky until sleep overtook me.

7 August 1945

I MUST have slept soundly because when I opened my eyes a piercing hot sun was shining in on me. There were no shutters or curtains to lessen the glare—and for that matter no windows.

The groans of patients assaulted my ears. Everything was in a turmoil.

Instruments, window frames, and debris littered the floor. The walls and ceilings were scarred and picked as though someone had sprinkled sesame seeds over their surfaces. Most of the marks had been made by slivers of flying glass but the larger scars had been caused by hurtling instruments and pieces of window casements.

Near a window an instrument cabinet was overturned. The head piece had been knocked off the ear, nose, and throat examining chair, and a broken sunlamp was overturned across the seat. I saw nothing that was not broken or in disorder.

Dr. Sasada, who had looked after me yesterday, lay on my left. I had thought he escaped injury, but now I could see that he was badly burned. His arms and hands were bandaged and his childish face so obscured by swelling that I would not have recognized him had it not been for his voice.

My wife lay to my right. Her face was covered with a white ointment, giving her a ghostly appearance. Her right arm was in a sling.

Miss Kado, only slightly wounded, was between me and my wife. She had nursed all of us throughout the night.

My wife, seeing that I was awake, turned and said: "Last night, you seemed to be suffering."

"Yes," said Miss Kado, chiming in. "I don't know how many times I examined your breathing."

I recognized Dr. Fujii's wife sitting motionless on a bench near the wall. Her face bore an expression of anguish and despair. Turning to Miss Kado, I asked what the matter was, and she replied: "Mrs. Fujii was not hurt very much, but her baby was. It died during the night."

"Where is Dr. Fujii?" I inquired.

"Their older daughter is lost," she answered. "He's been out all night looking for her and hasn't returned."

Dr. Koyama came in to inquire how we were. The sight of him, with his head bandaged and an arm in a sling, brought tears to my eyes. He had worked all night and was even now thinking of others before himself.

Dr. Katsube, our surgeon, and Miss Takao, a surgical nurse, were with Dr. Koyama, who was now deputy director. They all looked tired and haggard, and their white clothes were dirty and blood-stained. I learned that Mr. Iguchi, our driver, had contrived to rig up an emergency operating light from a car battery and headlight with which they had managed to operate until the light went out just before day.

Dr. Koyama, observing my concern, remarked: "Doctor, everything is all right."

Dr. Katsube looked me over and after feeling my pulse, said: "You received many wounds, but they all missed vital spots."

He then described them and told me how they had been treated. I was surprised to learn that my shoulder had been severely cut but relieved at his optimism for my recovery.

"How many patients are in the hospital?" I asked Dr. Koyama.

"About a hundred and fifty," he replied. "Quite a few have died, but there are still so many that there is no place to put one's foot down. They are packed in everywhere, even the toilets."

Nodding, Dr. Katsube added: "There are about a half dozen beneath the stairway, and about fifty in the front garden of the hospital."

They discussed methods for restoring order, at least to the extent of making the corridors passable.

In the space of one night patients had become packed, like the rice in *sushi*, into every nook and cranny of the hospital. The majority were badly burned, a few severely injured. All were critically ill. Many had been near the heart of the city and in their efforts to flee managed to get only as far as the Communications Hospital before their strength failed. Others, from nearer by, came deliberately to seek treatment or because this building, standing alone where all else was destroyed, represented shelter and a place of refuge. They came as an avalanche and overran the hospital.

There was no friend or relative to minister to their needs, no one to prepare their food.* Everything was in disorder. And to make matters worse was the vomiting and diarrhea. Patients who

* It is customary in Japan for the hospital patient to provide his own bedding, food, cooking utensils, and charcoal stove or *konro*. A member of the family or a friend stays with the patient to prepare the food and provide practical bedside nursing.

could not walk urinated and defecated where they lay. Those who could walk would feel their way to the exits and relieve themselves there. Persons entering or leaving the hospital could not avoid stepping in the filth, so closely was it spread. The front entrance became covered with feces overnight, and nothing could be done for there were no bed pans and, even if there had been, no one to carry them to the patients.

Disposing of the dead was a minor problem, but to clean the rooms and corridors of urine, feces, and vomitus was impossible.

The people who were burned suffered most because as their skin peeled away, glistening raw wounds were exposed to the heat and filth. This was the environment patients had to live in. It made one's hair stand on end, but there was no way to help the situation.

This was the pattern conversation took as I lay there and listened. It was inconceivable.

"When can I get up?" I asked Dr. Katsube. "Perhaps I can do something to help."

"Not until your sutures are out," he answered. "And that won't be for at least a week."

With that to think about they left me.

I was not left long with my thoughts. One after another the staff came in to express their concern over my injuries and to wish me a speedy recovery. Some of my visitors embarrassed me, for they appeared to be as badly injured as myself. Had it been possible, I would have concealed my whereabouts.

Dr. Nishimura, President of the Okayama Medical Association, came all the way from my native city,* ninety miles away, to see me. He had been crew captain of the boat team when we were classmates in Medical School. As soon as he saw me, tears welled up in his eyes. He looked at me a moment, and then exclaimed: "I say, old fellow, you are alive! What a pleasant surprise. How are you getting along?"

Without waiting for an answer, he continued: "Last night, we

* Dr. Hachiya was born and educated in Okayama, a large city and cultural center near the Inland Sea east of Hiroshima.

heard that Hiroshima had been attacked by a new weapon. The damage was slight, they told us, but in order to see for myself and to lend a hand if extra physicians were needed, I secured a truck and came on down. What a frightful mess greeted us when we arrived. Are you sure *you* are all right?"

And again, without stopping for me to reply, he went on to tell about the heartbreaking things he witnessed from the truck as he entered the city. These were the first details any of us had heard, so we listened intently.

While he talked, all I could think of was the fear and uncertainty that must be preying on my old mother who lived in the country near Okayama. When he had finished, I asked Dr. Nishimura if he would get word to my mother, and also to a sister who lived in Okayama, that Yaeko-san and I were safe. He assured me that he would, and before leaving he also promised to organize a team of doctors and nurses to come down and help as soon as he could get them together.

Dr. Tabuchi, an old friend from Ushita, came in. His face and hands had been burned, though not badly, and after an exchange of greetings, I asked if he knew what had happened.

"I was in the back yard pruning some trees when it exploded," he answered. "The first thing I knew, there was a blinding white flash of light, and a wave of intense heat struck my cheek. This was odd, I thought, when in the next instant there was a tremendous blast.

"The force of it knocked me clean over," he continued, "but fortunately, it didn't hurt me; and my wife wasn't hurt either. But you should have seen our house! It didn't topple over, it just inclined. I have never seen such a mess. Inside and out everything was simply ruined. Even so, we are happy to be alive, and what's more Ryoji, our son, survived. I didn't tell you that he had gone into the city on business that morning. About midnight, after we had given up all hope that he could possibly survive in the dreadful fire that followed the blast, he came home. Listen!" he continued, "why don't you come on home with me? My house is certainly nothing to look at now, but it is better than here."

It was impossible for me to accept his kind offer, and I tried to decline in a way that would not hurt his feelings.

"Dr. Tabuchi," I replied, "we are all grateful for your kind offer, but Dr. Katsube has just warned me that I must lie perfectly still until my wounds are healed."

Dr. Tabuchi accepted my explanation with some reluctance, and after a pause he made ready to go.

"Don't go," I said. "Please tell us more of what occurred yesterday."

"It was a horrible sight," said Dr. Tabuchi. "Hundreds of injured people who were trying to escape to the hills passed our house. The sight of them was almost unbearable. Their faces and hands were burnt and swollen; and great sheets of skin had peeled away from their tissues to hang down like rags on a scarecrow. They moved like a line of ants. All through the night, they went past our house, but this morning they had stopped. I found them lying on both sides of the road so thick that it was impossible to pass without stepping on them."

I lay with my eyes shut while Dr. Tabuchi was talking, picturing in my mind the horror he was describing. I neither saw nor heard Mr. Katsutani when he came in. It was not until I heard someone sobbing that my attention was attracted, and I recognized my old friend. I had known Mr. Katsutani for many years and knew him to be an emotional person, but even so, to see him break down made tears come to my eyes. He had come all the way from Jigozen * to look for me, and now that he had found me, emotion overcame him.

He turned to Dr. Sasada and said brokenly: "Yesterday, it was impossible to enter Hiroshima, else I would have come. Even today fires are still burning in some places. You should see how the city has changed. When I reached the Misasa Bridge † this morning, everything before me was gone, even the castle. These

* A village on the Inland Sea about 10 miles southwest of Hiroshima.
† A large bridge which crosses the Ōta River not far from the old Hiroshima Castle in the northern part of the city and only a few blocks from the Communications Hospital.

buildings here are the only ones left anywhere around. The Communications Bureau seemed to loom right in front of me long before I got anywhere near here."

Mr. Katsutani paused for a moment to catch his breath and went on: "I *really* walked along the railroad tracks to get here, but even they were littered with electric wires and broken railway cars, and the dead and wounded lay everywhere. When I reached the bridge, I saw a dreadful thing. It was unbelievable. There was a man, stone dead, sitting on his bicycle as it leaned against the bridge railing. It is hard to believe that such a thing could happen!"

He repeated himself two or three times as if to convince himself that what he said was true and then continued: "It seems that most of the dead people were either on the bridge or beneath it. You could tell that many had gone down to the river to get a drink of water and had died where they lay. I saw a few live people still in the water, knocking against the dead as they floated down the river. There must have been hundreds and thousands who fled to the river to escape the fire and then drowned.

"The sight of the soldiers, though, was more dreadful than the dead people floating down the river. I came onto I don't know how many, burned from the hips up; and where the skin had peeled, their flesh was wet and mushy. They must have been wearing their military caps because the black hair on top of their heads was not burned. It made them look like they were wearing black lacquer bowls.

"And they had no faces! Their eyes, noses and mouths had been burned away, and it looked like their ears had melted off. It was hard to tell front from back. One soldier, whose features had been destroyed and was left with his white teeth sticking out, asked me for some water, but I didn't have any. I clasped my hands and prayed for him. He didn't say anything more. His plea for water must have been his last words. The way they were burned, I wonder if they didn't have their coats off when the bomb exploded."

It seemed to give Mr. Katsutani some relief to pour out his

terrifying experiences on us; and there was no one who would have stopped him, so fascinating was his tale of horror. While he was talking, several people came in and stayed to listen. Somebody asked him what he was doing when the explosion occurred.

"I had just finished breakfast," he replied, "and was getting ready to light a cigarette, when all of a sudden I saw a white flash. In a moment there was a tremendous blast. Not stopping to think, I let out a yell and jumped into an air-raid dugout. In a moment there was such a blast as I have never heard before. It was terrific! I jumped out of the dugout and pushed my wife into it. Realizing something terrible must have happened in Hiroshima, I climbed up onto the roof of my storehouse to have a look."

Mr. Katsutani became more intense and, gesticulating wildly, went on: "Towards Hiroshima, I saw a big black cloud go billowing up, like a puffy summer cloud. Knowing for sure then that something terrible had happened in the city, I jumped down from my storehouse and ran as fast as I could to the military post at Hatsukaichi.* I ran up to the officer in charge and told him what I had seen and begged him to send somebody to help in Hiroshima. But he didn't even take me seriously. He looked at me for a moment with a threatening expression, and then do you know what he said? He said, 'There isn't much to worry about. One or two bombs won't hurt Hiroshima.' There was no use talking to that fool!

"I was the ranking officer in the local branch of the Ex-officer's Association, but even I didn't know what to do because that day the villagers under my command had been sent off to Miyajima † for labor service. I looked all around to find someone to help me make a rescue squad, but I couldn't find anybody. While I was still looking for help, wounded people began to stream into the village. I asked them what had happened, but all they could tell me was that Hiroshima had been destroyed and everybody was

* The next village towards Hiroshima from Jigozen.
† Miyajima, or "Sacred Island," one of the seven places of superlative scenic beauty in Japan, where the magnificent camphor-wood *torii* of the Itsukushima Shrine rises majestically from the sea as a gateway to the island, is plainly visible to the south of Jigozen.

leaving the city. With that I got on my bicycle and rode as fast as I could towards Itsukaichi. By the time I got there, the road was jammed with people, and so was every path and byway. "Again I tried to find out what had happened, but nobody could give me a clear answer. When I asked these people where they had come from, they would point towards Hiroshima and say, 'This way.' And when I asked where they were going, they would point toward Miyajima and say, 'That way.' Everybody said the same thing.

"I saw no badly wounded or burned people around Itsukaichi, but when I reached Kusatsu, nearly everybody was badly hurt. The nearer I got to Hiroshima the more I saw until by the time I had reached Koi,* they were all so badly injured, I could not bear to look into their faces. They smelled like burning hair."

Mr. Katsutani paused for a moment to take a deep breath and then continued: "The area around Koi station was not burned, but the station and the houses nearby were badly damaged. Every square inch of the station platform was packed with wounded people. Some were standing; others lying down. They were all pleading for water. Now and then you could hear a child calling for its mother. It was a living hell, I tell you. It was a living hell!

"Today it was the same way.

"Did Dr. Hanaoka come to the hospital yesterday? I saw him cross the streetcar trestle at Koi and head in this direction, but I can't believe that he could have made his way through that fire."

"No, we haven't seen him," someone answered.

Mr. Katsutani nodded reflectively and went on: "I left Koi station and went over to the Koi primary school. By then, the school had been turned into an emergency hospital and was already crowded with desperately injured people. Even the playground was packed with the dead and dying. They looked like so many cod fish spread out for drying. What a pitiful sight it was to see them lying there in the hot sun. Even I could tell they were all going to die.

* A railroad station on the very western limits of the city where the slopes of Chausu-yama merge with the Hiroshima delta.

"Towards evening, I was making my way back to the highway when I ran into my sister. My sister, whose home had been in Tokaichi, must surely have been killed. But here she was—alive! She was so happy, she couldn't utter a word! All she could do was cry. If ever anyone shed tears of joy, she did. Some kind people lent me a hand in making a stretcher and helped carry her back to my home in Jigozen near Miyajima Guchi. Even my little village, as far removed as it was from Hiroshima, had become a living hell. Every shrine, every temple was packed and jammed with wounded people."

Mr. Katsutani had said all he had in him to say. He left our room, but instead of going home, he stayed to help with the wounded.

The stories of Dr. Nishimura, Dr. Tabuchi, and Mr. Katsutani left no doubt in my mind about the destruction of Hiroshima. I had seen enough to know that the damage was heavy, but what they had told me was unbelievable.

When I thought of the injured, lying in the sun begging for water, I felt as though I were committing a sin by being where I was. I no longer felt quite so sorry for those of our patients who were obliged to lie on the hard concrete floors in the toilets.

My thoughts turned to myself.

"If only I hadn't been hurt," I mused, "I could be doing something instead of lying here as a patient, requiring the attention of my comrades. Wounded and helpless. What a plight, when all about me there is so much to do!"

Fortunately, my dismal thoughts were interrupted. Who should make an appearance but Dr. Hanaoka, our internist, whom Mr. Katsutani had just told us was last seen at Hatsukaichi.

"Dr. Hachiya, you don't know how happy I am to see you!" exclaimed Dr. Hanaoka. "After seeing what has happened to Hiroshima, it's a miracle anyone survived."

"We have been worrying about you, Dr. Hanaoka," I replied, "because Mr. Katsutani told us only a few minutes ago that he saw you disappear in the direction of Hiroshima while he was at the

Koi station yesterday. Where have you been, and how did you get here?"

"Now that I'm here, I wonder myself," said Dr. Hanaoka. "Let me tell you, if I can, what happened. Somebody told me that a special, new bomb was dropped near the Gokoku Shrine.* If what I was told is true, then that bomb must have had terrific power, for from the Gokoku Shrine clean out to the Red Cross Hospital † everything is completely destroyed. The Red Cross Hospital, though badly damaged, was spared, and beyond, going towards Ujina the damage is slight.

"I stopped by the Red Cross Hospital on my way here. It is swamped with patients, and outside the dead and dying are lined up on either side of the street as far east as the Miyuki Bridge.

"Between the Red Cross Hospital and the center of the city I saw nothing that wasn't burned to a crisp. Streetcars were standing at Kawaya-cho and Kamiya-cho and inside were dozens of bodies, blackened beyond recognition. I saw fire reservoirs filled to the brim with dead people who looked as though they had been boiled alive. In one reservoir I saw a man, horribly burned, crouching beside another man who was dead. He was drinking blood-stained water out of the reservoir. Even if I had tried to stop him, it wouldn't have done any good; he was completely out of his head. In one reservoir there were so many dead people there wasn't enough room for them to fall over. They must have died sitting in the water.

"Even the swimming pool at the Prefectural First Middle School is filled with dead people. They must have suffocated while they sat in the water trying to escape the fire because they didn't appear to be burned."

Dr. Hanaoka cleared his throat, and after a moment continued:

---

* A shrine near the southern border of the Hiroshima Military Barracks in the center of the city and less than 200 meters from the hypocenter of the atom bomb explosion. As the name of the shrine implies, it is dedicated to the defense of the fatherland.

† One of the modern hospitals in Hiroshima, opened around 1940, capacity 400 patients, it was badly damaged and many of its doctors and patients killed although fully 1500 meters from the hypocenter.

"Dr. Hachiya, that pool wasn't big enough to accommodate everybody who tried to get in it. You could tell that by looking around the sides. I don't know how many were caught by death with their heads hanging over the edge. In one pool I saw some people who were still alive, sitting in the water with dead all around them. They were too weak to get out. People were trying to help them, but I am sure they must have died. I apologize for telling you these things, but they are true. I don't see how anyone got out alive."

Dr. Hanaoka paused, and I could see he was anxious to get to work. With what there was to do, it would have been criminal to detain him.

Gradually, what these visitors were telling me began to fit into a pattern. A few comments from this one, a few remarks from another, were beginning to give me a picture of what Hiroshima was like.

Dr. Hanaoka had barely left when Dr. Akiyama, head of obstetrics and gynecology, came in. He was unhurt but looked tired and worn.

"Sit down and rest a few minutes," I said. "You must have been through a great deal. Where were you when the bombing occurred?"

"I was just leaving my home when it went off," said Dr. Akiyama in a tremulous voice. "A blinding flash, a tremendous explosion, and over I went on my back. And then a big black cloud, such as you see in the summer before a storm, began to rise above Hiroshima. 'Yarareta,' I shouted; and that was it. What a hodgepodge was made of my house. The ceilings, the walls, the sliding doors—everything—ruined beyond repair.

"Almost at once, injured people began to line up before my gate, and from then until a little while ago, I stayed and treated them. But my supplies are all gone, and there is nothing left to treat them with. Twenty or thirty people are still lying in the house and there is nobody to take care of them. There is nothing anybody can do, unless I find some more supplies."

Dr. Akiyama, ordinarily easy-going and happy, had the look of a man distraught. Dr. Koyama came in while Dr. Akiyama was talking and so heard most of what he had been saying.

"Knowing you, I can imagine what you have gone through," said Dr. Koyama.

"I don't know," sighed Dr. Akiyama. "Today it's the same as it was yesterday. There is no end to that stream of miserable souls who stop at my house to ask for help. They are trying to reach Kabe,* but they will never get there. And there is nothing I can do; nothing anybody can do."

Since Dr. Akiyama's home was in Nagatsuka, I got a general idea of what that suburb was like. The problem there was the same as in the Koi area. I could picture in my mind the wounded people walking in silence, like lost spirits, and answering, when questioned, that they had come "this way" and were going "that way." I could see them begging for water, hear their moaning, and see them dying. I might have been there myself, so vividly had my friends recounted to me what they had seen.

It was reported that none of the patients had any appetite and that one by one they were beginning to vomit and have diarrhea. Did the new weapon I had heard about throw off a poison gas or perhaps some deadly germ? I asked Dr. Hanaoka to confirm if he could the report of vomiting and diarrhea and to find out if any of the patients looked as if they might have an infectious disease. He inquired and brought word that there were many who not only had diarrhea but bloody stools and that some had had as many as forty to fifty stools during the previous night. This convinced me that we were dealing with bacillary dysentery and had no choice but to isolate those who were infected.

Dr. Koyama, as deputy director, was given the responsibility of setting up an isolation ward. He chose a site on the grounds beyond the south side of the hospital, and with the help of some soldiers who happened along he managed to construct what amounted to a crude outdoor pavillion. What we were trying to do probably was not worth much, but it helped our morale to think we were doing something.

* A town about 10 miles north of Hiroshima up the Ōta River valley.

Dr. Katsube and his staff had an impossible task. There was scarcely a patient who was not in need of urgent surgical care. The doctors and nurses were all busy helping him. Even the clerical staff and janitors, and those among the patients who could so much as get about, were organized and instructed to help. If progress was made, it was hard to see. How Dr. Katsube did what he did was a miracle.

The corridors were cleared enough to be passable, but in a little while they were as crowded as before. One difficulty was the influx of people looking for friends and relatives.

Parents, half crazy with grief, searched for their children. Husbands looked for their wives, and children for their parents. One poor woman, insane with anxiety, walked aimlessly here and there through the hospital calling her child's name. It was dreadfully upsetting to patients, but no one had the heart to stop her. Another woman stood at the entrance, shouting mournfully for someone she thought was inside. She, too, upset us.

Not a few came in from the country to look for friends or relatives. They would wander among the patients and peer rudely into every face, until finally their behavior became so intolerable that we had to refuse them entrance to the hospital.

A new noise reached us from outside. On inquiry, I was told that Dr. Koyama had procured a company of soldiers to clean out the fire-damaged Communications Bureau, so that it could be put in use again as an annex to the hospital.

The pharmacy came to life. Our meager supply of drugs was sorted and prepared for use under the watchful supervision of Dr. Hinoi and Mr. Mizoguchi.

A little order was appearing; something positive was being done. Perhaps in time we could get control of the situation.

Mr. Sera, the business manager, reported. He told me that sixteen patients had died during the night and that he had shrouded their bodies in white blankets and deposited them at the side entrance to the hospital.

"Can we spare those blankets at a time like this?" I thought to myself.

I was reluctant to object openly to what Mr. Sera had done because his action had been prompted by his sense of propriety and respect for the dead. When I discovered, however, that the army detail, dispatched to remove the dead, had thrown the bodies, blankets and all, onto the platform of a truck without any ceremony whatsoever, I seized on this indignity to suggest that our blankets be saved. The living needed the blankets more than the dead.

Patients continued to come from all directions, and since we were not far removed from the center of the explosion, those who came were in a critical condition.

Their behavior was remarkable. Even though the ones in the hospital fared little better than those on the outside, they were grateful for a pallet in the most crowded ward. It seemed to satisfy them if they could get so much as a glimpse of a white-robed doctor or nurse. A kind word was enough to set them crying. For the most trivial service they would clasp their hands and pray for you. All were sufferers together and were confident that the doctors and nurses would do their best for them. Later, word came that this hospital was considered a good place to be in. The remark pleased us, but we were never able to feel that we had done as much as we should.

Earlier in the day Mr. Imachi and those who worked with him in the kitchen managed to prepare some rice gruel which they brought in by the bucketful and dished out with big wooden spoons. For me, this simple gruel made the one bright spot in the day. It was served again that afternoon, and the mouthful I had, and the grain of rice that remained on my tongue, made me feel that I was going to get well. But there were many who were too weak or too sick to eat. In time, the weakness of hunger added to their misery.

Night approached and still the only beds were straw mats laid over the concrete floor. Wounds were becoming more painful, and there were not enough drugs to make them easy. Fevers rose and the patients became thirsty, but there was no one to bring cool water to quench the thirst.

Dr. Harada, one of our pharmacists, was brought into the hospital severely burned, and right after him, old Mrs. Saeki's son in the same condition. Miss Hinada, one of our nurses, had to be confined because of a severe diarrhea that had begun earlier in the day. Since there was no one to nurse her, her mother, despite being seriously burned, was trying to do the job.

Mr. Mizoguchi came in: "Dr. Hachiya, I must tell you that Miss Hinada and her mother have become worse. It doesn't look like either of them will live through the night, and old Mrs. Saeki's son is losing consciousness."

All day I had listened to visitors telling me about the destruction of Hiroshima and the scenes of horror they had witnessed. I had seen my friends wounded, their families separated, their homes destroyed. I was aware of the problems our staff had to face, and I knew how bravely they struggled against superhuman odds. I knew what the patients had to endure and the trust they put in the doctors and nurses, who, could they know the truth, were as helpless as themselves.

By degrees my capacity to comprehend the magnitude of their sorrow, to share with them the pain, frustration, and horror became so dulled that I found myself accepting whatever was told me with equanimity and a detachment I would have never believed possible.

In two days I had become at home in this environment of chaos and despair.

I felt lonely, but it was an animal loneliness. I became part of the darkness of the night. There were no radios, no electric lights, not even a candle. The only light that came to me was reflected in flickering shadows made by the burning city. The only sounds were the groans and sobs of the patients. Now and then a patient in delirium would call for his mother, or the voice of one in pain would breathe out the word *eraiyo*—"the pain is unbearable; I cannot endure it!"

What kind of a bomb was it that had destroyed Hiroshima? What had my visitors told me earlier? Whatever it was, it did not make sense.

There could not have been more than a few planes. Even *my* memory would agree to that. Before the air-raid alarm there was the metallic sound of one plane and no more. Otherwise why did the alarm stop? Why was there no further alarm during the five or six minutes before the explosion occurred?

Reason as I would, I could not make the ends meet when I considered the destruction that followed. Perhaps it *was* a new weapon! More than one of my visitors spoke vaguely of a "new bomb," a "secret weapon," a "special bomb," and someone even said that the bomb was suspended from two parachutes when it burst! Whatever it was, it was beyond my comprehension. Damage of this order could have no explanation! All we had were stories no more substantial than the clouds from which we had reached to snatch them.

One thing was certain—Hiroshima was destroyed; and with it the army that had been quartered in Hiroshima. Gone were headquarters, gone the command post of the Second General Army and the Military School for young people, the General Headquarters for the Western Command, the Corps of Engineers, and the Army Hospital. Gone was the hope of Japan! The war was lost! No more help would come from the gods!

American forces would soon be landing; and when they landed, there would be streetfighting; and our hospital would become a place of attack and defense. Had I not heard earlier that soldiers were coming to set up headquarters in the Communications Bureau? Would we be turned out?

Were there no answers?

Dr. Sasada, Miss Kado, and my wife were asleep. That was good, but there was no sleep for me.

I heard footsteps, and a man appeared at the door, outlined in the flickering darkness. His elbows were out and his hands down, like the burned people I had seen on my way to the hospital. As he came nearer, I could see his face—or what had been his face because this face had been melted away by the fire. The man was blind and had lost his way.

"You are in the wrong room!" I shouted, suddenly stricken with terror.

The poor fellow turned and shuffled back into the night. I was ashamed for having behaved as I did, but I was frightened. Now more awake than ever, every nerve taut, I could find no sleep.

To the east there was a perceptible lightening of the sky.

My shouting must have wakened my wife because she got up and left the room, I suppose to find the toilet. Before long she was back.

"What is the matter, Yaeko-san?" I asked, sensing she was upset.

"O-tōsan, the hall was so full of patients that I could find nowhere to walk without disturbing someone," she answered, trying to suppress her agitation. "I had to excuse myself every step I took. Oh! it was terrible. Finally, I stepped on somebody's foot, and when I asked to be excused, there was no answer. I looked down; and do you know what I had done?"

"What?" I asked.

"I had stepped on a dead man's foot," she said and with a shudder moved nearer.

8 August 1945

THE DAY began hot and clear. The sun was hardly up before my body was moist with oily sweat that dripped from my armpits and the inner sides of my thighs.

Smoke no longer rose from the second floor.

Dr. Sasada's face was more swollen this morning than yesterday, and blood-stained pus oozed from his bandaged arms and hands. I felt a wave of pity when I thought how he had used those hands to help me two days ago.

A noise outside the window caused me to recall a patient I neglected to mention yesterday. From time to time during the night I had heard him walking about, and this morning, he was walking again. You could hear him especially well when he stumbled into the fence or against the building.

"Has he been fed?" I asked Miss Kado.

"Don't worry, Doctor," replied Miss Kado. "There are plenty of potato leaves in the garden, so I don't think he'll be hungry."

The patient we were talking about was a horse who had been burned and blinded by the fire. Whoever saw him first did not have the heart to turn him away, so he was put in the garden under our window.

This garden had been a tennis court, but some time ago I thought it could be better used as a garden and I planted it in potatoes. My try at gardening caused no little amusement, and my potatoes came to be a joke.

"Miss Kado," I asked, "don't you think we had better dig up the potatoes? They must be quite big by now."

My companions laughed, and for a moment misery was forgotten.

My left ankle began to hurt. Looking down, I discovered that it had become wet and sticky through the bandage. Miss Kado saw my concern and offered to change the dressing, and when she finished, the ankle felt better. While she was changing the dressing though, I noticed a big blister on my left knee. This was a surprise because I could not recollect having received any burns. Later I remembered the hot ember that struck my leg while I was lying in the garden behind the Communications Bureau.

My appetite was better this morning and I seemed to be stronger. Even my spirits were improved, and the dark thoughts that beset me during the night were less oppressive.

Dr. Katsube came early. Instead of greeting him with a good morning, I asked him point-blank when I could get up. He told me again that it would be at least a week before he could remove the stitches and that I was to say no more about getting up until then.

"You are too impatient," he said. "You should be thankful that you are going to live."

That I might die had never crossed my mind, but now that Dr. Katsube had spoken so bluntly, I realized that I must have been hurt worse than I thought.

"Was I that bad off?" I asked, trying to appear nonchalant.

"We were all worried about you," Dr. Katsube stated. "Perhaps you don't realize how much blood you lost. Why, you remained comatose for the better part of the night! Your wife, Miss Kado, and Dr. Sasada, as well as Dr. Koyama and I, were, one or the other of us, at your side all night."

"No wonder I remember so little of what happened that night," I replied, trying to pass off his comments lightly.

I should have been content to rest. Dr. Koyama was certainly doing a good job of running the hospital, and I was in touch with things. Not only did he keep me informed, but he referred matters to me for opinion where he might have acted without doing me that courtesy.

A note, for example, came from Dr. Chodo, one of our dentists, which stated that he and his family were hiding in the hills behind Ushita. His family was unhurt, but he had been badly burned and asked if someone could bring him to the hospital. I sent for him, in spite of our critical shortage at the hospital.

Another report informed us that the Welfare Department of the Communications Bureau had between two hundred and three hundred sleeping mats or *tatami* * which could be procured for use in the hospital. Since these mats were roughly three by six feet in dimensions, the question arose, since we were so crowded, how we could get them under the patients. Mr. Sera and I felt that, crowded or not, the sleeping mats must be used, even if it meant clearing all the corridors.

* A *tatami* is a rectangular mat which measures approximately 6′ x 3′, made by the close weaving of a form of marsh grass called *i*, placed over a straw cushion of the same dimension to make the floor covering of a Japanese house. The size of a room or of a house is judged by the number of *tatami*; hence: a six *tatami* room or a ten *tatami* house. The Communications Hospital had introduced in some wards the innovation of Western beds.

A rumor that Mr. Yoshida, chief of the Communications Bureau, had been killed proved to be true. His charred body, identified by a belt buckle, was found near the hospital, and his remains were cremated in front of the Communications Bureau. In his death we lost a kind and loyal friend. Another prominent person to be killed was Mayor Otsuka.

I was startled to learn that I had been reported killed. The news was brought by two old friends, Mr. and Mrs. Nagao of Nishihara, who came looking for Yaeko-san and me this morning. We were happy to disprove the report of my death.

During the day, an effort was made to sort and rearrange the patients according to the nature and severity of their injuries, and not a few dead were found among the living, though fewer than yesterday. It irritated me when I heard the report, for I felt that the dead should be moved with greater dispatch in order to make room for the living. This is another example of my changed outlook. People were dying so fast that I had begun to accept death as a matter of course and ceased to respect its awfulness. I considered a family lucky if it had not lost more than two of its members. How could I hold my head up among the citizens of Hiroshima with thoughts like that in my mind?

Soldiers began to work again in the Communications Bureau. Dr. Koyama and I discussed the feasibility of getting them to help clear one of the floors for the patients quartered in the toilets and corridors. While we were talking, Dr. Hanaoka informed us that bloody diarrhea was increasing and that some had had as many as sixty stools since daybreak.

For the moment, a hospital annex in the Communications Bureau seemed less urgently needed than an enlarged isolation ward,* so the soldiers were asked to help with the latter.

The problem of how to reutilize the hospital came up for dis-

---

* It was perfectly logical to assume that the outbreak of bloody diarrhea represented the beginning of a dysentery epidemic and that the only possible way to control its spread would be to isolate the patients thus afflicted. The doctors in Hiroshima did not know that an atom bomb had been dropped, much less the fact that bloody diarrhea was a symptom of serious radiation sickness.

cussion because the fire-damaged second story had cooled down enough to be used. Before the fire there had been fourteen rooms above us, but since all the partitions were now destroyed, nothing remained but one single large room.

The question as to who among the patients should be moved upstairs provoked lively debate since it seemed at the time that the burned out second floor was far less desirable than the first, despite the crowding. It was finally decided that we, as staff members, should be the first to go up and leave the more desirable ground floor for patients from the outside.

I was moved first, and when my stretcher cleared the landing, my inquiring eyes fixed on the stark and twisted remains of thirty-odd iron bed frames, under each of which lay a white ash residue of the straw mattresses that had once covered them. There was not a sound bedframe on the floor, but after the two days spent lying on the concrete floor, the very sight of these beds was magnificent. Yaeko-san and I found beds near each other that were not too badly bent. Our sleeping mats were placed over the frames, and without further ado we were ready to resume life in our new quarters.

Dr. Sasada, Miss Susukida, and Miss Omoto joined us, and one by one other members of the staff were brought up until the big room became alive with people. One might have complained about the soot and ashes or about the pipes and curtain rods that hung crazily from the ceiling, but patients never lived in a hospital ward so nearly free of bacteria as this one that was sterilized by fire.

In all four walls were large casement windows which afforded a commanding view in every direction. There were no shutters, no curtains, nor even glass to impose the least obstruction to air or light. Looking east, south, and west, was an unobstructed view of Hiroshima and in Hiroshima Bay we could see the island Ninoshima.*

---

* Ninoshima is a small, saddle-backed, mountainous island, lying about 3 miles south of Hiroshima in Hiroshima Bay. Many survivors sought refuge on this island.

Near the center of the city, some fifteen hundred meters distant, one could see the blackened ruins of the two largest buildings in Hiroshima, the Fukuya Department Store * and the Chūgoku Press Building. Hijiyama,† the sacred and beautiful little mountain in the eastern sector of the city, looked almost close enough to touch. To our north no buildings remained.

For the first time, I could understand what my friends had meant when they said Hiroshima was destroyed. Nothing remained except a few buildings of reinforced concrete, two of which I have just mentioned. For acres and acres the city was like a desert except for scattered piles of brick and roof tile. I had to revise my meaning of the word destruction or choose some other word to describe what I saw. Devastation may be a better word, but really, I know of no word or words to describe the view from my twisted iron bed in the fire-gutted ward of the Communications Hospital.

I could see the soldiers working on our isolation ward. One took the lead in a work song and the others answered in chorus, verse for verse. In no time a ten *tsubo* ‡ addition to the ward was completed. Behind this they constructed an outdoor toilet with partitions of straw mats. From where I lay the mats provided no concealment.

A gentle breeze blew through the windows, bringing relief to

* The Fukuya Department Store was an eight-story, reinforced concrete building with brick veneer that stood 700 meters from the hypocenter. There are said to have been over 500 survivors in this building who showed evidence of radiation sickness. Persons in or near windows facing the explosion were killed.

† Hijiyama, once an island in Hiroshima Bay before the city of Hiroshima was claimed from the sea by dykes and filling, rises as a small flat-topped mountain 70 meters high in the eastern section of the city. A beautiful Shinto shrine and a park occupy its northern summit, a military cemetery its western face, while on an eastern point is a small cemetery with a monument erected by the Japanese in honor of a company of French and Dutch Marines who died at Hiroshima in 1900 of typhoid while helping defend Japan against Chinese pirates. Headquarters for the Atomic Bomb Casualty Commission, called locally *kamaboko goten* or "fishcake castle" for its similarity in shape and color to the Japanese fishcake, are now situated on Hijiyama.

‡ One *tsubo* measures 3.95 or roughly 4 square yards. It is a unit of land measure.

our fevered bodies. Gone were the confusion and disorder we had known downstairs. The abundant light from wide open windows and the distant vistas did something to our spirits. The very simplicity of our surroundings, contrasted with the chaos below, had a soothing effect.

We thought we had left the better part of the hospital for the patients downstairs, but now that we had moved in all agreed that ours were the better quarters. I resolved to have this room made available to the others as soon as possible.

Towards evening, a light southerly wind * blowing across the city wafted to us an odor suggestive of burning sardines. I wondered what could cause such a smell until somebody, noticing it too, informed me that sanitation teams were cremating the remains of people who had been killed. Looking out, I could discern numerous fires scattered about the city. Previously I had assumed the fires were caused by burning rubble. Towards Nigitsu was an especially large fire where the dead were being burned by hundreds. To suddenly realize that these fires were funeral pyres made me shudder, and I became a little nauseated.

Concrete buildings near the center of the city, still afire on the inside, made eerie silhouettes against the night sky. These glowing ruins and the blazing funeral pyres set me to wondering if Pompeii had not looked like this during its last days. But I think there were not so many dead in Pompeii as there were in Hiroshima.

For nearly three days the hospital staff had been laboring with scarcely a break, so tonight in order to give them a little respite, a space was cleared in our upstairs ward and alternate shifts were ordered to rest.

Dr. Koyama stopped to talk a few minutes before lying down and told me some of the things that had happened during the day.

In the morning a group of soldiers had come to the entrance, demanding bandages for the Second General Army, and despite the staff's assertion that our materials were low, made away

* During the summer months in the Inland Sea region a cooling southerly to southwesterly wind begins regularly each day around four in the afternoon and blows steadily until after nightfall.

with nearly all we had. These men behaved more like brigands than soldiers. Moreover, what they did was contrary to what we had been told to expect because the army had repeatedly promised to supply us with emergency goods in case of attack. These soldiers could not have come from the army that had been stationed in Hiroshima. There were not enough soldiers left in that group to help with the wounded soldiers brought to the hospital. The army was unable to provide for the wounded family of the local commandant whom we had made room for in one of the toilets. When the commandant's adjutant found them, he could find no better place to take them and was grateful when we managed to squeeze them into the janitor's office. The soldiers who got our supplies must have come from somewhere else.

We had further cause to worry. Dr. Koyama told me that soldiers from somewhere had been around all day cleaning out the Communications Bureau, and that rumors were current that an army headquarters was to be set up to direct a defense of Hiroshima in case of invasion. We both agreed that if an army should move in, our hospital would become a target for more bombing, and next time we would all be killed.

After Dr. Koyama left I continued to think along these lines, became upset, and could not sleep. I could hear every little sigh during the night, every plea for water, every groan. One of the dysentery patients who had been transferred to the isolation ward went to the back of the Bureau to get a drink of water. I heard a rude man scold him and tell him to go away lest he pass his dysentery on to him.

One voice called repeatedly for water, and as the night wore on the voice became weaker. I asked a nurse who the patient was, and she told me that he was a young officer who appeared to be from a decent family because every time she gave him a drink of water he thanked her politely.

Mention of the young officer called to mind a visit Yaeko-san and I had had on the second of August. A cousin, Captain Urabe, and his wife spent the day with us. Captain Urabe had been recruited as an army doctor shortly after he graduated from medical school, and when I saw him he had been eating army food for six or seven years in northern and central China. To me he appeared well-disciplined and courageous.

I was pessimistic about the outcome of the war and told him so. I confided that I thought we were going to lose because everything was becoming scarce, and the soldiers were no longer disciplined. I said that I was afraid Hiroshima was going to be bombed and that if it were the anti-aircraft guns would be useless. Our defenses had been prepared for incendiary bombing, and I considered it nonsensical to think the enemy would use incendiary bombs on a city with as many rivers and vacant lots as there were in Hiroshima.

To this my cousin listened calmly, and then replied: *"Niisan,* don't you worry for a minute. The chief of staff has said that no matter how much the nation criticizes the army, the army will reply with victory!"

As I lay there in the dark, I mumbled to myself, "Reply with victory." Where was my cousin now? If I could find him, he might be able to get us the medical supplies we needed. Captain Urabe must be busy, otherwise he would have come to see me before now.

9 August 1945

THE DAY began hot and clear, but upstairs the sun did not shine directly on us as it had downstairs. In addition, a cool breeze that blew right across the ward helped make our situation altogether more agreeable than it had been yesterday.

My mouth was more comfortable this morning so the healing of my lip and cheek must be progressing satisfactorily. Indeed,

I felt so much better that I asked if I might have some rice to eat instead of rice gruel. Miss Kado, always thoughtful, dug some of the sweet potatoes I had planted and prepared them for me. I do not think sweet potatoes ever tasted so good.

My wife, although still with her arm in a sling, was so much better this morning that she took care of me. I was amused to hear her ask for some white ointment which she put over her brows to conceal the fact that her eyebrows had been singed. Her returning vanity was a good sign.

Dr. Sasada was worse this morning. His temperature had increased, and he was weaker.

The sun had not been up long before visitors again appeared. One of the most welcome was a sturdy soldier, who staggered in under a load of bandages and drugs much too large for one person to carry. He had been sent by Lieutenant Tanaka of the Akatsuki Corps. Not only was I pleased to receive the badly needed medical supplies, but it was good to learn that Lieutenant Tanaka was alive. I had known this young officer through my cousin, Captain Urabe. His thoughtfulness was gratefully acknowledged by everyone.

There was another surprise. His excellency, Mr. Okamoto, head of the Western District of the Communications Ministry, came to see me. I had heard a good deal about him, naturally, but had not had an opportunity to meet him. He was a sociable, friendly man who immediately put me at ease. When we discovered by coincidence that I had followed him by six years in the same high school in Okayama, all barriers of authority disappeared, and we fell to talking of old times. He was on the way to Hiroshima when the bombing occurred and would have been here at the time had he not been stung by a bee near Kure, a city twenty-five miles south of Hiroshima, with the result that he stopped off for treatment. That bee saved his life.

During conversation with Mr. Okamoto, I sat up without thinking, from deference to my distinguished visitor. After he left, I suddenly realized that it had not hurt to sit up. If I could sit without pain, could I not stand? I waited until no one was looking and tried, but the stitches in my hip began to pull; so, somewhat crestfallen, I was obliged to lie down. Nevertheless, this experiment inspired me with confidence. Once my stitches were out, I was convinced I could be active again.

Today, Dr. Hanaoka's report on the patients was more detailed. One observation particularly impressed me. Regardless of the type of injury, nearly everybody had the same symptoms. All had a poor appetite, the majority had nausea and gaseous indigestion, and over half had vomiting.

Not a few had shown improvement since yesterday. Diarrhea, though, continued to be a problem and actually appeared to be increasing. Distinctly alarming was the appearance of blood in the stools of patients who earlier had only diarrhea. The isolation of these people was becoming increasingly difficult.

One seriously ill man complained of a sore mouth yesterday, and today, numerous small hemorrhages began to appear in his mouth and under his skin. His case was the more puzzling because he came to the hospital complaining of weakness and nausea and did not appear to have been injured at all.

This morning, other patients were beginning to show small subcutaneous hemorrhages, and not a few were coughing and vomiting blood in addition to passing it in their stools. One poor woman was bleeding from her privates. Among these patients there was not one with symptoms typical of anything we knew, unless you could excuse those who developed signs of severe brain disease before they died.

Dr. Hanaoka believed the patients could be divided into three groups:

1. Those with nausea, vomiting, and diarrhea who were improving.

2. Those with nausea, vomiting, and diarrhea who were remaining stationary.

3. Those with nausea, vomiting, and diarrhea who were developing hemorrhage under the skin or elsewhere.

Had these patients been burned or otherwise injured, we might have tried to stretch the logic of cause and effect and assume that their bizarre symptoms were related to injury, but so many patients appeared to have received no injury whatsoever that we were obliged to postulate an insult heretofore unknown.

The only other possible cause for the weird symptoms observed was a sudden change in atmospheric pressure. I had read somewhere about bleeding that follows ascent to high altitudes and about bleeding in deep sea divers who ascend too rapidly from the depths. Having never seen such injury I could not give much credence to my thoughts.

Still, it was impossible to dismiss the thought that atmospheric pressure had had something to do with the symptoms of our patients. During my student days at Okayama University, I had seen experiments conducted in a pressure chamber. Sudden, temporary deafness was one symptom everyone complained of if pressure in the chamber was abruptly altered.

Now, I could state positively that I heard nothing like an explosion when we were bombed the other morning, nor did I remember any sound during my walk to the hospital as houses collapsed around me. It was as though I walked through a gloomy, silent motion picture. Others whom I questioned had had the same experience.

Those who experienced the bombing from the outskirts of the city characterized it by the word: *pikadon.**

How then could one account for my failure and the failure of others to hear an explosion except on the premise that a sudden change in atmospheric pressure had rendered those nearby temporarily deaf: Could the bleeding we were beginning to observe be explained on the same basis?

---

* *Pika* means a glitter, sparkle, or bright flash of light, like a flash of lightning. *Don* means a boom! or loud sound. Together, the words came to mean to the people of Hiroshima an explosion characterized by a flash and a boom. Hence: "flash-boom!" Those who remember the flash only speak of the *"pika"*; those who were far enough from the hypocenter to experience both speak of the *"pikadon."* Another word less frequently used in Hiroshima, but no less expressive, is *gembaku,* which literally means "the place of suffering."

Since all books and journals had been destroyed, there was no way to corroborate my theories except by further appeal to the patients. To that end Dr. Katsube was asked to discover what else he could when he made ward rounds.

It was pleasing to note my scientific curiosity was reviving, and I lost no opportunity to question everyone who visited me about the bombing of Hiroshima. Their answers were vague and ambiguous, and on one point only were they in agreement: a new weapon had been used. *What* the new weapon was became a burning question. Not only had our books been destroyed, but our newspapers, telephones, and radios as well.

Dr. Chodo, our dentist, whom I spoke of earlier as having fled with his family to the Ushita hills, was brought in and assigned with his family to the waiting room of the Dental Department. I asked the nurse who helped bring him in how he was.

"Dr. Chodo is in a serious condition," she told me. "It is frightful to see all of him burned and glistening with oozing secretions. I don't believe he will live."

"How about his wife and daughter?" I asked.

"They weren't hurt," answered the nurse.

Poor Dr. Chodo. He and his family only recently came up from Okinawa and had no relatives here and few friends. What would happen to his family if he died?

While I lay there brooding over Dr. Chodo, old Mrs. Saeki came up quietly and stood by my bed. One look into her pale, careworn face and I knew what she had come to say. Her son was dead; her eldest son—her only child left in the world. She had been so hopeful yesterday when he was brought in, and now he was gone. Her son's wife and her second son had been killed on the day of the *pikadon*, and now no one was left. She put her hands over her eyes and cried, but her sobs were scarcely audible. I could not speak for a while because there was something in my throat.

"*Obāsan*," I said when I could control my voice, "don't worry. I will look after you hereafter."

Old Mrs. Saeki stood for a while, crying quietly. Then she said: "Please help me, doctor," and without saying anything more turned and went downstairs.

My thoughts returned to Dr. Harada. Except for the top of his head, every inch was burned, leaving his pus-glistening body red and raw. A circle of black hair covered the only surface that had not been cooked. From a distance it looked like he was wearing a cooking pot. He and Dr. Chodo were near the Asano Sentei Park * when the explosion occurred. Before the day was out Dr. Harada died, and his wife's family took his corpse to their home in Kabe.

Dr. Okura, another of our dentists, went out this morning to look for his wife, missing since the day of the bombing. He returned later with some bones that he picked up where she had last been seen. Mr. Yamazaki, in the business office, was still trying to find his daughter, but without success. Dr. Fujii finally found his daughter, but she was beyond help. She died in a friend's house in Midorii.

* The Asano Sentei Park was less than 500 meters from the hospital. It was situated on the west bank of the Kyōbashi-gawa and in earlier days had been a palace garden of the Asano family, the ruling princes or *daimyō* of what was then the province of Aki.

The name of the Asano family has remained famous because of an incident that occurred in 1701. Asano Naganori, then *daimyō* of Aki, drew his sword in the halls of the Shogun's palace in Yedo (Tokyo) and cut down Kira Yoshihide who, it was alleged, had insulted Asano while instructing him in the etiquette of a state ceremony. Asano was ordered to commit suicide for the double offence of unsheathing his sword in the palace and for assaulting a high official of the shogun. With Asano's death his forty-seven *samurai* were left without a master and thus became *rōnin* or soldiers without a leader.

Thinking to avenge the death of their *daimyō* these forty-seven *rōnin* waited patiently and secretly for two years until they found an opportunity on the snowy night of February 7, 1703, to invade the mansion of Kira and put him to death. The forty-seven *rōnin* then gave themselves up and were ultimately given the privilege of committing suicide. This vendetta on the Asano family has become famous in Japanese story and song, and the forty-seven *rōnin* are almost national deities.

The Asano family and the wife and son of Ōishi Yoshio, the famous leader of the forty-seven *rōnin*, are buried in Hiroshima at the family temple, the Kokutai-ji, not far from the Asano Sentei Park.

There was to be no more good news today. Dr. Morisugi, in our Internal Medical Department, was still missing, and since he had lived near the center of the explosion, we assumed that he and his entire family were killed. Three of our nurses had been killed and Miss Hinada, who seemed to be all right before her diarrhea started, was dying.

Towards evening, the young officer died whom I heard begging for water last night. His mother, coming all the way from Yamaguchi Prefecture, found him a few minutes after he had drawn his last breath.

A little girl was given the young officer's bed in the isolation ward. Her cries for her mother were heartbreaking.

Darkness came, and still there were no lights except the lights from the fires where the dead were burned. And again, the smell of burning flesh. The hospital was quieter, but in the isolation ward, the stillness of the night was broken again and again by the little girl.

"Mother," she would cry, "it hurts! I can't stand it. *Eraiyo!*"

Not until the eastern sky began to brighten did I fall into troubled sleep.

10 August 1945

THERE WAS a cool breeze when I awakened this morning. After an exchange of good mornings, I asked my companions how they had fared through the night. Those who could, raised their heads; the others, their hands. Happily, no one had expired.

Outside, people were combing the ruins in search of friends or relatives. To the south, along the streetcar line that had run between Hatchōbori and Hakushima, people walked in an unending stream, on their way to and from the hills and neighboring villages in search of people or possessions they had lost.

A message was brought me concerning Miss Yama, our head nurse in surgery. She was critically ill in a dugout near Yokogawa. I passed the news on to Dr. Katsube and Miss Takao because they were particularly close friends. The moment they learned where Miss Yama was they set out at once to find her. Miss Takao was in such haste that she followed Dr. Katsube in some old sandals that would not have lasted five minutes.

"Tomichan," I called out to Miss Takao, "you can't go out in those broken-down sandals. You'll never reach Yokogawa. Here, take my shoes."

Discarding her broken-down sandals, Miss Takao put on my shoes, and went clomping out after Dr. Katsube. How she kept them on was a miracle because she could have put both feet in one shoe. I could picture her toiling and panting to keep up with Dr. Katsube, the perspiration dripping from her chubby face. Easy-going and good-natured, and fat and roly-poly as Ebisu-sama, the god of wealth, she made a good companion for Dr. Katsube.

This morning I had boiled rice instead of rice gruel. What a difference it made! With solid food in my stomach I felt like doing something. Why should I not take advantage of Dr. Katsube's absence and try to walk again? To my delight, I found I *could* walk and even the stitches did not seem to pull too much. After a few steps, I was convinced that all I needed was practice.

While trying my wings, so to speak, I heard footsteps and turned to find Mr. Mizoguchi approaching my bed.

"Doctor, you had better be careful," he admonished, "or you will overdo it. May I have a few words with you?"

"Certainly," I replied, a little sheepishly since he found me out of bed.

"It concerns our medical supplies," stated Mr. Mizoguchi, politely ignoring my embarrassment. "They are almost exhausted. What few there are, we try to distribute equitably between the in-patients and the out-patients, but the out-patients have increased so that soon there will be nothing to give anybody. The bundle given you yesterday is the only addition to our stock since the bombing, and what emergency stores there are in Jigozen and Yaguchi can't be reached."

"Ask Dr. Koyama if he is busy," I replied. "Perhaps he could suggest some way out of this dilemma."

Dr. Koyama came up and I repeated what Mr. Mizoguchi had said and asked for his suggestions.

"No," answered Dr. Koyama, after a thoughtful pause, "I see no solution unless we can get someone to help us from the outside. The Prefectural Office promised help, you know."

"Then let's close the out-patient department!" I replied. "At least what little we have left can be saved for the in-patients."

"That would never do," replied Dr. Koyama. "Those who come as out-patients need help just as badly as those inside, and if we refuse them, where can they go?"

At this point, I lost my temper.

"Four days have passed," I shouted, "and still we have received no supplies. Even if the Prefectural Office keeps its promise and sends supplies, there still won't be enough. You have enough to do, worrying about problems in the hospital, without trying to care for every transient who comes to the door. You must close the out-patient department, I tell you; you must close it today!"

Dr. Koyama seemed to realize that my injuries, my insomnia, my brooding over hospital problems had made me unreasonable, for he tried to soothe me. I responded by showing contrition one moment and anger the next. In the end, perhaps for fear I would become completely unreasonable, he bowed to my insistent requests and promised to post a notice that the out-patient department would be closed.

The notice was hardly up before police and officials from the Prefectural Office appeared to ask why we had made such a rule. The effect was sensational. They begged us to continue the out-patient department for the sake of the Hiroshima citizens.

We would be glad to, we told them, but for the fact that our supplies were exhausted, and no one had made any effort to replace them. In answer, they promised to find us supplies if only we would reopen the clinic.

Perhaps my insistence that the notice be posted was not so unreasonable after all. Before they could change their minds, Dr. Hinoi was dispatched to the Sanitary Department of the Prefectural Office for the promised supplies. But what they gave him was scarcely worth mentioning. The bundle he returned with was no bigger than the tears of a sparrow.

There was no concealing our disappointment. The local officials understood our predicament. How could they expect us to treat patients without supplies? And to send a package like that! It was an insult!

Dr. Hinoi and Mr. Mizoguchi, less disturbed than the rest of us, listened patiently until we had vented our spleen and then pointed out that we had not been entirely outmaneuvered in our skirmish with the prefectural authorities.

"At least, we now know where the Sanitary Department is located," Dr. Hinoi said, "and we know that the chief of the department is alive and well. They told me that he was at home when the bombing occurred and suffered nothing more than a few fractured ribs. Why doesn't one of us go to see him, and explain the situation? I am sure he would help."

There did not seem to be any objection to this suggestion, so Dr. Koyama was delegated to call on the chief of the Sanitary Department at his home. Actually, I knew the man, for he and I had been classmates in school. Dr. Kitajima was his name.

Dr. Koyama found him at home, but Dr. Kitajima was anything but civil and not the least receptive to an explanation of our problems.

"You will continue your clinic by order of the Governor!" was Dr. Kitajima's terse reply.

"The mission of our hospital," Dr. Koyama answered, "is to treat the employees of the Communications Ministry and their families. We were voluntarily treating the citizens of Hiroshima for reasons of humanity and not because we are obligated to the prefecture. Our legal obligation is to the Communications Ministry, and not to the prefecture, so I see no reason to obey your order in the name of the Governor, even if he should sanction your arbitrary demand! All we ask for are supplies, supplies to treat any person who may need treatment, regardless of citizenship or connection."

Dr. Kitajima's manner changed and when he spoke, he lapsed into the soft tones of the Okayama dialect. "Dr. Koyama," he said, "don't say any more. Only please continue your clinic in the name of humanity, and I'll see that you receive medical supplies and all the doctors and nurses we can find to help you."

To use Dr. Koyama's expression, he saw no use wrestling with his mouth longer and returned to the hospital satisfied that Dr. Kitajima would be a man of his word. We were happy to have his promise. We had won our point, and the notice on the clinic was removed. The Kitajima-Koyama meeting had been a success.

Miss Yama was alive! They were bringing her in now. She had been on the way to the hospital when the *pika* occurred and, although partly shielded by a parasol, was badly burned. She had lost all of her clothes. Dr. Katsube held little hope for her.

Mr. Shiota, a Communications Bureau employee, had been wounded near Nigitsu * and was now in the home of a friend in Hesaka. A messenger came to ask if he could be brought to the hospital. Word was sent for him to come without delay.

People who had taken refuge in outlying villages and suburbs began to return. Word had reached them that the hospital was functioning, so in they came from temples, schools, houses, and even barns. None of these people had received any treatment, and all were weak with hunger.

To accommodate such an influx, room was needed, so, without delay, we tried to prepare the Bureau for a hospital annex.

Staff members of the Bureau and their families were given preference in the Bureau annex; others were accommodated in the hospital. Mrs. Yoshida, the wife of the Communications Bureau's chief who had been killed on the way to work, was admitted to

---

* Nigitsu or Nikitsu-jinja, a Shinto shrine 1700 meters from the hypocenter, about ½ mile from the hospital.

the annex. This poor woman, at first listed as missing, was injured and escaped to her home in Kō-machi. We placed her in the reception room next to the old office of her dead husband.

The influx increased until it became more than we could manage. Imagine our delight when Dr. R. Norioka from the Osaka Communications Hospital suddenly appeared with a group of assistants and all the supplies each of them could carry. His coming was like a merciful rain during drought. Dr. Norioka, who had the appearance and manner of a skillful, conscientious physician, went to work quietly, and in no time his skill as well as his optimism became an inspiration. Everyone quickly felt the strength of his presence.

What a contrast this man with his highly skilled team made with a group from a certain medical association who came later with protestations of help. The latter group did nothing, came empty handed, and were so in the way that I wanted to tell them they would be more appreciated if their expressions of good will could be shown in some practical way. Dr. Norioka and his group, by contrast, gave strength to the weary hearts of the patients.

Ever since the blast the screws of our hearts had been loose, but Dr. Norioka was tightening them up with his silent virtues. He worked hard. He was a man who noticed everything. Above all, he had sympathy and discernment, and he found time to teach us as well as to treat us. For the first time since the bombing I felt that we were beginning to catch up.

Night came, and it was the first night without the smell of death. Whether this was because of a change in the wind or whether cremations had become fewer, I do not know. Certainly, the number of our people dying each day had decreased, for today there were only two.

Mr. Mizoguchi brought me a light. It was a crude oil light, fashioned from an iron plate with a wick composed of bandage scraps, but the light seemed surprisingly bright. It lighted the ceiling, the walls, and even the corners of the big room. It was the first light we had seen since the *pika*. One forgets how bright a light can be at night.

Mr. Mizoguchi stayed for a few minutes to talk. He told me of a man he had interrupted trying to remove the leggings from a blinded soldier. He then told me about Miss Hinada and Miss Susukida.

"Time and again through the night," he recounted, in a soothing tone, "the woman who lay beside me talked in a soft friendly voice. It was not until morning that I discovered that it was Miss Susukida. Her face was so swollen I didn't recognize her until she told me. . . ."

I fell asleep listening to Mr. Mizoguchi.

11 August 1945

THE DAY dawned hot and clear. For the first time since the bombing I slept soundly all night and awakened refreshed.

Looking around, I discovered that Miss Yama had been admitted. Her bed was between Miss Omoto and Miss Susukida, both of whom were quite ill. Miss Yama was the only one who could not raise her head when I called the roll. I could only see the back of her head because she was facing away from me, so I called out: "If you can't raise your head, Yama-san, raise your hand. If you can do that, you'll be all right."

Miss Yama answered by raising her hand.

"Good for you," I said, trying to encourage her. "You'll come through. There's plenty of life in you if you can raise your hand, so keep up your courage. We'll help you get well."

No one had died during the night, and three of our folks came in whom we had given up for lost. Everyone seemed to feel better this morning. Breakfast tasted exceptionally good when Mr. Mizoguchi brought it up.

Not long after breakfast a strong wind sprang up and set the dust whirling. White chips of blistered paint and mortar, dislodged from the ceiling, settled over us like falling cherry blossoms. Dr. Sasada fared the worst because his bandaged hands made it difficult for him to protect his eyes and face.

"It would be much pleasanter to suffocate under a shower of cherry blossoms than under plaster from this ceiling," I said jokingly, trying to brush him off.

Until the wind stopped and we could halfway clean off the dust and grit we were pretty uncomfortable. My bald head felt rough and gritty and my matted whiskers were white as snow. Never have I wished so much for a bath and a good shave.

It is an ill wind that blows no good, though, for when Dr. Katsube made rounds and saw what a mess I was, he took pity and dressed my wounds. He must have been pleased because to my surprise he removed the stitches a day earlier than he had promised. What a difference my new dressings made. To be rid of the smelly old bandages and no longer feel the pull of stitches improved my whole outlook. The dust storm was forgotten.

While I lay enjoying my new comfort, Lieutenant Tanaka, the young officer who sent us the badly needed medical supplies day before yesterday, came up. After exchanging greetings, I expressed our gratitude for his unsolicited generosity and asked what had happened to his troops in the Second Corps who had been stationed in the barracks back of the hospital.

"Over four hundred medical recruits were stationed there," he answered, "most of them men sent up for punishment. Nearly all were killed."

"Have you heard from my cousin, Captain Urabe?" I asked.

"Someone told me Captain Urabe was wounded in the back of the head and had been sent to Ujina for treatment, but that's all I've heard. Communications are extremely poor, and survivors are so widely dispersed that we can't keep up with anyone."

One last question I was almost afraid to ask. A rumor was circulating that Russia had entered the war against Japan and was invading Manchuria like a tempestuous flood. Lieutenant Tanaka confirmed the rumor but did not elaborate.

This was unbelievable! We now had enemies in front of and behind us. Assuredly there was no hope. I felt as if a great weight were crushing my chest.

Later in the day news came that a mysterious new weapon had been used to bomb Nagasaki with the same result as in Hiroshima. It, too, had produced a bright flash and a loud sound.

Pikadon was accepted as a new word in our vocabulary, although some, like old Mrs. Saeki, who had been in the city at the time of the bombing, continued to say simply *pika*. Those who had been outside the city insisted on saying *pikadon*. The latter finally won out.

Following the news that Nagasaki had been bombed, a man came in from Fuchu * with the incredible story that Japan had the same mysterious weapon, but until now, had kept it a strict secret and had not used it because it was judged too horrible even to mention. This man went on to say that a special attack squad from the navy had now used the bomb on the mainland of America and that his news had come from no less a source than General Headquarters. The blow had been dealt by a squadron of six-engined, trans-Pacific bombers, two of which failed to return. Those bombers were assumed to have dived right into their targets to make certain of success.

If San Francisco, San Diego, and Los Angeles had been hit like Hiroshima, what chaos there must be in those cities!

At last Japan was retaliating!

The whole atmosphere in the ward changed, and for the first time since Hiroshima was bombed, everyone became cheerful and bright. Those who had been hurt the most were the happiest. Jokes were made, and some began singing the victory song. Prayers were said for the soldiers. Everyone was now convinced that the tide of war had turned.

* Fuchu is a township about one mile east of Hiroshima and cut off from the city by a low mountain ridge running from north to south (the hills of Ushita and Nigitsu).

I was determined to get out of bed, since my sutures were out, to see if I could expedite the moving of the medical supplies the Sanitary Office had promised us yesterday. The best course of action was to go directly to the Sanitary Department, which, as a subsidiary of the Prefectural Office, was quartered in a gutted bank building in Yamaguchi near the center of the city.

Dr. Hinoi was informed of my intentions, and knowing my weakened condition, offered to take me there on the back of his bicycle. For once I made no objection; and when he was ready, we set out.

The distance to the Sanitary Office from the hospital was about a mile, so I looked forward to this opportunity to examine this sector of the city at close range. Leaving the hospital, we passed the infamous outdoor toilet I mentioned earlier. It was disgraceful. Patients who could walk still insisted on coming here at night to relieve themselves, despite our begging them to use the latrine behind the hospital. The area was scrupulously cleaned each morning, but so much filth soaked into the ground the revolting odor remained.

Beyond the hospital the assault on our nostrils was replaced by an assault on our muscles, for we found the street so obstructed that we spent more time carrying the bicycle than riding it. The trolley wire and its supporting cables were down, so about every fifty feet we had to crawl over or under a cable, and between these tangles of telephone and electric wire had to be negotiated. Other obstacles were fallen poles and toppled walls, and if nothing else obstructed the way, there were always the holes. A track team would have been discouraged by the hurdles we faced.

If our destination had not been so clearly visible, our tedious journey would have been less frustrating. But there it was, in plain view across the rubble. Once, when we stopped to rest after a particularly troublesome detour, Dr. Hinoi remarked. "Doctor, will we ever get there? It looked like every detour we take only gets us farther away!"

I had ample chance to inspect the ruins on both sides of the street. There were tile walls and broken tubs to distinguish the homes that had once had bath rooms, and bits of china and fragments of crockery where kitchens had stood. The remains of vases with patterns of finely-wrought *cloisonné* reminded us that this had once been a prosperous residential district. Many of the inhabitants I had known, but the place was so strange to me now, that for the life of me, I could not have said where any of them had lived.

We saw charred bones, but only once or twice were we able to detect the sick-sweet smell of decaying flesh. These reminders of death were scarcely remarkable as we threaded our way through this wilderness. I was disturbed most by the sight of burnt toys in the ruins.

We finally reached the gutted bank building on Yamaguchi Avenue and paused to look back. To the north were the hospital and Bureau, alone and lonely, and beyond, the hills of Ushita, its slopes scorched and bare.

We entered the bank through a back door and found ourselves in a barren lofty room that dwarfed the host of little people scurrying about inside. This, I thought, looked more like the inside of a honeybee's box than a bank. Certainly it did not look like a Prefectural Office.

We found Chief Kitajima and a couple of assistants perched on broken chairs behind desks made from old orange crates. When Kitajima-san saw me, he looked surprised for a moment, and then his face lighted up. The next instant we were embracing and addressing each other in the Okayama dialect.*

"Luckily, I was at home when the bombing occurred," he told me. "All I got were a few broken ribs, but look at you. Are you all right? I guess we're both fortunate to be alive!"

While we chatted, Dr. Hinoi excused himself and began looking around. After a while he returned and gave me a wink. In no time

* The Okayama dialect, like dialects in other localities in Japan, is distinctive. It is characterized by a soft, gentle, almost musical accent pleasant to the ear. One Okayama native can recognize another, as can a native of Tokyo, Kochi, Matsue, by accent, inflection, and manner of speaking. This, of course, is no different the world over, but in Japan this feature of speech is impressive.

he had assembled the supplies we most urgently needed, and Dr. Kitajima promised early delivery.

Our mission was accomplished, so, thanking Dr. Kitajima, we excused ourselves and departed.

"Dr. Hinoi," I said, when we had reached the street, "Our patients are not the only ones with dysentery. Kitajima-san tells me that every hospital in the area is filled with dysentery cases. And something else he told me is that the basement of the Fukuya Department Store is being used as a first-aid station. Let's have a look before we return to the Bureau."

Dr. Hinoi nodded, so when we reached Fukuya's, we stopped. One peep into the basement was enough. It was so dark and forbidding that we changed our minds about going in and, instead, continued on to the corner and turned into the street which passed the Bureau.

For a while, we proceeded in silence, for both of us were tired and not a little depressed. The heat of the day, our exertions, the woeful destruction around us had acted cruelly on body and spirit. Nor did the scraps of news Dr. Kitajima had given us serve to improve our outlook. Eighty doctors out of 190 in Hiroshima were killed by the *pikadon*, and many of them had been my friends. I could not dismiss what I had seen at Fukuya's. The biggest department store in Hiroshima, the pride of the city, left a shambles, its windows blown in and its interior reduced to a dark gloomy cave. People who had once gone there to trade were now patients inside. I could still hear their moans and groans.

Our hospital was a paradise by comparison. Small? Yes, but there was light and good ventilation. Even in the toilets under the stairs the patients enjoyed better accommodations than the best in Fukuya's. Bad as things were, I was beginning to understand why patients appeared grateful and happy in our hospital. We had something to work for and to improve. My spirits began to revive.

"Dr. Hinoi, did you get what you wanted from Dr. Kitajima?" I asked.

"Yes," he replied, relieved that I had broken the silence. "I ran into Dr. Fujimura and he was not only sympathetic, but helpful. He told me we could have as much as we needed of anything they had. From now on I think we'll be all right."

As if to emphasize his own rising spirits, Dr. Hinoi smiled and peddled along quite jauntily until his peddling brought us again to the jungle of wires we had encountered earlier. But now, the wires seemed less formidable, and in no time we were home.

After a rest, I decided to make rounds. What the patients might think to see me, the Director of the Communications Hospital, in dirty pants, patched shirt, and looking worse than the chief of a hobo village, might have disturbed me before the *pikadon*, but not now. No one could look less like a doctor than I, but before I had gone far, it was easy to see that despite my disreputable appearance, I was one of the best dressed men in the hospital.

I felt ashamed to be as well dressed as I was when I witnessed the misery of the pitiful people around me. Here was an old lady, on the verge of death, in nothing but an undershirt, and a horribly burned young man, lying completely naked on a pallet. There was a dying young mother, with breasts exposed, whose baby lay asleep in the crook of her arm with one of her nipples held loosely in its mouth, and a beautiful young girl, burned everywhere except the face, who lay in a puddle of blood and pus. A soldier, naked except for shorts, lay on a mat smeared with blood. Others wore improvised articles of clothing made from curtains, tablecloths, or any other materials their friends had been lucky enough to pick up around the hospital.

I tried to encourage everyone I could.

"In spite of our accommodations and what we can provide for you," I would tell them, "this is the best hospital in Hiroshima. No less an authority than the chief of the Sanitary Department in the Prefectural Office told me so today. Please be patient."

I did not mean to boast. Our hospital *had* been complimented by the Prefectural Office, and if the other hospitals around the city were anything like what I had glimpsed at the Fukuya Department Store, the compliment was not altogether unjustified.

While we were uptown, I had run into Mrs. Yanagihara, the widow of an old friend. This poor woman was thin as a stork; her home, clothes, everything, had been destroyed in the blast; and she was alone in the world, far from her native home in Shikoku.*

"Where are you staying, Mrs. Yanagihara?" I had asked.

"At Fukuya," she answered, and tears welled up in her eyes.

The misery in her expression and the sadness of her voice as she said "at Fukuya" embarrassed me and left me fumbling to find a word of encouragement.

"Well; at least, I'm glad to see you weren't hurt badly," I finally replied.

"Yes," she answered sadly, "but I'm still at Fukuya."

What I had heard and seen today gave me conviction when I praised our hospital to the patients. If I had made rounds before going uptown, I would have been less sanguine.

Damage in the city was far greater than I had imagined. A force that could leave this reinforced concrete building shattered like a broken basket and turn the hospital safe completely around could not be expected to spare furnishings, fittings, or instruments.

A sudden flash, a blast, and then a cataclysmic earthquake—fire, lightning, earthquake—all the representatives of disaster and death, each following the other.

I went to bed intending to rest but soon discovered I was too keyed up to relax. The physical and emotional exertion of the day had excited that state of fatigue which leaves one intoxicated and restless and prey to thoughts that border on madness.

I walked to and fro in the big room, then lay on my bed for a few minutes, and then walked again. The wind began to blow, stirring up dust and scattering plaster in whirling, powdery clouds. This I enjoyed and seemed to lose all restraint. It suited my mood. Thoughts raced through my mind. I became annoyed by the end

* Shikoku, which means four provinces, is the fourth large island in the Japanese archipelago, and is directly across the Inland Sea to the south of Hiroshima. From Hiroshima it is an eight-hour boat trip to Matsuyama, the principal port in northwest Shikoku.

of an electric wire that protruded from an overhead pipe. Nothing would do but I must get on my bed and pull the wire out. I pulled and coil after coil appeared and piled into tangles around me, but there was no end to the wire. If I could just get rid of the wire and then the pipes, and finally the beds, a big open room would be left in which we could spread mats and accommodate fifty or sixty more patients. Then everyone downstairs could come up and enjoy the view, the wind, the light.

But I was alone; no one would help me.

Gradually, I became quiet. My senses returned and with them more rational thoughts. We did need more room, but the sensible thing would be to clean up the many rooms that were still cluttered and useless. By doing this a hundred patients or more could easily be accommodated in the two buildings.

I became quiet enough eventually to lie down, but my mind still kept reviewing the events of the day. My thoughts went again to poor old Mrs. Yanagihara, and I wondered how she would fare from now on. Seeing her had made me think of my own mother and set me to wondering if Dr. Nishimura had carried my message to her.

My thoughts returned to the scenes in the city I had glimpsed this afternoon. Never again would I be witness to such destruction and such a spiritless people.

I thought of the dead. Someone had done a good job disposing of the bodies. This, I recalled, had been done very soon after the *pikadon*, because Dr. Hinoi had told me that when he went out on the first night after the bombing to look for his relatives the dead bodies in the principal streets had already been removed.

I thought of stories I had heard the first day. What a weak, fragile thing man is before the forces of destruction. After the *pika* the entire population had been reduced to a common level of physical and mental weakness. Those who were able walked silently towards the suburbs and the distant hills, their spirits broken, their initiative gone. When asked whence they had come, they pointed to the city and said, "that way"; and when asked where they were going, pointed away from the city and said, "this way." They were so broken and confused that they moved and behaved like automatons.

Their reactions had astonished outsiders who reported with amazement the spectacle of long files of people holding stolidly to a narrow, rough path when close by was a smooth, easy road going in the same direction. The outsiders could not grasp the fact that they were witnessing the exodus of a people who walked in the realm of dreams.

A spiritless people had forsaken a destroyed city; the way and the means were of no importance. Some had followed the railways, some, as if by instinct, had chosen footpaths and paddy fields, whereas others found themselves shuffling along dry river beds. Each to his separate course for no better reason than the presence of another in the lead.

As the day ended I might as well have been suspended in time, for we had no clocks and no calendars.

12 August 1945

I AWAKENED at dawn but dozed off again until the faintly lighted sky had become bright day.

I had spent a restless night in penalty for the walking I did yesterday and this morning felt dull and sluggish. My muscles were sore, and every time I tried to move my stiff joints, I groaned with pain. For the first time since the *pika* I was content to stay in bed.

As I lay there mumbling and stroking my beard, Miss Kado came over and offered to give me a shave.

"Wherever would you find a razor?" I grumbled but, then becoming ashamed of my rudeness and at the same time wishing to be rid of my whiskers, added in a more civil tone, "Please! I would be grateful for a shave."

Miss Kado produced a pair of old scissors and went to work. I endured the onslaught with what grace I could muster and sympathized with the lamb who is shorn. Miss Kado had the worst of the bargain as the scissors were dull and my beard was matted and tangled. The other patients were not a little amused as they heard my cries of "Ouch!" and entreaties to stop, which only drew from Miss Kado the laconic reply: "*Mō sukoshi.* A little more."

An old friend, Captain Fujihara, another native of Okayama, who had trained in the naval school at Iwakuni * and risen to command a battleship, came to see me. Before his ship was sunk he visited us every time he touched port at the Kure naval base.† He regularly informed us of everything he was permitted to tell without betraying military secrets. Often, when I pressed him in that direction, he would simply throw up his hands and laugh. I had great respect for Captain Fujihara and knew him to be a bright, young officer with a brilliant future.

He approached the bedside and said, "Dr. Hachiya, it's a pleasant surprise to find you and your wife alive. What an experience you must have gone through!"

"It's a pleasant surprise to see you," answered my wife. "How did you escape the *pikadon?*"

"I had just gotten off the train at Iwakuni, when I heard the '*don,*' " he answered. "Looking east towards Hiroshima, I saw a great mass of smoke rising like a puffy cloud and guessed that you had been bombed."

Before Captain Fujihara could go on, my wife interrupted: "Ichiro-san, the peaches you brought us from Okayama the day before the *pika* were delicious. We only ate one apiece and were

---

* Iwakuni was a large naval training station and air base on the Inland Sea about 30 miles southwest of Hiroshima.

† Kure is a large naval base on the Inland Sea about 25 miles southeast of Hiroshima. Its navy yard had one of the largest drydocks in the world; e.g. the 73,000-ton battleship *Yamato* was built in this dock.

saving the others for a special treat, but like everything else, they were lost in the fire."

"Where were you when the explosion occurred?" asked Captain Fujihara.

"The doctor was in the *hanareya* resting, and I was standing under a glass window in the kitchen. This is what happened to me," continued my wife, showing him her scars from the flying glass.

Captain Fujihara had stopped to visit us on his way down from Okayama the day before the bombing and had brought us a basket of the peaches for which Okayama Prefecture is famous. He spent the night, and next morning did not even stop to wash his face in his haste to catch an early train to Iwakuni. I remembered the peaches and my mouth watered as I thought about them.

"Loss of the peaches is a small thing," remarked Captain Fujihara. "It is a miracle you survived. After all, the explosion of an atom bomb is a terrible thing."

"An atom bomb!" I shouted, sitting up in bed. "Why that's the bomb I've heard could blow up Saipan, and with no more than ten grams of hydrogen."

"That's true," affirmed Ichiro-san. "I got my information at the naval hospital in Iwakuni where they are studying and treating victims from Hiroshima who seem to have some dreadful disease."

Ichiro-san, not being a doctor, could not tell us much about the disease, but he was sure one symptom was a low white blood count. I thought to myself that Ichiro-san must have been misinformed, but until I learned better, I should listen to him.

I quizzed him at length but learned no more, and I could not shake him from his statement that atom bomb victims in the Iwakuni hospital had low blood counts.

Before he left, he opened his briefcase and presented us with a bottle of whisky and some cigarettes.

"This isn't much," he said apologetically, "but these things are getting hard to find."

After Captain Fujihara left, I determined to get a miscroscope and see if what he said was true. But to find a microscope was another matter. The hospital scopes were useless; the lenses and even the supporting frames were broken.

I remembered that Dr. Morisugi had kept a microscope locked in the hospital safe. When I went to look for it the carrying case was lying on the floor and in the recesses of the safe stood the microscope—broken and useless. I later discovered that all of our counting chambers were broken as well. If I expected to lay hands on a microscope I could use, it would have to come from somewhere else than Hiroshima.

Dr. Sasada was worse. His face, badly swollen, looked like a glazed bun sprinkled with white powder. Blood-stained pus oozed through the dressings on his hands and forearms.

Miss Susukida was the same way, although her hands were not so swollen. Her face resembled a comic mask.

Mr. Shiota, who was admitted during the night, looked like a drowned man who had been too long in the water. His face, trunk, and extremities were swollen and he labored for breath. No one was so badly burned except possibly Miss Yama. Better than half of her body was burned, leaving her like some dirty plaster doll tossed on a trash heap. Her condition could scarcely be better than hopeless.

Miss Omoto's burns were not as extensive as Miss Yama's but they were deep enough to expose muscle.

These people were far worse off than Miss Sasaki or my wife. *Momochan*, as we called Miss Sasaki because her cheeks were pink and downy as a peach, had incurred a head injury but now was almost well. My wife, who received mild burns as well as lacerations, was making a gratifying recovery. Her missing eyebrows gave her a sinister look, and her arm was in a sling, but she insisted that she was *"sukoburu genki"*—"very well."

Dr. Koyama, who had worked unflaggingly as deputy director since the *pikadon*, still wore bandages around his head and arm.

In our ward, those who had been cut were improving, whereas those who were burned seemed to be worse.

I could not get Dr. Sasada off my conscience because if he had not protected me as he did, he would not have been hurt. Nor could I forget that he treated many other patients before the seriousness of his injuries was discovered. Here I was improving while he became worse.

Dr. Sasaki came down from our hospital in Osaka to relieve Dr. Norioka. He, too, was one of the best men on the staff there and proved a fitting replacement for Dr. Norioka. Not only were we indebted to these doctors for their care of the patients, but we could thank them for the medical supplies and the competent assistants they brought with them.

Later, an aunt of mine from Saijo, Mrs. Shima, visited us.

"Why do you stay here?" she asked Yaeko-san and me. "We have ample room in our home, and your uncle insists that you come back with me."

They had heard the explosion in Saijo,* miles across mountainous country from Hiroshima.

"Later," she said, "we were told that Hiroshima had been bombed. That didn't disturb us at first, but when we were told we were to provide shelter for the wounded, and that truck convoys would bring them in, the town was thrown into turmoil."

Mrs. Shima was like a phonograph which shows no signs of running down.

I asked about Eizo-san, her son, and she stopped long enough to answer, "Oh! he came home all right and without a scratch. Late in the night, it was. How he got back and what route he took, I don't know because he didn't stay long enough to say. The next day he went back to Hiroshima. You know Mr. Watanabe, who works in my husband's store, and his son. Well, they got burnt in front of the Hiroshima Station, and bad, too; so bad nothing can be done for them."

Despite her long-windedness, it did me good to see my aunt

---

* Saijo is a town about 20 miles east and slightly north of Hiroshima, well up in the mountainous country characteristic of the greater part of Japan. Saijo is known locally for the excellence of its *sake*, the abundance and flavor of its *matsutake*, a delicious mushroom gathered from pine groves in the early fall, and its festival folk dances commemorating the rice harvest each year. There were many sick and injured who crowded into Saijo after the bombing.

if for no other reason than to know of her offer to take care of Yaeko-san and me. If I could not accept the invitation, I knew where I could send Yaeko-san as soon as she recovered enough to travel.

When things quieted down, my thoughts returned to my conversation with Captain Fujihara. To think that Hiroshima had been hit by an atom bomb. That *was* news! And I passed it on to everyone I saw.

Towards evening, I made rounds downstairs.

The burned patients were about the same as those upstairs. Those who had complained earlier of anorexia, belching, vomiting, diarrhea, and bloody stools were better. In two or three patients, however, gastro-intestinal symptoms had become worse, and the severity or the presence, even, of injury did not seem to be related with the gastro-intestinal symptoms. This was also true for another symptom now becoming apparent in the injured and uninjured alike. Not a few were developing foul, painful, bleeding ulcers in the mouth and throat.

They all had fever, but since there were no thermometers, we could not tell how much. Wounds were healing well, except in patients with compound fractures. These latter showed a tendency to bleed, and amputation of an arm or leg had to be done on several to prevent fatal hemorrhage.

One old woman I saw on rounds annoyed me because she kept asking us to end her life. She had not been injured, was in no pain, and, out of respect for her age, everyone tried to make her comfortable, but her only response was to ask everyone who came near to end her misery.

"Please let me die!" she would say in a dull monotonous voice. "If the Buddha won't come to me, send me to him. Let me visit Buddha. Please let me go to his side!"

Her family had been killed, and she was alone in the world, but others were also bereaved and managed to contain their grief in consideration for others.

In the corridor, I ran into Mr. Kitao who worked in the business office with Mr. Sera. He had a bed upstairs but was gone so much I wondered what kept him so busy. I now found that he ran the hospital crematory, and while we were talking, Mr. Yamazaki appeared to ask if the night's cremation was ready to start.

"Everything is ready," Mr. Kitao answered, and, turning to me, remarked, "Dr. Hachiya, I beg your pardon, but would you care to see how we do the cremations? I've done so many, I'm an expert."

Mr. Kitao's nonchalant manner upset me, but I made no comment and motioned for him to lead the way.

A makeshift crematory was set up about thirty meters beyond the hospital fence, hard by an outside bath and water pump used by the hospital employees.

A patient who died earlier in the day was brought from the morgue by Mr. Kitao and Mr. Yamazaki, using a door for a bier. The body was placed on a pile of broken desks, packing cases, and anything else that would burn, and two nurses arranged the shroud. A large slab of sheet zinc was then laid on top of the corpse and the fire lighted.

As the flames leaped up I unconsciously clasped my hands in prayer. One must excuse the perfunctoriness of this cremation by remembering that so many had died that the ritual normally accorded the dead was an impossible luxury. But even so, the fact there was not a priest to say a prayer for this departed soul disturbed me.

My thoughts were interrupted by a loud voice from the bath-tub.

"How many have you cremated today?"

"Only one!" answered Mr. Kitao.

"Is cremation so commonplace that a man can take his bath next to a funeral pyre and ask a question like that?" I exclaimed aghast.

"Yes, I suppose we have become pretty calloused," replied Mr. Kitao apologetically.

I started to say how rude I thought everyone was but said nothing. My one consoling thought was that patients who died in the Communications Hospital were at least cremated separately.

I had been strongly attached to the patient they were cremating tonight. For years Hiroshima had been an army town, and this poor woman had been the widow of a retired army officer who, like many other service people, was never happy unless he was in earshot of mustering troops, the roll of drums, and the call of bugles. Hiroshima had been a pleasant place for these people, and near our hospital had lived a community of army and government pensioners.

This woman had been loved and respected by her neighbors, and to the soldiers in the Second Corps she was the *baba-san* of Hiroshima. Her meagre pension as well as her savings had been spent to help one soldier or another. Her round, shapeless figure had cast a friendly shadow in the neighborhood and on the wards of our hospital. Many were the times when she and another *baba-san* had brought cheer to the sick and lonely. In a small army of army wives this woman had been "General" by popular acclaim. Even the detention barracks were open to her, and the roughest soldier became as gentle as a child in her presence.

Shortly before she died I recalled stopping at her pallet to comfort her. She could not see me because her eyelids were swollen shut, but she recognized my voice.

"*Baba-san*," I said, "your friends are around you. Hiroshima has been a good place to live in because you have been here to think of others before yourself. Death is approaching, but like an old soldier you can die with dignity in the knowledge that your wounds were received in line of duty."

The old lady died quietly, and now, looking on her dead face, I wondered if the other *baba-san* had been spared to take her place.

I returned to the hospital, but it was useless to think about sleep. I was depressed. This had been a hot day and tonight the air hung close and sultry because the cooling wind which usually blew in from the sea towards evening was missing. In no time my body became moist with sweat. I pitied the man with work to do.

No one else in the ward was inclined to sleep, so conversation there in the dark became general.

"Why were so few people in the streets today?" I asked of no one in particular.

"Probably because today is Sunday," someone answered.

"Sunday!" I exclaimed. "I wouldn't have guessed it. Without a calendar and one day so like another, I am thoroughly confused."

"Because today is Sunday isn't the only reason so few people are about," remarked another voice. "Somebody told me that the people who have been coming into Hiroshima since the *pika* have taken sick. Some have even died!"

"Yes," agreed another, "I heard rumors that a gas is loose in Hiroshima that will kill anyone who breathes it."

Others took up the argument, so I lay silent and listened and thought.

That a poison gas or deadly germ had been loosed in Hiroshima, I had finally dismissed, but these rumors were disturbing. Perhaps a gas bomb had been dropped. I could think of people who had died within two or three days who earlier appeared perfectly well. I recalled persons who died while they nursed the sick. I had heard of people on the outside of a house who died although they had incurred no apparent injury, whereas others inside the house and severely injured, survived. If a poison gas had been used, it should have killed everyone. Whatever killed these people, therefore, could not have been a poison gas. But it was easy to see why rumors were going around. The more I thought, the more confused I became.

I was still in doubt when sleep overcame me.

13 August 1945

ANOTHER HOT, sunny day.

After breakfast I borrowed a bicycle and pedalled to the Prefectural Office. The experience was altogether different from the one I shared with Dr. Hinoi because I was stronger and my wounds no longer hurt so much. To feel well enough again to go about unassisted was a pleasant experience. The electric wires, the power lines, all the other obstructions of day before yesterday, were still present but no longer seemed insurmountable.

I examined a gutted streetcar and discovered with surprise how simple the motor was. Curiosity deserted me though when my eyes fastened on the remains of a blackened body slumped in a corner. Such an unexpected encounter with grim death in broad daylight startled me so that I did not regain my composure until I had put a considerable distance between me and the streetcar.

Since the bomb was said to have exploded near the *torii* of the Gokoku Shrine, I pedalled in that direction and was surprised to find the *torii* still standing. Even the medallion in its center remained, but everything else in the area was either destroyed or badly damaged.

The Aioi Bridge,* whose structural steel arches spanned a wide branch of the Ōta River, was so buckled and sprung that its re-enforced concrete surface had been thrown into waves; it was so

---

* The Aioi or "T" Bridge, which spans the Ōta River near the center of the city, is generally given as the hypocenter for the atom bomb. There is reason to believe that the bomb actually exploded approximately 50 meters southeast of the Aioi Bridge where the Shima Hospital stood, because concrete columns flanking the entrance of this hospital were driven straight into the ground. At any rate, the editor has used the Shima Hospital as the approximate hypocenter whenever reference to radial distance is made in this account.

cracked and shattered that gaping holes exposed the river below. It was a pitiful sight to see how this beautiful bridge had been destroyed.

Below the bridge, on the east bank of the river, had stood the bronze-domed Museum of Science and Industry.* This building, symbolic of the poetic name of Hiroshima—*Mizu no Miyako* (The City or Metropolis of Water)—had been the most beloved structure in Hiroshima. Its bronze dome was gone, its sturdy walls of brick and stone cracked and crumbled, and its interior devoured by fire. For some time, I studied these ruins and they became the symbol and epitome of a destroyed city and its people.

Backtracking, I followed the streetcar line until I reached the Prefectural Office. My reason for going here this morning was to obtain news, so both ears were cocked and ready when I reached my destination.

The staff had increased since day before yesterday, and among the newcomers were many familiar faces. After an exchange of amenities, I asked if I could see Dr. Kitajima and was promptly directed to his office.

After thanking him for his prompt compliance with our request for more doctors and nurses, I started to ask if we could have some more supplies when I saw he was upset.

"Is something the matter?" I asked, fearful that the news I had been so anxious to get might not be welcome news.

"You've no doubt heard that an 'atom bomb' was dropped on Hiroshima?" Dr. Kitajima answered. "Well, I've learned that no one will be able to live in Hiroshima for the next seventy-five years."

"One of our nurses died suddenly, yesterday," I answered, as if to confirm the ominous import of his words.

After I had spoken, I was annoyed at having given credence to what my mind recognized only as an ugly rumor. Yesterday I determined, after my talk with Dr. Fujihara, that I would think

---

* The ruins of this building have been preserved as a monument to the atom bombing of Hiroshima and as such has become a pictorial symbol of atomic destruction.

and act calmly whatever the news, and here I was, the next day, jumping to conclusions without knowing facts.

"What about the war in Manchuria?" I asked, trying to change the subject.

"Things aren't going well," replied Dr. Kitajima. "The enemy is already in Korea."

I left the Prefectural Office depressed and lonely and, nourishing a renewed doubt, returned to the hospital to hide my grief and despair.

What should I do about the patients? What about my staff and their families? Should I tell them to flee because I was over-- burdened with responsibility? After thinking for some time, I concluded that no problem could be settled by flight.

Think how many days have already passed since the *pika*, I said to myself. More than a week, and none but the one nurse on our staff is dead yet. My own wounds are healing, and I feel stronger every day. How preposterous to believe that Hiroshima will be uninhabitable for seventy-five years! Such a statement cannot be true. It is an enemy stratagem aimed to deprave a people already demoralized. To believe such a thing is sheer nonsense because here I am, improving day by day, despite having been so near the center of the *pika*. Mumbling and talking, I gradually reconquered my spirits.

Nothing is so unstable as a man's mind, especially when it is fatigued. Regardless of the direction one's thoughts take, the mind is ever active, ever moving, at times slowly, at times with lightning rapidity. My mind was a confusion of strength and weakness, sometimes fused, sometimes separated.

"If you must die, die like a man," I would tell myself.

Then, I would look myself over and find no part that appeared to be dead.

"So far, so good. You are still alive, so lie down and rest your mind," my stronger nature would argue. If the stronger won, I would become calm until weakness reared its head again.

Someone with a long beard was standing near the door looking around the room. His eyes finally rested on me, and he approached the bed. For a moment this stranger stared with a wry face, and then, closing his eyes, began to mumble in his beard. It was Mr. Kajitani, the postmaster of a small post office in Yamagata County, whom I had visited years ago when he was critically ill. I could not understand him but guessed he was inquiring about my health. When it dawned on me that this kind, warmhearted, sympathetic man had come all the way from his home in Yamagata County to see me, something welled up in my heart.

Conversation was difficult for Mr. Kajitani, and the harder he tried to express his wish to help, the more confused and embarrassed he became. Finally, he thrust his *bentō* into my hand and despite my protests, insisted that I eat it all. A simple lunch never tasted so good. It was a *hinomaru bentō*,* made of cooked rice balls filled with red-coloured, sour plums.

Dr. Horie, from the San-in District northwest of Hiroshima, paid me a visit today and was as surprised as others had been to find how much greater the damage had been than he had been led to believe.

When Dr. Horie left, I went downstairs and found the patients discussing the rumors I had heard at the Prefectural Office, but no one seemed very excited.

"What nonsense!" someone said, "to be told that Hiroshima will be uninhabitable for the next seventy-five years."

Dr. Chodo, the dentist, was worse. He was not able to recognize me, so my feeble words of encouragement made no impression.

I was told that Mrs. Yoshida, who occupied a room on the third floor of the Bureau, had taken a turn for the worse. Using a cane, for I was still quite weak, I went up to her room. Old Mr. Ushio,

---

* *Bentō* refers to a lunch put up in a flat, rectangular box of metal or lacquer and may consist of cooked rice with meat, egg, fish, or pickles. Fancy *bentō* may contain slices of meat or boiled rice and other foods flavored with vinegar, called *sushi*. The traveller may purchase *bentō* put up in disposable thin wooden boxes from vendors on trains or in stations; or hotels and inns may pack them for the convenience of their departing patrons. The *hinomaru* is the flag of Japan, a red sun centered in a square of white. Rice rolls stuffed with red plums are thus called *hinomaru bentō* because of their resemblance to the flag.

head of General Affairs, introduced us, and I learned that she had been injured at her home in the small southeast suburb of Komachi. She had sustained multiple glass wounds to both arms, but no burns. None of her wounds measured longer than five centimeters, and they appeared to be healing. Notwithstanding, she was extremely pale and her face had a mottled, cyanotic, unhealthy appearance. In addition, she had a weak pulse, pain on swallowing, and a persistent, non-bloody diarrhea. Except for slight inflammation, I could detect nothing unusual in her throat or mouth. I was at a loss to understand her condition and answered Mr. Ushio evasively when he asked my opinion.

"There isn't much to worry about now, and her condition isn't bad. But be on the lookout!" I said, more like a fortune teller than a doctor who should know what he is doing. What else could I say?

After I left the room it occurred to me that Mr. Ushio looked sicker than Mrs. Yoshida, and I wondered who would die first. He had certainly aged during the last ten days.

Near the entrance to the Bureau I met an old friend, Mr. Kobata, who despite his age, had been searching for his brother ever since the *pika*. He had an astonishing reserve of energy. We chatted for a while and he related some of his experiences in the city. One story remains vivid in my mind.

"I ran into four middle-school students near the hypocenter in Tenjim-machi who were badly burned," recounted Mr. Kobata. "Desperately ill and forlorn, they sat in a small circle beside the road, and I stopped to ask one where his home was. He replied that this was his home and asked that if I should encounter his mother or sister would I tell them not to waste time looking for him or his companions because they were all going to die. The others nodded in agreement. The lot of these boys was all the more tragic because nothing *could* be done for them, and so there they sat under the hot sun in dust and rubble. Tears came to my eyes.

"One boy asked if I would make some shade for them, and by borrowing a few straw mats and sheets of galvanized iron from some soldiers, I made them a shelter. I asked another boy where his home was, but he was too weak to say anything but 'ya' so I couldn't discover whether he was from Yano, Yagi, or Yaga.

"Some tomatoes I had for my lunch I cut into halves and squeezed the juice into the boys' mouths. They could hardly swallow but all mumbled '*oishii!*'—'delicious!'

"One boy begged for water and as I had no container with me I told him I would try to get some in my hat. This I did, and finally left with the promise I would try to find a first-aid squad to come to their assistance. I had a few pieces of Jintan, and this I divided among them.

"I couldn't find a first-aid squad, search as I might, so all night the thought of those poor boys was on my mind. When I left home the next morning I took some things I thought might add to their comfort, and searched until I found them. I found them all right, but they were dead, huddled in the same small circle I had left them in the night before."

Mr. Kobata had many such stories to tell.

On returning to my bed I found the General Chief of the Western Bureau had come to visit for the second time since I was hurt. He complimented my trim whiskers and remarked that I looked better. He tried to be cheerful and optimistic about the war, but before he left he confessed that Japan's only chance of winning was with thousands of planes and atom bombs. No comment was required. I asked if he could get some medical supplies for us from the Western Army and he promised to do what he could.

During the early evening, most of the talk centered on opinions as to why Hiroshima should not be habitable for seventy-five years. This rumor was given emphasis and a note of credence by the fact that many people who appeared to be healthy and had escaped uninjured were beginning to die with symptoms of vaginal bleeding, nose bleed, bloody sputum, bloody vomitus, and hemorrhages beneath the skin and in the tissues. The most popular explanation was still that some poison gas had been liberated and was still rising from the ruins. My conjecture that deaths were due to the effects of a germ bomb causing dysentery

I had to discard because diarrhea and bloody stools were decreasing. I was forced to fall back on my earlier thesis that the dead and injured had suffered the devastating effects of a sudden change in atmospheric pressure incident to the tremendous blast and intense heat.

There was not a breath of air stirring and my *tatami* was hot and uncomfortable. Like everyone else I was sweating. My head was itchy and my ears felt flushed and hot. Perhaps I had done too much thinking.

"*Atsui ne!*" I sighed. "It is really hot."

"Isn't it?" replied Dr. Sasada, turning towards me.

Mr. Shiota, who lay nearby, voiced his agreement. He had managed to procure some *shōji* * which arranged around his bed afforded a degree of privacy as well as protection from the slanting rays of the setting sun.

"Shiota-san, are you all right now?" I queried.

"Thank you, I'm much better," he replied.

"What are you doing behind that old, torn *shōji?*" I asked.

"Doctor, you are incurable!" he answered, laughing.

Somebody giggled behind the screen. It was Mr. Shiota's wife.

From the kitchen down the corridor I heard laughing voices, and going to investigate, found old Mrs. Saeki and Mr. Mizoguchi. I joined them and we sat talking until late in the night.

* *Shōji:* paper-covered, sliding doors, which are a common feature of Japanese house construction.

14 August 1945

ANOTHER HOT day!

At an early hour, the air-raid alarm sounded, and fearing that some of us may not have heard it a man from the Bureau ran through the wards warning us to take cover.

No one attempted to leave his bed but lay calmly looking out the windows. In every mind must have been the same thought. Could this happen again after what we had been through?

Soon, we could hear the noisy clamor of planes and as the sound became louder, we guessed they were coming in over Hiroshima Bay from the south. I tried to glimpse them from behind a window frame, but someone outside saw me and shouted for me to get down. The sound was deafening.

The ambulatory patients sought shelter, but the ill ones were obliged to remain in their beds. What a helpless feeling to realize we could do nothing for them. I had one consoling thought. I had seen that the staff of the Communications Bureau and their families were hospitalized on the first floor of the communications building.

For a few minutes, I lost my head and hastened to the basement where others were assembled. None of the staff was there and I realized if I stayed with so many lying helpless on the wards, I would set a bad example and disgrace the hospital. If death were to visit this hospital again, my place was on the wards. Regaining composure, I left the basement and told everyone I found to get down there as quickly as possible and carry with them all who could be moved. I then took a station in the middle of the hospital. Those who were left gazed out of the windows and listened to the frightful din of planes as they flew over the city.

My legs began to shake and instinctively I sought the protection of a big pillar. Suddenly, the earth trembled and I heard the frightening sound of bombs exploding and anti-aircraft guns firing. To our relief, however, the din of crashing bombs and answering anti-aircraft came from the west, so it became apparent that the air raid was directed at the naval air corps base at Iwakuni.

The sound lessened and finally died. Calm was restored and there was no one who did not feel grateful that his life had again been spared. For some time I lay quietly in bed, with many thoughts in my mind. How hard for a man to die whose life has once before been miraculously spared. On the day of the *pika* I gave no thought to my life, but today I wanted to live and death became a spectacle of terror.

Later in the morning, Mr. Sasaki, a neighbor whose home had been across the street from ours, paid me a visit, bringing a present of *ayu*.* You can imagine how delighted I was to receive so delectable a gift. The succulence and excellent flavor of these small fish are a gourmet's delight.

Mr. Sasaki was at a friend's home in Yamaguchi, where the Sanitary Department of the Prefectural Office had its headquarters, when the bomb exploded. Luckily, he managed to flee from the house before the roof fell and guided his bicycle through the darkening streets halfway across town before the increasing fires caught up with him. When he reached Hakushima, where our hospital stands, and near where we lived, the fires made further progress impossible. Like others from our neighborhood he fled to the hills of Ushita. When his house collapsed, my wife and I had just reached the street in our flight from our home. Mr. Sasaki's mother was killed but other members of his family, though injured, escaped. If I had not been injured, I might have saved his mother because their house collapsed at my feet.

Mr. Sasaki informed me before he left that an important radio broadcast had been announced for tomorrow. Everyone was urged to listen, so we could guess that an announcement of tremendous importance was in the offing.

* *Ayu* are small, fresh-water trout caught at this time of year in the swift mountain streams by trained cormorants. Not only are the fish delicious, but the birds, dignified, willing, and capable, command admiration and respect.

A dining room had been improvised on the second floor from a storage room previously used by the Pharmacy Department. In one corner there still remained a quantity of bicarbonate of soda blackened and ruined in fifty-kilogram bags. Near the entrance an alcove for cooking had been fashioned and meals were served on desks, benches, and boxes in the center of the room. The ambulatory patients ate here regularly out of dishes salvaged from the ruins. Bed patients were served from improvised trays.

This noon, I lunched with my wife and Miss Kado. All we could talk about were the delicious *ayu* Mr. Sasaki provided. The bed patients had a real treat in store for them.

It had become my custom to take a short rest after lunch and then make ward rounds. My rounds had nothing in common with rounds you see in university hospitals where assistants and nurses laden with paraphernalia trail behind the doctor. I made rounds alone and, clad in old pants and shirt, presented anything but a dignified, professional appearance. My dress was in keeping with my surroundings, and since we were all clothed in the best the city relief agencies could provide, we had no reason to complain.

My rounds were hardly professional in the strict sense of the word because there was little I could do other than cheer this patient, encourage another, or make a little joke with a third.

Mrs. Yoshida I visited first, as usual. After bowing I took her pulse. Yesterday she had responded to my bow, but today, she was unable to answer. Since it is customary for a patient to acknowledge a doctor's entrance with a small bow or nod of the head or to return a greeting initiated by the doctor, the fact that Mrs. Yoshida failed to greet me was a bad sign. She was worse this morning, and her face had an ashen, blue color.

Downstairs, I visited the other patients. About fifty or sixty members of the Communications Bureau staff and their families were quartered together, and since we knew each other well, I felt as though they were members of my family. Their sleeping mats were arranged on *tatami* placed in groups of two, four, or six. Fortunately, most of them had minor wounds and were thus able to nurse those who were critically ill. The beautiful young girl whom I spoke of earlier lay on a *tatami* separate from the others. Although her condition was critical, she smiled for me and expressed a courage and optimism lacking in people far less badly hurt than herself. Her burns were not caused by the *pika* but by fire as she tried to rescue members of her family from their burning house. She still lay in a puddle of old blood and pus, and her legs and flanks were soiled with urine and feces. Before leaving, I persuaded someone to take over her care and make her as clean and comfortable as possible.

I next saw to the change of bandages on burned patients who were unable to care for themselves. This tedious and painful task required over an hour. The lack of skilled help during the early days after the bombing prompted us to place a crock filled with Remaon's solution * near the entrance of the hospital, and notices were posted instructing patients to soak their dressings in the solution before covering their wounds. This practice was instituted on the day after the bombing and at any hour people could be found lined up waiting their turn to obtain some of the solution. One *koku*, a measure of about 180 liters, was prepared each day. The patients and their attendants became diligent in changing dressings each day because they learned if this were not done the dressings would become crusted and painful and cause bleeding when removed. Today, there was a large gathering around the crock: some standing, others reclining, and a few in grotesque postures as the result of painful reflex contractions. The seriously burned patients were dressed by the professional staff.

Leaving the annex, I returned to the hospital. The old woman was still sitting in the corridor watching and waiting for someone to come.

"*Sensei-san*,† no one has come for me," she declared in a sad voice. "Please, sir, when can I go?"

---

* Remaon's solution is a trade name for acrinol, a mild germicidal solution similar to acriflavine.

† *Sensei* as used here means "doctor" or "physician." It also means "professor." An elder statesman, sage, or the respected town or village father is addressed as *sensei*.

"Old lady, try to be patient," I remonstrated as gently as I could. "We must not forsake life because we are ill."

It was easier to walk the corridors today because the number of patients had decreased, but too many were still quartered in the toilets or beneath the stair wells. Some arrangements would have to be made to transfer these patients to the second floor.

After rounds, I left the hospital with the intention of procuring a toilet bowl I had espied on one of my jaunts. While looking for it, I discovered a quantity of china and tableware in the burned-out kitchen of the house where I had seen the toilet. I found two good rice bowls and a hatchet without its handle. These I carried back to the hospital and presented to Mrs. Saeki.

"*Baba-san,* I made a find a little while ago. There is a quantity of china in the ruined houses hereabouts, so why don't you get someone to collect for you? Your kitchen and dining-room could stand some additions."

I went out again and in my excitement to find more dishes forgot about the toilet. Digging in the ashes, I discovered many bits and pieces of what had once been precious vases, cups for formal tea ceremony, and other extravagant items, but none that were sound or capable of repair. Wearying finally, I gave up my search for art treasures and consoled myself with the thought that treasures are never found by looking—only by accident.

My roommates were busily discussing Mr. Sasaki's announcement of the important broadcast to be made tomorrow, and each tried to guess what the news would be. I refused to enter the discussion because I felt there was enough to worry about without trying to anticipate the future. Besides, we had no radio. To me, this was something of a blessing, for being without some of the so-called advantages of civilization gave me a freedom of spirit and action others could not enjoy with their telephones, radios, and newspapers. Having lost everything in the fire and being now empty-handed was not entirely without advantage. I experienced a certain light-heartedness I had not known for a long time.

Towards night, I saw Mr. Mizoguchi disappear into the dining room with a lighted candle. Following him, I found old Mrs. Saeki already there. In this small room, dimly lighted by the flickering flame of the candle, we enjoyed a coziness and feeling of camaraderie impossible in the big open ward. Conversation, as usual, turned to the *pika*, and since Mr. Mizoguchi was disposed to talk, we listened.

"*Baba-san*, the wind changed directions while I was in the Bureau garden, and balls of fire began coming towards me. Frightened, I ran out through the back gate and with some girls barely managed to reach the bank of the Ōta River. I never saw so many people. One could hardly move for the crowd. Nearly everyone was badly burned and the spectacle they made was horrible. I felt the sorriest for the women who were completely naked." He turned to me. "You were naked, too, Dr. Hachiya. You can sympathize with them. It is my opinion that their dresses must have been torn off when they crawled from under the fallen houses."

While he talked, old Mrs. Saeki sat blinking her eyes, and now and then emphasizing a nod of her head with "*ah sō*" or "*ahano*."

"Doctor, what were you doing at that time?" Mr. Mizoguchi asked me.

"Yes, doctor, what were you doing?" echoed old Mrs. Saeki.

"I was at home," I replied, "and I believe I had on my underwear. But when I escaped from my house, I didn't have a stitch on. Even my *fundoshi* was gone. I was on duty at my air-raid post from the evening before until 4:00 in the morning and after leaving my post I went home to try to rest. For some reason I couldn't sleep, so I was lolling about absent-mindedly in the *hanare*. You recall an air-raid alarm was sounded that morning and I was getting ready to put on my air-raid clothes when the alarm was called off."

Before I could go on, Mr. Mizoguchi interrupted: "*Baba-san*, there was something peculiar about one's experience with clothing after the bombing. Just consider for a moment Miss Omoto's arms. Her clothes were light except for some black patching on her sleeves and that's the only place she was burned. If her dress had been completely white she wouldn't have been burned at all.

Doctor, colored things are no good, are they? I am told they will catch on fire right away!"

"Mr. Mizoguchi," I replied, "did you hear what Dr. Hinoi had to say? An instant after the *pika*, he saw a soldier running whose clothing was in a light blaze. Dr. Sasada's hands were badly burned and he remembers them catching on fire. He remembered nothing else though; perhaps that minor point may have something to do with why his burns are so bad."

"Probably so," sighed Mr. Mizoguchi.

Old Mrs. Saeki stroked her face with both hands and muttered: "Terrible! Terrible!"

She poured some tea and we sat a while, smoking. After a while Mr. Mizoguchi, whom we all admire as a storyteller, went on with his narrative.

"And so, *baba-san*, the fire extended right down to the river and before long flames were leaping all about us. We had no means of crossing the river and so there we huddled under the bank until that young girl from Seno who worked in the Bureau had the presence of mind to shout to us to swim for it. She jumped into the river and we followed her.

"There was little reason for our having tried to cross the river because flying embers, carried by high winds, set fire to houses on the opposite bank and we were caught between two walls of fire. Fortunately, the water was shallow near the opposite shore so we were able to lie on the bottom and splash water over our heads and so escape the searing heat. Really, *baba-san*, I was never so scared in my life."

Old Mrs. Saeki nodded and from time to time punctuated his remarks with such expressions as "*geni*" or "*makoto-ni*."

I simply listened.

"Hundreds of people sought refuge in the Asano Sentei Park. They had refuge from the approaching flames for a little while, but gradually, the fire forced them nearer and nearer the river, until at length everyone was crowded onto the steep bank overlooking the river.

"Standing waist-deep in water on the opposite shore was a half-naked officer brandishing his sword and shouting in threatening tones to the people crouching on the opposite bank of the river.

" 'Don't try to cross the river!' the officer shouted. 'If anyone tries, I shall kill him with this sword!'

"For a moment I thought the officer had lost his mind, but then I realized he was trying to save these people and was wise as well as brave. Doctor, you know very well the river at that point is deep and the current swift. Every year many people drown who try to cross there. It is my belief that the officer was trying to prevent the people from jumping into the river at that treacherous point.

"Even though the river is more than one hundred meters wide along the border of the park, balls of fire were being carried through the air from the opposite shore and soon the pine trees in the park were afire. The poor people faced a fiery death if they stayed in the park and a watery grave if they jumped in the river. I could hear shouting and crying, and in a few minutes they began to fall like toppling dominoes into the river. Hundreds upon hundreds jumped or were pushed in the river at this deep, treacherous point and most were drowned. The sight was unbelievable. For myself, I lay there in the river and splashed water over my head when the heat from the licking flames became unbearable."

Mr. Mizoguchi's narrative upset old Mrs. Saeki, and I was afraid he would stop in deference to her feelings.

"What happened next?" I asked, so anxious was I to hear all I could from Mr. Mizoguchi.

"Dousing ourselves with water now and then, we slithered along in the shallow water until we reached the relative security of the Tokiwa Bridge.* As we made our way, I encountered one poor man lying in the water who was so weak, probably from loss of blood, that he was unable to keep himself wet down. He begged me to douse him with water, and I stopped long enough to dig a

* The Tokiwa Bridge crosses the Kyōbashi branch of the Ōta River 150 meters east of the Communications Hospital.

hole and cover him with wet sand. I have no doubt though that when the tide came in he drowned like thousands of others.

"When the fires abated, I made my way back to the hospital in company with two girls I ran into from my native village. Meeting them was a stroke of fortune because I had already sent my wife and family to my native home. When Mr. Kitao later took the girls home, he visited my folks and told them I was all right. Since then, my wife has visited me and tells me that our little village, Seno,* is crowded with sick and injured."

I gave Mr. Mizoguchi a cigarette and after a few puffs he asked me where I got them.

"A naval officer brought them to me," I replied.

"Doctor," commented old Mrs. Saeki, "you are indeed fortunate. Someone brings you cigarettes. Today, Mr. Sasaki brought fish, and this evening Mr. Nagao brought you tomatoes. You may not have anything, but you have nothing to worry about. You are a fortunate man and for your many friends you should be thankful. If you weren't, it would be a sin against heaven."

"*Baba-san*, you have a boil on your face," remarked Mr. Mizoguchi, sensing my embarrassment.

"It's only a little boil, but it's so hot I'm hardly aware of it," replied old Mrs. Saeki, scratching.

"As for me," she went on, not wishing to be left out, "I was cleaning the sewer in front of the hospital. A white light burst before my eyes and I got down flat on the ground. The next moment it became so dark I thought the hospital had collapsed on me, so I tried to make myself as little as possible. After a bit, I peeped out through my fingers and found I could still see, and you don't know how glad I was to find I was still alive. That's one time I thought I had died. Yes, indeed!" she exclaimed, a happy ring to her voice.

---

* Seno is southeast of Hiroshima on the road to Kure.

15 August 1945

THIS WAS the day for the broadcast.

Despite my resolve to avoid speculation or conjecture I succumbed to a personal debate and finally concluded that the broadcast would announce an enemy invasion on our shores. General headquarters would order us to fight to the bitter end. What a hopeless situation.

I could escape to the hills, but what route should I take? To follow the Sanyō Line * would be dangerous. The safest bet would be to follow the Hamada or Geibi Line into the Chūgoku Mountains. I had friends in many of the little mountain towns: Miyoshi, Shobara, Seijo, Tojo, Uji, Yoshii. It would be best, perhaps, to go to Uji where my son had been evacuated or to Yoshii where my mother was living, but what difference did it make? More than once I had heard Dr. Akiyama, my old friend who participated in the Shansii operation, say that the side which escaped to the mountains lost the war.

The army had been losing the war since April. Many soldiers had no guns and morale was bad. Only children and old people were permitted to leave the cities, and among those who remained all under forty were assigned to the civil defense corps. In case of emergency we would all be drafted. Our comments and actions

* The island of Honshu, the principal island of Japan, extends for the most part east and west. Its southern shore which borders the Inland Sea is warmed in the winter by the long rays of the southern sun and the currents and southerly breezes from the Japan current, while its northern shore, separated by a mountain range from the sun and warmth of the south, is exposed to the cold north winds that sweep down across Siberia, Manchuria, and the Japan Sea. In the old days, the road skirting the southern shore was called the *sanyō-dō* or the "road of sunshine and warmth," while the road along the northern shore was called the *sanin-dō* or "the road of shadow and cold." The names and the roads persist.

were watched by the military police and during recent months their domination had become more and more oppressive. In areas designated as fire lanes or escape channels the houses had been ruthlessly destroyed.

Everything had gone wrong, and now, an enemy was to land in Japan. The mere thought made me feel sick.

Hiroshima was destroyed, and here we were working our hearts out to sustain life in the ruins. We had no army barracks and no army. The army had escaped and deserted us. Even the few soldiers left to police the area deserted their posts every time an air-raid alarm sounded. Many hid behind the hospital.

Even before the *pika*, the arsenal and most of the barracks were empty. As early as April the officers' families had been evacuated, but after April civilian evacuation was prohibited. My petition was certainly denied.

Whether or not the army had barracks and fortifications built in the mountains, one thing was certain; we were deserted and undefended. Things I should not think about kept crowding into my mind.

Word came to assemble in the office of the Communications Bureau. A radio had been set up and when I arrived the room was already crowded. I leaned against the entrance and waited. In a few minutes, the radio began to hum and crackle with noisy static. One could hear an indistinct voice which only now and then came through clearly. I caught only one phrase which sounded something like, "Bear the unbearable." The static ceased and the broadcast was at an end.

Chief Okamoto, who had been standing by the radio, turned to us and said: "The broadcast was in the Emperor's own voice, and he has just said that we've lost the war. Until further notice, I want you to go about your duties."

I had been prepared for the broadcast to tell us to dig in and fight to the end, but this unexpected message left me stunned. It had been the Emperor's voice and he had read the Imperial Proclamation of Surrender! My psychic apparatus stopped working, and my tear glands stopped, too. Like others in the room, I had come to attention at the mention of the Emperor's voice, and for a while we all remained silent and at attention. Darkness clouded my eyes, my teeth chattered, and I felt cold sweat running down my back.

After a bit, I went quietly back to the hospital and got into my bed. Over and over the words "a lost battle!" rang in my ears.

The ward was quiet and silence reigned for a long time. Finally, the silence was broken by the sound of weeping. I looked around. There was no look of gallantry here, but rather, the faces of all showed expressions of despair and desperation.

By degrees people began to whisper and then to talk in low voices until, out of the blue sky, someone shouted: "How can we lose the war!"

Following this outburst, expressions of anger were unleashed.

"Only a coward would back out now!"

"There is a limit to deceiving us!"

"I would rather die than be defeated!"

"What have we been suffering for?"

"Those who died can't go to heaven in peace now!"

The hospital suddenly turned into an uproar, and there was nothing one could do. Many who had been strong advocates of peace and others who had lost their taste for war following the *pika* were now shouting for the war to continue. Now that surrender was an accomplished fact, irrefutable and final, there was no soothing the people who had heard the news. With everything lost and no fear of losing more they became desperate. I began to feel the same way—fight to the bloody end and die. Why try to live with a scarred body? Would it not be better to die for one's country and crown life with perfection rather than live in shame and disgrace?

The one word—surrender—had produced a greater shock than the bombing of our city. The more I thought, the more wretched and miserable I became.

But the order to surrender was the Emperor's order and to this we could not object. His injunction to bear the unbearable could mean but one thing. As a nation we must be patient. I repeated his words again and again to myself, but no matter how hard I tried, I could not rid my mind of despair. Finally, I found myself thinking of something else.

When war was declared four years ago, no one was unhappy about the consequences, but no one then had thought of this day. Why had the Emperor not been requested to speak then? He was not requested because Tojo was the only actor on the stage and did what he pleased. I can still hear his high-pitched voice ringing in my ears.

To myself, I began denouncing the army: "What do you fellows think about the Emperor? You started the war at your pleasure. When the outlook was good, you behaved with importance; but when you began to lose, you tried to conceal your losses, and when you could move no more, you turned to the Emperor! Can you people call yourselves soldiers? You have no choice but to commit *harakiri* and die!"

As if echoing my thoughts, someone shouted: "General Tojo, you great, thick-headed fool; cut your stomach and die!"

Goaded by the tumult in my mind and the general excitement, I thought I must flee and had reached the back gate of the Bureau when I was stopped by a voice that exclaimed: "Doctor, what's the matter?"

This question brought me to my senses and I became ashamed that I had been on the verge of fleeing. I returned to the Bureau and my patients.

My rounds were not professional today. I could not focus mentally on the patients' problems, but I went to each bed and did what I could to calm their fears.

"Things don't look good, but the Emperor has so ordered," I repeated to everyone I saw.

The nurses were going about duties as if nothing had happened. These innocent figures working calmly seemed to achieve an air of greatness and their presence did much to calm my feelings.

I missed the old lady who had lain near the hospital entrance, so I went to the business office and asked Mr. Sera and Mr. Kitao where she was. After a pause one of them said: "She died last night. *Ba-san* died without knowing about the surrender and we are glad she did."

In the corridor, a soldier stopped to ask: "Doctor, what shall we do?"

"I don't know where your headquarters are," I answered, "but you may stay here until you are recovered. Don't worry; leave the responsibility to me."

"When will *they* land?" he asked.

"It won't matter if they do," I rejoined. "You are a patient. Leave me to explain the situation. If the need arises, I might even help you escape, but for goodness sake don't be upset. You might relay the message to the other soldiers."

"Sir, I will relay your orders!" replied the soldier, a look of relief on his face. Saluting smartly, he withdrew, dragging his blood-soaked trousers.

Supper was served, but having no appetite, I drank a cup of hot water and went to bed. What little spirit I had declined with the setting sun. Everyone on the ward was worrying about the Emperor and I, too, had a feeling of sorrow when I thought of him. Slipping out of bed, I went up to the balcony and, bowing toward the east, prayed for his peace of mind.

I walked about for a while and then sat down on a ventilator where I could gaze out over the ruins. The night was lonely with the *obi*-like * Ōta River glittering faintly as it made its tortuous way through the dark city. The pitch-black outlines of Futabayama stood out against the dark eastern sky. Even in a nation defeated, the rivers and mountains remained the same. I became overwhelmingly lonely as I experienced the emotions of defeat and thought of the future before us.

* An *obi* is a long, wide sash worn around the waist.

16 August 1945

THE DAY began bright and clear.

Our ward had a restless night. The desire and will to go on were submerged by the sorrow and sadness of defeat. We wondered when the enemy would come. All were uneasy.

During the night the "Double Zero" air force detachment from Hiro * distributed hand bills which read: "Continue the war!" "Don't surrender!"

As these tokens of resistance were brought in, news came that the Imperial Fleet was attacking in the waters of Shikoku. There were some who considered this good news, but I feared it to be an attempt by some of the younger officers to show an act of bravado to satisfy a grudge. Some patients shouted with joy, but I felt sorrow for those who chose death to surrender.

The hospital was divided into two groups, one which confirmed the surrender and the other which denied it.

This morning we had a visit from one of Dr. Sasada's classmates who worked with the broadcasting station in Tokyo before the surrender. He informed us that negotiations leading to surrender had been under way since August 10 and that he left Tokyo with the express purpose of changing his currency into material assets for fear it would be frozen and devalued as in Germany.

I did not have to worry on that score because I had lost everything. Except for my sorrow over defeat, that was one reason I could live so free from worry and enjoy the generosity and bounty of my friends. Before the bombing, there had been some compensation in my position which others in the profession could

---

* A naval air training station, supply and fuel dump, and plane assembly plant were located at Hiro, a suburb of Kure, about 25 miles south of Hiroshima.

not share. Employed by the government on a meager salary, I did not have to worry about living expense. Nor was there the mad incentive to struggle for gain because I knew what my salary was and could expect a check each month.

Had I been a businessman or a practicing physician in the community, I would have been more impressed with his story. All things considered, as a government employee, I had much to be grateful for.

I was busy part of the morning trying to tighten up on the records of patients still in the hospital. It had been impossible to think of records earlier because everyone had all he could do to take care of the urgent demands of patients. I mentioned the overwhelming burden of work Dr. Koyama and the staff performed to save the hospital, without thought for themselves and little rest. At my request, Dr. Katsube took the responsibility for recording as precisely as possible all objective and subjective findings. Dr. Hanaoka and Dr. Akiyama assisted him. We had no microscope, no laboratory reagents, and no laboratory, but what history and clinical findings we could record might someday be important. Nowhere before in the history of the world had a people been subjected to the devastating effects of an atomic bomb.

Mrs. Yoshida became so much worse that I was called to see her before regular rounds. Her condition was indeed critical. The inside of her mouth was swollen and ulcerated and her tonsils severely inflamed. Her wounds, which appeared to be healing earlier, had reopened and become crusted with dirty blood clots. Her body was covered with pinpoint subcutaneous hemorrhages. The paleness and blueness of her face had increased, if that were possible, and her pulse was barely perceptible. There was no question but that she was hopelessly ill.

Mr. Mizoguchi and Dr. Hinoi went out with a cart early today to gather food, and when old Mrs. Saeki, Miss Kado, my wife, and I gathered for supper they still had not returned. I was apprehensive for their safety, and old Mrs. Saeki tried to reassure me.

"They will soon be back," she remarked, blinking.

Sitting there in the dark, I was told that a disturbance had occurred at the Hiroshima station yesterday following the surrender. It seems that the station master and all his staff had worked diligently to keep the military supplies moving as quickly as possible. But after the surrender, the station master and everyone in the place, after pilfering a quantity of bottled *sake*, got riotously drunk. Knowing the station master for a jolly old man, I could imagine the disturbance he made. Carousals like this must be occurring all over Japan.

Miss Kado and my wife returned to the ward. I lingered in the dining room while *baba-san* washed the dishes. It is easy to be cheerful during the day when there is light and people are about, but when night falls, and darkness closes about you, gloomy thoughts are hard to avoid. What turmoil there must be in Tokyo. Soldiers fighting among themselves, without law or order, plundering and pillaging. Officers and soldiers who could not stand to think of surrender were committing *harakiri*. What must the Emperor think of this?

My thoughts seemed to be echoed by old Mrs. Saeki because she stopped her washing and, with a finger touching her one remaining tooth, commented reflectively: "Doctor, I'm sorry for the Emperor. He didn't start the war."

I agreed and found myself hating the military authorities with whom I had been in sympathy. They had betrayed the Emperor and the people of Japan. Even here in Hiroshima they had tried to conceal the fact that we had been devastated by an atom bomb. And when they knew we were losing the war, they ignored us when they should have kept us informed.

Mr. Mizoguchi returned late in the evening, sad and discouraged. He told us that riot and disorder were rampant in the city.

17 August 1945

ANOTHER clear day.

I slept poorly last night. I worried about the Emperor and confess that his welfare loomed larger in my mind than the spectacle of defeat. He had been victimized by the military clique who, in defeat, were prepared to thrust the entire responsibility on his shoulders. Insidiously, and by degrees, the military group, professing allegiance to the Emperor, had come to dominate the entire nation.

The name of the Emperor was invoked as a national allegiance and a means for deriving power long before an unsuspecting people could see the results. An officer class developed that was dedicated to reckless bravado and swagger. Even the cadets in the military schools were taught to believe that they were superior and in a class apart. Spuriously infected with a sense of power and an inflated pride, they trampled rough-shod over everyone beneath them. Young cadets, just out of school, never addressed a common soldier but by the inferior title of: "You," or "You there!"; and the dignity of a man as an individual was disregarded.

If a common soldier tried to think for himself, his officer would, likely as not, go into a rage and not infrequently subject him to physical violence. If objection were made, officers as low as the cadet level would arrogantly reply: "My orders are the Emperor's orders! Always keep that in mind."

Thus, the military man had his way whether he was right or not. The higher officers became godlike in their power. Under such a regime, those who bragged, boasted, and threatened the most reached the top, and from such material came the brains of the general staff. Common sense and discretion were unknown. Like wild boars they charged in all directions, ignorant of reality, until their uncontrolled energies were exhausted. Even then they would not give in or listen to reason for fear of losing authority and their fearfully-held reputations.

Under such a yoke the common soldiers and the people suffered most and with them the Emperor. Otherwise, why should the Emperor have been obliged to announce the surrender and take responsibility for what the military group had sponsored?

I made rounds early this morning. Mrs. Yoshida was still alive but weaker. When Mr. Ushio asked me what I thought, I did not have the courage to tell him and I left the room with the feeling I was running away from a friend.

To our delighted surprise, Dr. Hiroshi Moriya, an old classmate of mine on the staff of the Tokyo Communications Hospital, came in with a generous shipment of relief supplies. He was president of our class in primary school nearly thirty years ago when I last saw him.

"What a treat to see you!" he exclaimed. "In Tokyo, we didn't know whether you were dead or alive. The only news we had was that Hiroshima was completely destroyed. Dr. Hasegawa and Dr. Miki were worried for your safety and will be happy to know you are alive. I brought some medical supplies," whereupon he opened one of the bundles which contained forceps, scissors, and rubber goods.

He even had his camera and after learning about my wounds asked if he could take a picture of me standing beside my bed.

"Moriya-san, if the military police find you taking pictures in Hiroshima, you may get into trouble," I warned, but this did not frighten Dr. Moriya.

After he had taken my picture, minus shirt and pants, he took a number of shots from the windows and, as a favor to me, pictures of our staff. He then went out to look over the city.

I learned from Dr. Moriya that things in Tokyo had calmed down. Furthermore, he informed me the Emperor had made the surrender broadcast of his own accord and for the reason that he did not want the nation to suffer any more. This news moved me deeply and was entirely contrary to my original supposition.

A number of visitors came during the afternoon, but whether they brought news or rumor I could not tell. One told me the war minister was chased by some young officers and finally hid in a toilet in the Imperial Palace where he committed *harakiri*. Another informed me the Imperial Counsel was called to discuss terms of surrender and the war minister tried to get the Emperor to retract the proclamation of surrender, the Emperor refusing on grounds that he was concerned more about the nation than himself or the army.

I made rounds again in the late afternoon and discovered that one in every five or six patients had developed petechiae * like the ones observed on Mrs. Yoshida. In some patients these subcutaneous hemorrhages were large and in others small. Patients with small subcutaneous hemorrhages had not recognized them, but those who had large ones asked me what they were.

I soon discovered the tendency to subcutaneous hemorrhage was greatest in those who had been near the center of the explosion and that many who appeared to be uninjured were now showing petechiae. Since the spots were neither itchy nor painful, I was at a loss to explain their presence.

I told Dr. Sasada and Mr. Shiota about my findings after I returned to bed, and they suggested I have a look at myself. Much to my relief my skin was clear.

I learned at supper that a contingent of girl students from the country was coming to help us tomorrow. Other assistance was promised by aid squads organized in adjoining prefectures. I also learned that people were flocking to Hiroshima to loot and scavenge.

* Petechiae are pinpoint subcutaneous hemorrhages that show on the skin like flyspecks on a white wall. They are caused by hemorrhage or bleeding from small blood vessels in the skin.

18 August 1945

THE DAY began clear, but clouds soon gathered and we had a much needed shower.

I began my rounds early. The number of deaths had decreased significantly, but each day one or two patients died and in each instance petechiae developed before death.

The number of patients with petechiae was increasing. In Mrs. Yoshida's case, they were more numerous than yesterday, and the look of death was on her face. Her wounds were no longer wet and bloody, but dry and crusted. I told Mr. Ushio that I did not think she would live until night.

The out-patients were developing petechiae, and today, another symptom became apparent. Many patients were beginning to lose their hair. These people had a bad color and it occurred to me that if we had a microscope, a blood examination might cast some light on the cause for their appearance.

I found Dr. Sasada minutely examining his chest when I went back to bed. When he saw me, he covered himself up as though he did not want me to know what he was doing. I made no comment because I did not wish to embarrass him or intrude on his privacy, although I knew, without his saying a word, that he had petechiae and wished to keep the fact from me. But there was no mistaking the worried look on his face. Thinking it best to leave him undisturbed, I made a pretense of fetching something from my bed and left the ward.

Downstairs, I ran into Mr. Hirohata sitting on a bench and sat down beside him. Mr. Hirohata had been employed in the Telephone Bureau and was at work in the building when the explosion occurred. Despite the fact that he was less than four hundred meters from the hypocenter, Mr. Hirohata escaped injury.

"How did you avoid injury when nearly everyone around you was killed or hurt?" I asked.

"The thick concrete wall of the building protected me," answered Mr. Hirohata, "but people standing near the windows were killed instantly or died later from burns or cuts. The night shift was just leaving and the day shift coming on when the explosion occurred. Forty or more were killed near the entrance. About fifteen employees in the construction department, stripped to the waist, were outside taking gymnastics. They died instantly.

"Doctor, a human being who has been roasted becomes quite small, doesn't he? Those people all looked like little boys after the explosion. Is there any reason why my hair should be falling out and I feel so weak? I'm worried, doctor, because I have been told that I would die and this has already happened to some people I know who didn't seem to be hurt at all by the *pika*."

"Mr. Hirohata, I don't believe you need worry about yourself," I answered, trying to be reassuring. "Like so many others, you've been through a dreadful experience, and on top of that have tried to work night and day here at the Bureau. What else could one expect? You must go home, stay absolutely quiet in bed, and get all the good nourishing food you can."

There was something about this poor old man, the way he sat, his manner of speech, and color of his skin, that told me he was going to die. But what could one do?

The girl students came to help this morning and under the supervision of the nurses thoroughly cleaned the wards. Everything became neat and tidy.

Outside, a gentle rain was falling.

Our beds were moved to a new room this morning, so the big ward could be used for downstairs patients. The room we moved into was smaller, but quite serviceable. Five beds were placed in a row next to the windows and three beds along the wall adjacent to the corridor. Dr. Sasada's bed was placed near the wall so that he would not be in a draft. His wounds were still painful and hurt more if he were in a draft. My bed was placed opposite Dr. Sasada's where I could get a good breeze. Yaeko-san had the bed next to me and Miss Kado the one beyond her. The bed between Miss Kado and Dr. Sasada was reserved for the doctor on duty, although during the day, his bed was used as a seat for visitors. Mr. Shiota, Miss Yama, and Miss Susukida occupied the beds along the corridor. Our new room had two entrances, and a broken-down chair and desk were placed beside the entrance nearest me to serve as office and reception room. The whole arrangement was quite cozy. Being closer together gave us a feeling of intimacy and security.

The view from the windows was an east-southeasterly one, a change in bearing of ninety degrees from the former room. I could see the Hiroshima station * and on beyond the Kaita station, the third stop from Hiroshima on the road to Kure. Seno and Hachihonmatsu could be seen in the hazy distance. The mountains along the Sanyō Line were visible, and by looking at the hills I could picture the villages nestled at their bases. The sky and the hazy outline of the mountains made me think of the mountain village near Okayama where my mother and son were living.

With everything in the foreground destroyed the railway tracks were clearly visible as they wound around the northeast edge of the city. While I looked out the window, a train came along and stopped. Never have I seen a train so overcrowded, although "overcrowded" is hardly adequate to describe the situation. People hung on in clusters like swarming bees or like a tree overburdened with fruit. Even the coal tender was overrun.

The moment the train stopped, some on the inside began urinating from the windows and others got off to urinate along the right of way. While I was watching this dismal spectacle, grateful I did not have to endure such crowding, the engine whistle gave two sharp blasts and the train began to move again. Not a few were left behind, but to be left seemed to make no difference. They continued their way on foot, slowly and painfully. How humble human beings become after they are defeated in war.

* Hiroshima station, about 1000 meters southeast of the Communications Hospital, was 2000 meters from the hypocenter. The massive brick and reinforced concrete structure was badly damaged by blast and fire.

Trains were daily becoming more crowded, if that were possible. Even the freight trains swarmed with human cargo.

My new window was over the hospital entrance, so I could see everyone who came or went without leaving my bed. One woman, about thirty, came to the entrance and cried out a bitter denunciation of her husband and the Communications Bureau. Her husband was apparently employed by the Bureau and she was complaining that his salary was so small she could not get enough to eat. The poor thing must have suffered in silence during the war and, now that defeat had come, was giving voice to all her pent up emotions. It sounded as though she had lost her mind.

The good news came that Mr. Okura's wife was alive! When the blast occurred, Mr. Okura and his wife were pinned beneath their house. He managed to extricate himself and heard Mrs. Okura crying for help, but before he could reach her the house became a blazing inferno, and he was forced to abandon his efforts to save her. When the fire subsided, Mr. Okura returned to the ruins of his house and found some charred bones near where he had last heard his wife's voice. Mr. Okura, believing these bones to be those of his wife, brought them back and laid them before the hospital altar.

The other day Mr. Okura took the bones to his wife's family home in the country where he found his wife, safe and unharmed. She had somehow escaped the burning house and was picked up and carried to safety by a passing army truck.

This story was unbelievable, but it made me realize we should never give up hope.

Towards evening, I made rounds again, and found that the patients with petechiae were not doing well. Everyone had begun to examine one another for these ominous spots until it seemed we were suffering a "spot phobia." I, too, became afraid. When I got back to my bed, I examined every inch of my body and you can imagine the relief I felt when I found no petechiae. So far, I was all right.

19 August 1945

GENERALLY clear with occasional clouds and the sound of thunder in the distance.

The railway tracks were no more than one hundred meters from the hospital and each time I heard a train, I sat up in bed and looked out. Trains passed in both directions crowded with demobilized soldiers and made the reality of defeat more emphatic.

Here at the Bureau, the soldiers who had been around the hospital in numbers were gone. The urge to move, to go home, became infectious so that even civilian patients, many of whom were barely able to move, left the hospital. Many fled to escape the unseen figure of the enemy.

Mr. Shiota was in high spirits, and I knew why. For days he had been constipated and today, his bowels moved.

I had told him he was too anxious and that his bowels would not move for that reason. Every day, I lectured him on the technique of defecation. He and the people around laughed when I talked, but if he had listened to me, he would not have had his trouble.

Feces will never come out if you are impatient. It will only come if you relax. The more impatient you are, the more it becomes stuck. Patience is, therefore, of the utmost importance. You should try to defecate only when you have the urge for a movement. Moreover, you should strain down as long as the urge is present and when peristalsis stops, you should relax and wait until peristalsis again occurs. Force must be combined with peristalsis and the trick is to join the two naturally. Today, Mr. Shiota obeyed my instructions, and he had a big bowel movement.

"*Mā, mā!*" he exclaimed, returning to the ward with a big smile on his face which was as brown as fried bean curd. "I feel better," he told me. "Doctor, I owe it to you and I thank you."

His wife smiled indulgently while she wiped his sweating brow.

Miss Yama, extensively burned, was entirely covered with bandages. She scolded every time her sister, a nurse, changed the bandages. I could appreciate her feelings, but after a while I felt sorrier for her sister than for Miss Yama.

Mrs. Susukida on the other hand, although not so extensively burned, gritted her teeth and kept quiet while her dressings were changed. She was in no way as perverse as Miss Yama even though her burns caused pain and endangered her life. Mrs. Susukida's daughter changed her dressings and I do not recall her scolding once. It was interesting, in a way, to observe two women similarly hurt, one always scolding, the other calm.

Dr. Katsube changed the dressings for Dr. Sasada, my wife, and me. I suffered most from having my hairs pulled out by the roots while adhesive tape was being removed. To avoid hurting me, Dr. Katsube would remove the tape slowly, but as far as I was concerned it was an unwelcome favor. To escape this prickly pain I would jerk off my tapes as fast as I could when my turn came for dressing.

Mrs. Yoshida died today, and one of her last complaints was visual disturbance. Throughout the hospital there were more dying patients. They almost invariably had purpura, a condition manifested by extensive, severe hemorrhage throughout the body. Against this terrifying symptom we were helpless. As far as patients with petechiae were concerned they seemed to be doing all right but we still worried about them.

Tonight, as I lay in bed I could hear the high-pitched voice of the insects coming from the basement, and the cricket was chirping as if calling for autumn and he sounded very lonesome. I was almost asleep when, suddenly, a piercing shriek came up from the ward below. Rushing down, I found that one of our patients, a woman, badly injured, had gone mad. Standing like a shadowy giant in the darkened ward, her hair disarranged, she screamed at the top of her voice. She caused the patients around her to become terrified. In the meantime this woman's brother was trying frantically to soothe her.

"Sister, everyone is asleep," the brother admonished in hoarse whispers. "Please be quiet! You are disturbing other people!"

Realizing it would be impossible to quiet her, I ordered two injections of morphine from the treatment room. Shortly thereafter, she vomited twice and lapsed into a profound sleep. I felt sorry for her brother; he sensed that her breakdown was a sign of impending death.

Wide awake and unable to sleep, many thoughts crowded into my mind.

Following the *pika*, we thought that by giving treatment to those who were burned or injured recovery would follow. But now it was obvious that this was not true. People who appeared to be recovering developed other symptoms that caused them to die. So many patients died without our understanding the cause of death that we were all in despair. They all had symptoms which we could not explain and during the past few days spots began to appear. These were cause for greater alarm.

Hundreds of patients died during the first few days; then the death rate declined. Now, it was increasing again. Symptoms common to the ones who died during the first four or five days after the *pika* were general malaise, anorexia, eructation, diarrhea, and vomiting. Of these symptoms, general malaise and anorexia were the commonest and more patients had diarrhea than vomiting. The critically ill patients had all five. As time passed, anorexia and diarrhea proved to be the most persistent symptoms in patients who failed to recover.

Another observation was that the severity of gastro-intestinal symptoms appeared to bear no relation to the extent of burns and other injuries. Many patients with severe wounds recovered rapidly whereas there were patients with the symptoms described who did not appear to be injured at all but who, nevertheless, died.

Among those who died many had a bloody diarrhea similar

to that seen in dysentery, and others had bloody urine or sputum. Severe uterine hemorrhage, which at first we mistook for derangements of menstruation, was common among the women. Some, who lingered as long as a week, died with stomatitis or gangrenous tonsillitis. Now, with the death curve rising again, stomatitis appeared and with it petechiae. The occurrence of petechiae followed the same pattern we had observed in patients with gastro-intestinal symptoms. They bore no relationship to the type or severity of injury, and those who appeared to be uninjured and had even felt well enough to help in the care of other patients were beginning to show these blood spots beneath the skin. We had several instances of presumably healthy people who developed petechiae and died before persons who were obviously critically ill. You can understand what an ominous portent the development of petechiae had for us.

It was now obvious that epidemic dysentery had nothing to do with the bewildering symptoms we witnessed. The thesis was advanced that the symptoms could be explained on the basis of a decreased white blood count and that the decrease could be explained as a sequel to the toxic effects of gangrenous tonsillitis. It did not occur to me that the gangrenous tonsillitis might be caused by a reduction in white blood cells.

Why should leukopenia occur?

That was as far as I could go. There was no making heads or tails to this puzzle. But what were we to do? What would happen next? Was there no answer? These thoughts kept me awake until morning.

20 August 1945

TEMPORARILY overcast, but generally clear.

The much desired microscope I had requested arrived this morning from the Communications Hospital in Tokyo. It had been sent down by a special messenger at the behest of Chief Ikuta, a former head of the Communications Bureau.

No time was lost setting up the microscope and making preparation for blood counts. The six people in our room were found to have white blood counts in the vicinity of 3,000, a little less than half the normal count of 6,000 to 8,000.

The blood studies were under the supervision of Dr. Katsube and Dr. Hanaoka, and everyone worked feverishly to examine as many patients as possible. Some patients had a count of only 500-600, although the majority ranged around 2,000. One critically ill patient had a count of 200, and died shortly after his blood was taken. It became apparent very quickly that patients whose blood counts were low were the ones with the poorest prognosis.

In the burned and injured patients with severe suppuration one would have expected their blood counts to be elevated, but these, too, had low white counts. My suspicions were confirmed. The patients were suffering with a blood disease characterized by agranulocytosis, or in other words, a suppression of the white blood cells, and some toxic substance must be responsible. It was hard to keep a note of exaltation from my voice when I remarked:

"We are dealing with agranulocytosis due to an unknown cause and that's what caused the gangrenous tonsillitis!"

I made a check on each patient and was surprised to find that many lived near the hospital. I also discovered there were more relatives of patients in the hospital than patients. How we were to cope with this situation I did not know. It was hard enough to get food for patients, let alone their relatives, but since there was nowhere for them to go there seemed no alternative but to keep them. No wonder the hospital and Bureau continued to look like a slum. The situation was no better elsewhere, a fact I learned from a friend of mine, Mr. Sagara of Jigozen, when he appeared bringing me a new shirt, hiking pants, and a pair of shoes. Every surrounding shrine, school building, and house, he told me, was packed with *pika* victims. They were much worse off than we were since they had no medicine, no clothes or dressings, and little food. By contrast, our people did have doctors and nurses, and somehow, Dr. Hinoi and Mr. Mizoguchi managed to find us medicine and food.

Rather than appear ostentatious, I continued to wear the knee length pants and hand sewn shirt the city had given me and felt grateful that the patients and their families thought well enough of us to stay here.

21 August 1945

A CLEAR day.

Visitors increased daily and all had something to tell of what they had seen, heard, or thought. By now, I was bored listening to stories they insisted on telling from morning until night, but my boredom did not worry my visitors.

"Doctor, where were you at the time of the *pika?*" they would ask and, without giving me a chance to get a word in edgewise, would proceed to recount their experiences; and in each instance tried to convince me that theirs had been unique. Some did have unusual stories to tell.

"The first-aid station the Labor Service set up at Hijiyama," recounted one visitor, "was in a turmoil. There were so many burned that the odor was like drying squid. They looked like boiled octopuses. I have never seen so pathetic a spectacle.

"Doctor, do you think a man could see with a protruded eyeball?" this visitor continued. "Well, I saw a man whose eye had been torn out by an injury, and there he stood with the eye resting in the palm of his hand. What made my blood run cold was that it looked like the eye was staring at me. Doctor, the pupil looked right at me. Do you think that eye could see me?"

Not knowing what to answer, I replied, "Could you see your face reflected from the pupil?"

"No," replied the visitor, "I didn't look that close."

Fortunately, this conversation was interrupted by an old friend, Dr. Yasuhara from Tamashima, who was chief of our surgical service until two or three years ago.

"Doctor, this place is not safe for you!" he began. "Come on and go home with me. You will never recover staying in a place like this!"

Dr. Yasuhara was so impulsive I knew if I did not stay on guard he might have me in a car and gone before I knew it. He calmed down when he recognized my wife, Mr. Shiota, Miss Yama, and Miss Susukida. The sight of these old friends made him realize I was not the only one in trouble.

"I have brought you a little present: a box of peaches," he informed us in a subdued voice and with tears in his eyes.

After asking about other friends in the hospital and Bureau, Dr. Yasuhara informed us that my cousin, Captain Urabe, was dead and that our old friends and classmates, Dr. Onoda, Dr. Akamatsu, and Dr. Osugi were missing. I had to learn this sad news sometime, but it did nothing to boost my spirits at the present.

For lunch, we had the delicious Okayama peaches Dr. Yasuhara had brought.

I intended during my afternoon rounds to record as much as I could of the patients' histories, but everything was so confused I hardly knew where to start. The woman who went mad last night was up again, shouting meaningless words. The patients with petechiae had increased and some complained that their hair was coming out in handfuls.

I did record a few short notes:

Mr. Sakai, fifty-three-year-old male, entered the hospital with complaint of discomfort in chest. On both arms, several distinct petechiae present, each as large as the tip of the little finger. Temperature 100.4°. Considerable amount of hair gone. Condition critical.

Mrs. Hamada, female, forty-seven years. Exposed in house at Teppocho, one kilometer from hypocenter. Vomiting, weakness, headache, and thirst immediately following the bombing. Symptoms continued for about four days, accompanied by malaise and diarrhea. Gradually improved and believes she had completely recovered by 15 August except for slight malaise. Acute exacerbation of malaise on 18 August 1945 which has become worse day by day. On admission yesterday, skin found to be dry with numerous petechiae over chest, shoulders, and both arms. Complains of pain on swallowing and breath has a fetid odor. Condition critical.

Miss Kobayashi, female, nineteen years. Exposed on street at Hatchōbori, 700 meters from hypocenter. Vomited several times while attempting to escape. Severe weakness during next three days with anorexia and diarrhea. Like Mrs. Hamada, she made gradual recovery and regained good appetite, but because of malaise and insomnia remained in bed. General condition worsened around August 18, so she was admitted to hospital. On admission, had generalized petechiae with complete epilation. Pulse rather good, so not listed in critical condition group.

Falling hair!

This was an unusual symptom, but undeniable. Unconsciously, I grabbed some of my hair and pulled. I did not have much hair in the first place, but the amount that came out made me feel sick.

Prompted by this unpleasant discovery, I took care to examine each patient's head and found epilation to be present in some degree in all the patients. Miss Kobayashi and Mr. Sakai had epilated the most.

The patients now had another symptom to worry about, but none was more worried than I.

The beautiful young girl who was burned everywhere but her face showed no signs of epilation. She still lay in a puddle of pus * and appeared neither to improve nor become worse. Since there was no one to care for her, I always gave her special attention on my rounds and tried to get other patients to help. She seemed to appreciate my concern and smiled with pleasure when I came around. Even though her face and body were black with dirt and filth, there was something beautiful about her when she smiled. Perhaps her glittering gold teeth accounted for this. She reminded me of the Indians with their golden ornaments.

Returning to bed, I told my neighbors about how patients were losing their hair and tried to pull out some more of my own. Following my example, everyone began to tug at his hair, but none would come out. Even mine failed to come lose this time. Reassured, we convinced ourselves that we were moving under full sail towards recovery.

We had a peach by way of celebration and as I ate mine, it felt as if I had cleaned the soot from my throat. Thereafter, when I so much as thought of those delicious peaches, my mouth watered.

Yaeko-san appeared to have a cold and was running fever. I gave her aspirin.

* Persons with extensive second and third degree burns will ooze body juices and white blood cells from the raw surfaces. This exudate, or pus, will continue to escape until healing or crusting is complete.

22 August 1945

A CLEAR day.

I awakened long before day and was unable to go back to sleep. While my companions slept, I slipped out of bed and went up on the balcony to see the sun rise. It was clear and crisp, and I stayed on the balcony until the sun was well in the sky. This would be a good time, I thought, to examine the ruins of the second corps area and the headquarters detachment that had been stationed in the old Hiroshima castle.

On the way to these ruins, I had the urge to urinate, and, looking for a place to go, I found an intact tiled toilet. I was delighted because it was cleaner than the hospital toilet which, as I stated earlier, was simply a board covered hole in the ground surrounded by straw mats. Since this toilet was a short distance from the hospital, I determined henceforth to use it.

Stopping at the ruins of an army storehouse south of the hospital, I discovered the burnt and twisted frames of two motorcycles covered with broken bricks and roof tiles, but no weapons. How well the army had evacuated, I thought. A wooden storehouse which stood near the south side of the Bureau before the bombing had been the first to catch fire and nothing remained except scattered roof tiles. Flames from this building set fire to the hospital and Bureau. The army had needlessly destroyed many houses in the area as a precaution against fire but left this tinder box intact. Every other house within fifty meters of the hospital had been demolished. That was why the hospital had not been completely consumed, but a useless wooden storage house left at the edge of the army compound had been the cause of needless damage to our buildings and hurt to ourselves.

You can understand our contempt, indeed, hatred of the army

leaders. Their ruthlessness and stupidity knew no bounds. Our personal rights were violated and we never knew when we might say something to provoke their irascible and vindictive natures. Mr. Mizoguchi was once questioned at the Hiroshima station by a military policeman, and when it became apparent to this low-grade martinet that no valid charge could be leveled, he slapped Mr. Mizoguchi with the excuse that he looked like a Korean.

Leaving the ruins of this detested area, this symbol of oppression, I returned to the hospital for breakfast.

Old Mrs. Saeki's eyes were round with excitement when she served me rice.

"*Sensei-san*, I've heard the engineering corps will give you as many shirts and uniforms as you wish!" she exclaimed. "Why don't you and Mr. Mizoguchi go and get some? They have lots of them! The army has everything!"

Spreading her arms as far as she could, *baba-san* went on, "They will give you this much. They have blankets and uniforms and shoes all stacked up as high as a mountain. They really do. The army has everything!"

Mr. Mizoguchi, who had already investigated this rumor, broke in, "*Baba-san*, some of these things were available until the 18th, but now they won't give you anything. We might try again though." He turned to me. "There is still quite a stockpile, and perhaps if we went to the commanding officer and explained that we wanted goods for the hospital, he might do something for us. At any rate, it won't hurt to try."

I agreed with Mr. Mizoguchi and we planned to go to engineering headquarters this afternoon.

The clinic was filled with patients requesting blood examinations. I saw two waiting in the corridor who had noticeably thin hair. Near the janitor's room, I encountered Mrs. Maeoka who once worked in the hospital as a nurse. Her husband was dead and she had come in for examination because she was not feeling well.

One could look at this poor woman, frail and thin, with ashen face and lusterless eyes and know she was doomed. She came expecting help, yet there was nothing we could do.

No significant change could be detected in the in-patients today. Since I had been making rounds regularly, I had learned to distinguish the patients from their families, and there was no question but our census counted more family than patients. Many went out to work during the day and returned to the hospital at night. Our wards were thus more like an apartment filled with patients than a hospital. Each family arranged its various *tatami* in little groups to simulate a living room and in this area its members would gather around the *hibachi* * and cooking utensils. Rations were divided and shared in a neighborly fashion.

The improvised wards in the Bureau were supervised by Mr. Numata and the hospital wards by Mr. Kimoto. Under their excellent direction everything went smoothly. This is another example of the diligence my staff exercised in an effort to accommodate the confusion of people under our roof.

Epilation—loss of hair—was now more fearfully regarded than petechiae. Indeed, some had forgotten their spots altogether.

Mrs. Hamada was worse today. All of her hair was gone and her petechiae had increased.

Miss Kobayashi had a fever of 102°. Her throat was sore and she complained of weakness and discomfort in her chest and pain in her abdomen. Her head with the hair gone looked like a yellow pumpkin, and her body was covered with petechiae of various size. She and Mrs. Hamada were critically ill.

Mr. Sakai, a patient I spoke about yesterday, looked as though his head had been shaved. Miss Kobayashi, whose hair was lost earlier, now had a fine growth of black under-hair which made her head look as though it was painted with *sumi*.† These three patients: Mrs. Hamada, Miss Kobayashi, and Mr. Sakai, were all

---

* A *hibachi* is a wooden, metal, or earthenware container partly filled with ashes, usually of straw, in which is placed a small charcoal fire. Except in unusual circumstances it is used more for heating than for cooking.

† *Sumi* is a word for a black writing ink, also charcoal.

epilated and all had petechiae. I wondered which one would die first.

There was no way to estimate accurately the prevalence of petechiae because unless symptoms were present they might pass undetected. Likewise, there was no way to determine a relationship between the onset of petechiae and epilation because within a few hours both might appear. When both symptoms occurred together they were sooner or later accompanied by symptomatic signs of illness.

After lunch, Mr. Mizoguchi and I visited the commanding officer of the engineering corps. I tried to look presentable but it was difficult in my dirty pants and shirt.

Headquarters for the 5th Engineers Battalion was situated in the suburb of Hakushima on a peninsula between two branches of the Ōta River directly north of the hospital. My home had been in Hakushima and before the bombing I thought of Hakushima as a large suburb, but with the houses gone it now appeared quite small. Not all the houses were destroyed although the few left were badly damaged.

The corps' main supply dump was across the river and accessible by way of the Kohei Bridge. A guard standing watch at the other end of the bridge knew Mr. Mizoguchi and offered to take us to the commanding officer.

We walked through an open area piled high on all sides with arms and other supplies until we came to the mouth of a cave dug into a hillside. Here the guard asked us to wait and disappeared into the cave. After a while he came out with the commanding officer. I was impressed that neither the guard nor the officer were armed, and I must confess seeing these soldiers stripped of their guns and swords depressed me, for nothing could be more symbolic of defeat.

The commanding officer was an old man and so woebegone that he struck me with pity. For a moment I was at a loss to know what to say. I bowed and Mr. Mizoguchi introduced me. The introduction restored my composure, and I proceeded to tell him of our hospital and its work, sparing no detail from the day of the *pika* to the present. I ended by asking his aid.

The old officer listened with polite attention; and when I finished speaking he answered me in low, grave tones: "Until around the 17th I had orders to distribute army clothing and other material but since then the policy has changed. I am now under order to turn the goods over to the city office who will assume the responsibility for distributing them to the citizens."

"Would it be possible, then," I asked, "to give the city office clothing, blankets, and other goods necessary for two hundred patients with the stipulation that they be distributed at our hospital?"

The old officer said my suggestion would be entirely agreeable to him and that he would do what he could to assist us.

We thanked him for his kindness, bowed, and departed.

On the way out we examined the supplies piled up like treasures. There were many, many things: saws, axes, navigation lamps, cooking utensils, desks, and chairs. Boxes labeled "shoes" were stacked sky-high. There were mountains of blankets, army uniforms, underwear, and big boxes containing leather goods. To us, it seemed that all the citizens in Hiroshima could be clothed with goods to spare.

If only we could get some for our hospital! What we had done for wounded soldiers should entitle us to something. On the way back, I searched my mind for the right person, perhaps some friend, who would intercede for us. I could think of no one, so we decided that Mr. Mizoguchi should go to the city office, explain our meeting with the commanding officer of the engineers corps and ask for their help before the whole business got tied up in red tape.

After supper, Dr. Katsube and Dr. Hanaoka gave me the results of their first blood studies on our patients. The microscope could be used only during daylight since we had no electricity, so I was impressed to learn they had examined some fifty cases.

The white blood count in persons exposed in the Ushita area, between two and three kilometers from the hypocenter, ranged from 3,000 to 4,000. Patients nearer the hypocenter, although fewer in number, had counts around 1,000. Severely ill patients had counts lower than 1,000, and the nearer the hypocenter the patient had been the lower the white count.

If we could examine the blood of several hundred patients, we should be able to prove a relationship between distance and white blood count.

The precise location of the hypocenter was in doubt. Since the A-bomb had not exploded on the ground but in the air, there were no precise landmarks. Some said the bomb had exploded over the Aioi Bridge, popularly called the "T" Bridge; others located it variously over the Hiroshima post office, the Shima Hospital, the Museum of Science and Industry, or the great *torii* at the entrance to the Gokoku Shrine. Short of asking the bomb itself, there was no way of telling.* A majority opinion favored the great *torii* at the Gokoku Shrine, but it was my belief that the hypocenter was more to the south, and that is where we arbitrarily placed it.

Our preliminary blood findings filled us with excitement and the feeling that for the first time we were coming to grips with this unknown enemy, the atom bomb.

My excitement was so great, I hardly slept a wink all night.

---

* Heat shadows were cast by the intense flash of light attending the detonation and these shadows were etched into concrete, stone, or metal. By triangulating from many points, the convergence of projected shadow lines fixes the approximate ground location and height of the bomb. However, even where hundreds of projections are made, the diameter of the center could not be reduced to an area much less than 100 meters, or the height more accurately fixed than between 500 and 700 meters. The center was probably more nearly over the Shima Hospital. As already mentioned, concrete columns flanking the Shima Hospital entrance were driven some distance into the ground. Had the driving force not been overhead, the columns should have toppled.

23 August 1945

A CLEAR day with occasional clouds and a refreshing breeze.

I started by visiting the elegant toilet I found yesterday. When I got back to the room, I found Mr. Shiota grinning. He had watched me from the window.

Mr. Shiota was our manager and for several days had been back at his post. When he was able to walk, one of the first things he did was to show up with two bags, each of which contained fifty packages of cigarettes. Where and how he got them I will never know, but you can imagine our surprise and delight. I had never seen so much tobacco outside a tobacco store and never dreamed so many cigarettes would come into our possession. For a while, we kept the packages on display the better to enjoy this unexpected bounty. Throughout the hospital habitual smokers drew a breath of relief. Why, a good, strong, working man could do more work with a pack of cigarettes. By the same token, the efficiency of our student helpers could be measurably increased. We could do anything as long as we had an abundant supply of cigarettes. This luxury had become exceedingly scarce in Hiroshima because of its value in barter. We were amazed at Mr. Shiota's ability.

"I can get as many as I want," he exclaimed with confidence, "so smoke as much as you wish! When these are gone, I'll get more."

We smoked and puffed to our hearts' content and came to life again.

Dr. Sasada was better today. It was possible to see his childish face peeping from behind the red-brown crusts. He was far from well; but he was better. The petechiae on his chest he had tried to hide were now gone.

Miss Yama's burns still hurt her, but she showed no signs of petechiae or epilation.

Miss Susukida's oedema was subsiding and her face looked better.

My wife's fever was down, but she still complained of chills. Whatever she had, she did not appear too sick.

We were all more cheerful. The fact that Dr. Sasada's petechiae had disappeared indicated that petechiae did not *always* mean death. This thought cheered us.

Around 10:00 I was visited by a friend, Mr. Isono, and was surprised to learn that he was the new Chief of the Communications Bureau. He was Chief of the Health Section in the Communications Ministry when I started working for the Communications Bureau and I respected him deeply for his knowledge and for his ability as a hospital administrator. He was worried about the rumors that Hiroshima would be uninhabitable for seventy-five years, so I hastened to reassure him.

The atmosphere in the wards, this morning, was in sharp contrast to that in our room. Patients who had not epilated were so worried they were pulling at their hair all the time. Those who had epilated were convinced they were going to die. I must confess I could not help sharing their worry despite Dr. Sasada's having impressed me that petechiae were reversible and not necessarily a sign of death.

A patient stopped me and asked: "Doctor, your hair is thinner, isn't it?"

"I was born with sparse hair," I retorted, "and time hasn't kept it from becoming thinner. You know as well as I do that falling hair has nothing to do with longevity."

My comments were motivated by pride as well as fear. I did not tell the patient I had been guilty of pulling my own hair like everybody else. In my mind, I was really worried. This show of bravado fooled no one, and the more I tried to conceal my apprehension the more it showed on my face.

As rounds progressed, I discovered those who had only epilated appeared to be better. A man in the Out-Patient Clinic who was completely epilated showed no signs of illness. Epilation, *per se*, could not mean, therefore, that death was inevitable.

I went back through the wards trying to reassure patients more as a comforter than a physician. The Chinese character which means physician also means comforter.

The three patients I described yesterday were weaker and had more petechiae. Whether it was because of his age, I do not know, but Mr. Sakai was the sickest of the three. He and Miss Kobayashi were now completely epilated, but Mrs. Hamada's hair had only thinned slightly, so it was hard to say whether she had epilated or not.

Among the less seriously ill were some whose petechiae had disappeared like Dr. Sasada's. There were others whose petechiae were on the decrease. There was still no indication that falling hair and hemorrhage beneath the skin were related. Perhaps epilation was related to one's general constitution. Perhaps not.

This morning, I made another entry for the clinical record:

Mr. Otani, male, aged fifty years, exposed on the second floor of the food distribution corporation at Hatchōbori, 750 meters from the hypocenter. Vomited about fifteen times immediately after the bombing and complained of headache and weakness. Began to feel better after a week's rest and was able to walk again. Developed inflamed gums (gingivitis) two or three days ago. Became critically ill. No epilation, but numerous petechiae.

This man's history was typical of many who appeared to improve at first and then became worse. If this were true, people who now appeared well should be on their guard.

Lunch was over when I finished rounds, and there was no one in the dining room but old Mrs. Saeki.

"*Baba-san*," I said, sitting down, "the critically ill patients are increasing. Those whose hair is falling don't worry me, but I am concerned about those with sore throats and fever. They don't seem to improve. You can't feel safe even when they look better because you can't tell when they are going to get worse again."

Baba-san, who listened patiently to all our troubles, paused from her tea making: "*Sensei-san*, you must take better care of yourself! Overwork at this time is a bad thing and you are working too hard. I don't like the color of your face. You must get someone to help you."

Baba-san set a cup of tea before me. After drinking it, I smoked a cigarette and returned to our room.

"It's heaven up here!" I remarked to Dr. Sasada and Mr. Shiota. "It's heaven up here, but down where the critically ill are it's terrible. You should see the flies. There are so many on the ceiling that it looks like sesame seed have been sprinkled about. When you pass the toilets, they come up in noisy swarms. Old Mrs. Saeki calls them *nimbai* (human flies). Do you know why? She calls them that because she says human beings are hatching them."

My audience laughed.

"If you think I'm lying, go down and see for yourselves," I replied, somewhat nettled.

"We know that very well," answered Mr. Shiota. "We weren't laughing at you but at old Mrs. Saeki's funny expression: '*Nimbai*.' She's probably right."

"So that's why you made your toilet out in the ruins!" Mr. Shiota kidded me.

"Try it yourself, Shiota-san," I replied. "See which is the better toilet, mine or the hospital's. But a word of advice: If you wish to defecate, you had better wait until night."

Dr. Koyama came in while we were laughing and joking about the toilet and old Mrs. Saeki's "*nimbai*." He looked harassed.

"I'm at my wit's ends," he exclaimed. "Trying to manage these first-aid teams is impossible. I can't get work out of them, for they sit and gossip or pry into matters that are none of their business. But enough of that."

Changing the subject, Dr. Koyama gave me an account of the professional organization in the hospital. Dr. Fujii, the dentist, was in charge of the Out-Patient Surgery Clinic and Dr. Hanaoka was running Out-Patient Medicine. Dr. Akiyama was in charge of the hospital wards, the Bureau annex, and directed the outside doctors who came in to help. Dr. Katsube ran the operating room and cared for the patients in our ward. The nurses worked in one place or another, depending on where they were most needed. Dr. Koyama ran the Eye Clinic in addition to his administrative duties.

I asked Dr. Koyama what his findings had been in patients with eye injuries.

"Those who were watching the plane had their eye grounds burned," he replied. "The flash of light apparently went through the pupils and left them with a blind area in the central portion of their visual fields.

"Most of the eye-ground burns are third degree, so cure is impossible."

Those who were burned on the face or body were fortunate, I thought. Even if we should have ugly scars, at least we had not been blinded.

My wife had fever and complained of chills. I gave her aspirin and pyramidon.

24 August 1945

GENERALLY overcast.

The night had been close with many mosquitoes. Consequently, I slept poorly and had a frightful dream.

It seems I was in Tokyo after the great earthquake and around me were decomposing bodies heaped in piles, all of whom were looking right at me. I saw an eye sitting on the palm of a girl's hand. Suddenly it turned and leaped into the sky and then came flying back towards me, so that, looking up, I could see a great bare eyeball, bigger than life, hovering over my head, staring point blank at me. I was powerless to move.

I awakened short of breath and with my heart pounding. I must have held my breath during this horrible dream. The story about the man at the Hijiyama first-aid station who held the eye in his hand had been a little too much.

I lay there trying to recall the name of the man who told me the story, but I could not remember his name. I knew the man well and knew where he worked, but I still could not remember his name.

This blindness for names had troubled me before because there were many friends whose names I could not recite since the *pika*. At times names would come and then they would escape completely. Sometimes, I could remember names but not faces. I thought that if this maddening disturbance continued I would go crazy.

I recalled Dr. Koyama's account of patients who had been blinded by looking directly at the *pika*. Their blindness was understandable because their eye nerves had been scorched. My exposure was indirect. I had seen only the flash, but the heat rays had not reached me so the "mirrors" in my eyes were not injured. Perhaps the *pika* had caused damage even though it reached me indirectly. Maybe my eye nerves were weakened by the *pika*. I could not believe I had retrograde amnesia. Can one get an optic amnesia? Could that account for my inability to remember names and faces? Would I improve, or would this go on the rest of my life? When morning came, I was in a proper state, convinced I would never improve.

Breakfast did little to dispell my gloomy forebodings, so I returned to my bed and stared vacantly out of the window. A truck drove up and my troubles were forgotten.

The supplies had come, the goods we requested from the Engineering Corps. The unloading was done with dispatch and soon there was a great heap of articles in front of the hospital. There were such necessities as saws, axes, cooking utensils, ropes, buckets, lamps, shoes, hatchets, knives, desks, and numerous other items. What an abundance!

Everybody who could walk turned out to unload the truck and then began to help themselves. Cooking utensils were the most popular. I helped myself, too. I chose a white rice bowl with a blue star in its center * and a white dish with a cherry blossom design.

The whole hospital was filled with joy. The wards, where sorrow and gloom had ruled since the day of the *pika*, became noisy with talk and laughter. Patients who, up to now, had been using tin cans and fire-blackened bowls had a happy time lining up new bowls and dishes beside their pillows. Our maintenance crews were happy with their new saws and axes. Gleefully, they went through the motions of sawing and chopping great trees for firewood. For the first time since the *pika*, we had decent cooking equipment and eating utensils as well as the tools necessary to get firewood.

Ward rounds were impossible in the morning, so it was late in the day when I went around.

Mr. Sakai died, complaining of shortness of breath and blindness. Mrs. Hamada died the same way.

Miss Kobayashi, with a temperature of 104°, was still holding on. Her painful, infected, ulcerating mouth was worse. She complained of shortness of breath and since morning had been suffering with severe abdominal pain. Whether she had peritonitis from obstruction or perforation, we could not tell.

Mr. Onomi was weaker, his petechiae increasing, and since morning he had been suffering from a prolapsed anus.

Patients completely epilated or continuing to lose hair still showed few or no subjective symptoms. This was reassuring. Epilation signs could no longer be called the halo of death.

Dr. Sasada and Mr. Shiota continued to improve. Miss Yama and Miss Susukida remained seriously ill, but they appeared to

* White dishes decorated with the blue star were made expressly for the Japanese army.

be stable. My wife was still having fever and chills which I treated with aspirin.

After supper, Mr. Mizoguchi, Miss Kado, old Mrs. Saeki, and I lingered in the dining room. I learned people were looting the supply dump at the engineering corps. Vandals even came with carts and hauled away everything they could carry. Some of the supplies we received this morning had already been stolen right out of the hospital. Hiroshima was becoming a wicked town. Without police I was not surprised, but I was ashamed.

A flickering light sprang up outside my window later in the night and, looking out, I discovered that Mr. Sakai and Mrs. Hamada were being cremated. The silhouette of the bath tub loomed in the foreground.

25 August 1945

OVERCAST early in the day, then clear.

I awakened and went to my toilet. Returning, I stopped where Mr. Sakai and Mrs. Hamada had been cremated. The skull and hip bones are not always completely consumed in the cremation fire, but this time, the job had been well done. Nothing remained but white ashes, so I surmised that a bountiful supply of wood had been used thanks to our new saws and axes.

Around the hospital entrances were thousands of flies and each step one took caused them to rise in black swarms. The noise of their wings was terrific. Here and there they formed small black mountains. Poking with a stick I uncovered a denuded fish bone and beneath it discovered a mass of white maggots. As soon as I removed the stick the bone became black with flies again. These flies were not "*nimbai*" as old Mrs. Saeki contended, but no matter. They were all around the hospital, inside and out, and there was nothing we could do. With the recent weather and the filth, flies had increased to an appalling degree. They were less troublesome on the second floor of the hospital than downstairs but were still an annoyance. Immediately after the *pika* there was not a fly to be seen, but now we had flies *and* mosquitoes.

I brought the subject up at breakfast hoping someone might have a suggestion for getting rid of them, but old Mrs. Saeki shook her head and said: "They are human flies, so there's nothing you can do about them. Why, downstairs they're all over the kitchen and if you open your mouth, they'll fly right in."

We considered burning their breeding grounds with gasoline, but since gas was more precious than human blood, it was out of the question. Anyway, the flies were hatching in ruins all over the city, so local efforts would not do any good.

We received another load of military goods from the engineering corps today, but except for two huge cooking pots, an iron field stove, and a few battered desks, this shipment was not as useful as the one yesterday. Today, there were several boxes filled with red and white signal flags and others filled with khaki-colored life preservers. A few boxes contained small articles, the most useful of which were little flashlights in leather cases.

People entering or leaving the hospital picked up one or more flags. The small khaki-colored life preservers were appropriated for pillows. The children enjoyed the flags and ran up and down to make them flutter, shouting and laughing happily.

From my window, I watched the people who picked over the goods. There were various ways to take things, I learned. Some would glance furtively about before they took something, whereas others would take an article and then look about. Some would come up, shouting loudly, and rummage through the goods with an air of contemptuous disdain, and seize everything they touched and depart in haste. This little human drama seemed to express the character and training of these people. There were a few who, on seeing the goods, inquired if they might have some. These people made me believe there were still refined people left in the world and I made a mental note to be careful of my behavior.

On rounds this morning I found that all the in-patients now had petechiae and epilation. Their conditions had not worsened though, so there was greater optimism in the wards.

Many asked if their hair would grow again and although I could not honestly say, I told them it would. To say this without knowing was a deception, but I believe I will be excused because of the pleasure it gave the patients.

A few with petechiae and epilation had developed sore mouths and rising temperatures. These patients were worse and, incidentally, all had low white counts.

Mr. Onomi was still in pain because of his anal prolapse and the petechiae on his chest had increased. His mouth was worse and his temperature had risen. Altogether, he looked bad.

Miss Kobayashi was worse. She still had abdominal pain and was quite distended. My examining hand met no resistance but did cause intense pain. Her mouth and throat were so sore and swollen that she could not swallow. Her fever was 102°. She begged for death.

Mr. Onomi and Miss Kobayashi were nauseated and had no appetite after the *pika*. Vomiting and diarrhea followed but improved a week later. They developed petechiae and epilation four or five days ago and later painful, swollen, ulcerating mouths. It suddenly became apparent that this combination of symptoms plus a low blood count, which both had, must govern prognosis.

Dr. Sasada was so much better we considered letting him leave the hospital. Miss Yama and Miss Susukida held their own.

Mr. Kadoya, chief of the Communications Bureau Welfare Section was admitted with diarrhea. He was transferred to the Hiroshima Communications Bureau after the *pika*. My wife was moved to a bed in the corridor, so Mr. Kadoya could have her bed. He had considerable abdominal pain with his diarrhea, but I guessed he would be all right because he had not been in Hiroshima when the bomb exploded.

After supper, talk turned to the effects of the bombing. It was still believed that if gas emanating from the bomb were inhaled, death would ensue. Someone remarked that there were people who came into Hiroshima after the *pika* and developed symptoms like those of the people who had been in Hiroshima on the fateful day. A case was cited of a man from Gion who came into Hiroshima after the *pika* and later died.

I could only comment that stomatitis, or sore mouth, was an ominous symptom and that it had developed in uninjured persons nursing the sick.

It was rumored that a number of people in concrete buildings near the center of the explosion were protected and thus escaped injury. That they were now beginning to die was attributed to their having later worked in the ruins.

Worry broke out again and it was no longer possible to reassure those who were epilated or had petechiae. Their fears must be allayed.

Six days had passed since the first blood examination and tomorrow it was to be repeated. I determined to post the results in each ward and issue a statement summarizing the signs and symptoms our patients had with a note describing their progress. Perhaps this would help to restore calm.

Convinced that a concise statement, based on what we had observed, would do much to relieve tension and fear, I went to bed. For the first time I could remember I had a sound night's rest.

26 August 1945

Rain with overcast skies through the day.

I was working on my notes after breakfast when a nurse rushed in to inform me that Miss Kobayashi was dying. By the time I reached her she was dead.

She had continued to complain of intense abdominal pain earlier this morning although her abdomen was but slightly distended. We did not believe she had peritonitis or intestinal obstruction. Could she have had pancreatic necrosis or a ruptured ectopic pregnancy? Other patients had mentioned abdominal pain, but hers had been a leading complaint. Dr. Katsube and I discussed the differential possibilities and ended up no better than we started. There was only one way to find out.

"Dr. Katsube, we must do an autopsy," I said. "That is the only way we can hope to clear up this case."

"I quite agree," replied Dr. Katsube, who was deep in thought.

The time for our blood examination came, so Dr. Katsube and I went downstairs to the Out-Patient Department.

Dr. Hanaoka informed us that those who were near the hypo-center still had low white counts, but those from 3,000 to 4,000 meters no longer showed a decrease. I was happy to learn that my count had increased from 3,000 to 4,000.

"Dr. Hanaoka," I exclaimed, "whoever heard such an absurd story as the rumor that Hiroshima will be uninhabitable for seventy-five years!"

Dr. Hanaoka patted my shoulder modestly and replied: "Doctor, everything is all right now."

Returning to my room, I told everyone that my white blood cells had increased and urged them to go down for an examination at once. My announcement had a good effect.

While I sat chatting happily, word came that Chief Isono wished to see me. Going to his office, I found him dejected and worried.

"Dr. Hachiya, are you all right?" he asked, unceremoniously. "The color of your face is not good. Is it true people will die who came to Hiroshima after the *pika*? Should we leave the Bureau and go somewhere else? My staff is worried and many are failing to show up for work. What do you think?"

"Chief Isono, I think you are worried because you came here from another place," I answered. "Those of us who were here at the time have gotten used to things and are no longer bothered. Like yourself, I've heard it said that no one can live here for seventy-five years, but that is nonsense. Look at me! I've been here through the whole affair and injured to boot, but I am recovering. The same is true for the rest of the staff. Not a one has died. Your poor attendance record is probably due to the fact that many of your employees have urgent business at home. You know as well as I do that every home has one or more members who were hurt.

"As for those who are dying, they are invariably people who were nearest the hypocenter. Some delayed effect of the bombing is responsible because almost invariably an earlier appearance of health has been followed by the development of petechiae and loss of hair. We are going to autopsy such a patient today. It is about these patients that we are worried and not those who came to Hiroshima later. I must confess we don't know the cause and we don't know what to do."

I had tried to reassure Chief Isono, but obviously I was not very successful.

"If we don't do something," he continued, "the staff will become smaller still and there'll be no one to work. I think the best thing we can do to restore confidence is to move the Bureau to a safer place. There still may be poison left in the city."

"I know there are people who say this, but it's a lie!" I replied heatedly. "This hospital is a good example because not one of us has died and no one of us is going to die!"

"I wonder!" Chief Isono replied, a doubting note still in his voice.

"Chief, I tell you again, everything will be all right!" I exclaimed emphatically. "It's my intention to post a statement where everyone can see in an effort to allay the fears that have been provoked by the reckless rumors bandied about."

"That's good!" answered the Chief less desperately. "Please do it."

Poor Chief Isono wanted to believe me but found it difficult. His thoughts were divided.

"Leave it to me," I answered and left the office.

I must lose no time with my plan. The findings must be posted for everyone to see by tomorrow morning.

I had lunch and was on the way to my room when old Mrs. Saeki called: "Doctor, Dr. Katsube is looking for you, I left him standing in front of the X-ray room, so you might find him there."

I found Dr. Katsube in the X-ray room with the dead patient on the Bucky table * ready to begin the autopsy. I bowed in respect to the dead and moved up to the table.

The abdominal cavity was opened and found to be filled with bloody fluid.

"That's funny!" I exclaimed. "Is it pancreatic necrosis, Dr. Katsube?"

"I don't believe it's the pancreas," said Dr. Katsube, shaking his head as he searched the abdominal cavity with his hand.

The spleen was small. The liver was dark brown in color, its substance congested, and covered with small, hemorrhagic spots. The blood vessels of the stomach and intestines were dilated, and the intestines, like the liver, presented numerous submucosal

---

* Bucky table—A St. Louis radiologist named Gustav Bucky invented an X-ray grid in 1913, composed of thin strips of lead alternating with wood which, placed between the X-ray tube and the object to be X-rayed, greatly increases the sharpness of the picture, by admitting only those rays perpendicular to the object. A "Bucky" or a "Potter-Bucky" attachment to an ordinary X-ray table has become so useful and so widely used that the table itself is now often referred to as the "Bucky table."

hemorrhagic spots. Between the iliac arteries * was found a large amount of bloody fluid, and each time Dr. Katsube moved his hand, a little would spill out.

The reason for this poor woman's abdominal pain was apparent and very likely the cause for her death. Petechiae developed not only on the body surface but in the internal organs as witnessed by the changes apparent on her stomach, intestines, liver, and the lining of the abdominal cavity—practically all her internal organs. Petechiae were an ominous sign.

We made one further observation. The blood in the abdominal cavity had not coagulated, even though some time had passed since death. Perhaps the coagulating power of the blood was decreased. Perhaps the blood platelets were decreased as well as the white blood counts. Giving voice to my thoughts, I remarked to Dr. Katsube: "I think we must make platelet counts. Perhaps their absence may have something to do with the failure of this woman's blood to coagulate."

Dr. Katsube agreed.

From one autopsy we had learned a great deal. If we had begun to do autopsies sooner, perhaps we would not have been so in doubt about our patients' signs and symptoms. It never occurred to me as forcibly as now how important and necessary autopsies are.

The rest of the day I worked on my report. Night found me still at work on our information relating distance from the hypocenter to white blood count and trying to formalize in a concise statement what I had seen and heard and what could be gathered from our meager records. I found it difficult to express my thoughts on paper and time and again I tore up what I had done and started over. It was late when I finally finished.

The following statement I submitted to Mr. Mizoguchi with the request that he have it copied on big sheets of paper and posted before day throughout the hospital and Bureau:

---

* Between these blood vessels lies the deep pelvic recess where fluid or other material spilled into the peritoneal cavity accumulates.

Notice Regarding Radiation Sickness
Hiroshima Communications Hospital

1. No abnormal blood counts have been found in persons working in the city since the A-bomb who were not in the city at the time of the *pika*. No abnormal counts have been found in persons who were in the basement of the Telephone Bureau during the *pika*. Persons in this category are requested to continue their work as usual.

2. It has been found that those with low white blood cell counts were near the center of bombing, that is: employees of the Telephone Bureau, the Telegraph Bureau, and members of their respective distribution departments. The white blood counts are either normal or slightly decreased in persons who were working at the Communications Bureau when the bomb exploded.

3. There does not appear to be any relation between severity of burns and decrease in white blood cells.

4. Loss of hair does not necessarily have an unfavorable prognosis.

5. Persons whose white blood counts are low must take care to avoid injury or exertion because their body resistance is low.

6. Those with wounds must take pains that they do not become infected. Those with infection should receive treatment at once to prevent a spread of the infection to the blood stream.

7. According to reports by authorities from Tokyo University there does not appear to be any residual radiation from uranium.

THE END

(*Signed*): Michihiko Hachiya, Director
Hiroshima Communications Hospital

I found it difficult to get to sleep because my bed was wet from the rain. Most of the night I spent slapping at mosquitoes.

27 August 1945

RAIN. LATER cloudy.

The 210th day * was approaching, so we could expect a rainy spell. Since there was no glass in the windows the building soon became thoroughly wet. Here and there, water puddled on the floor, and bedding became damp and musty. Mosquitoes and flies increased our discomfort.

I had not bathed since the *pika* because of my wounds. My thigh wound still looked as if the flesh had been scraped away like paper from a *shōji*. Accumulated sweat and fat gave me an awful odor and I loathed myself every time my arms and knees came close to my nose.

It was sticky this morning and I sweated heavily. After breakfast, I asked old Mrs. Saeki if she would sponge me with hot water. We had no soap, but a little rubbing sufficed to remove masses of dirt and filth adhering to my skin. After the sponge bath, I felt very much better.

Alone, I thought of many things. Here were the black, burnt ceilings, the walls without paint, and the glassless windows. The *konro*, our small charcoal cooking brazier, stood under the sink supporting a battered and blackened teapot whose top was covered by a dish in lieu of a lid. Army rice bowls and ceremonial tea cups were indiscriminately stacked in a bamboo basket. All these things recalled the pity of war.

On the other hand, I thought, where could one find another room so colorful? Everything we used had been christened by an

---

* In the old calendar the 210th day marked the approach of the autumnal equinox, characterized by windy, rainy days. Since this calendar was reckoned from around the 4th of February it would correspond closely with the 1st of September in our calendar.

A-bomb. Everything was broken or burnt. Our mess table was an ordinary, battered old office desk, its surface etched and marked where glass fragments had scarred it. Little bits of glass were still imbedded in the wood as though placed there by an inlay worker. Boxes, containing berry-colored army flags, cluttered one corner. Old Mrs. Saeki used these flags for dishclothes and floor mops. On a shelf stood a thermos bottle Mr. Mizoguchi brought back from his home in Seno a couple of days ago. He returned with it filled with *matcha*,* stating the vitamin C would be good for me. Drinking some of that tea brought back memories of better days. Even the broken tea cup and the old *hashi* with which I stirred the tea could not mar its flavor or aroma. The memory of it was still in my mind this morning and caused me to think of my home and the tea cups I had had before the bombing. Such thoughts made me sad.

On rounds yesterday, it occurred to me that we had had no tetanus, even in patients whose wounds contained filth and dirt. Why had that been? Had the tetanus germs been killed by the *pika* or had we overlooked tetanus when everything had been confused and chaotic? I must try to answer this question, I thought to myself.

Mr. Kadoya's diarrhea was not improving. Some believed he had dysentery whereas others contended it was catarrh of the colon, but whatever the cause he continued to frequent the toilet. Mr. Kadoya had a good sense of humor, though, and always managed to laugh when someone joked about his time in the

---

* *Matcha* is a finely powdered green tea prepared by placing a small quantity in a tea cup with scalding hot water and whipping it briskly with a flexible bamboo whisk. The tea ceremony, together with the art of landscape gardening and flower arranging, was introduced into Japan during medieval times by Zen Buddhist monks from China.

No one has expressed the ceremony more fittingly than Reischauer, who states: "... an aesthetic spiritual ritual in which a beautiful but simple setting, a few fine pieces of old pottery, a slow, formalized, extremely graceful ritual for preparing and serving the tea, and a spirit of complete tranquility all combine to express the love of beauty, the devotion to simplicity, and the search for spiritual calm which characterize the best in Zen."

toilet. I am afraid those of us who went through the *pika* developed a rather coarse sense of humor.

"Don't worry, Mr. Kadoya," I remarked, making amends for our shortcomings. "You have only one more day to bear your abdominal pain and diarrhea. You will be well tomorrow if you don't eat."

Dr. Sasada left in the early afternoon. Since he had nothing to take with him, his leaving required no preparation.

"Your turn will be next, Mr. Shiota," Dr. Sasada said in farewell. This little remark cheered Mr. Shiota.

Today, a contingent of nurses and doctors came in from the Okayama Medical School. They were led by Dr. Yadani, an old classmate, who studied with me under Professor Inada. There were eight nurses and two students. Among the nurses I recognized several familiar faces.

When I found the group was to be with us for a week and had even brought their own microscope, I felt as though a great army had come to help. To have so much help was like the old saying, "arming the devil with an iron bar." Their coming made me so happy I neglected proper greetings.

Mr. Sera, Mr. Kitao, and Mr. Mizoguchi saw they had the best we could provide in food and sleeping accommodations. Dr. Katsube and other healthy staff members gave up their beds and moved to a shed near the hospital. There still being insufficient room to accommodate everybody, we made beds in the examining rooms and operating room of the gynecology department.

To accommodate our visitors in this way may not appear hospitable, but it was the best we could do. Consider Dr. Katsube, for example. He had been on a burned and scarred old bed in one of the second floor toilets, the walls streaked with blood, the floor littered with fragments of glass and debris, and the iron window shutters broken and sagging. Into these accommodations he moved without comment or complaint. Others on the staff slept wherever they found an empty spot each night; sometimes on the top of a desk, sometimes in a chair—rarely two nights running in the same place.

Even the matter of bedding was a problem and when we despaired of finding enough to care for fifteen additional people the city office came through with blankets, sheets, and uniforms. "It's a long lane that has no turning," I thought. There were blankets and to spare. Two came my way, one of which I fastened across the window to keep out the rain and the other I used as a rug on the damp floor beside my bed.

There was so much excitement today it was night before I realized I had not made rounds. Now, it was too late. Moreover, when I found myself quiet for the first time since our visitors arrived, I noticed pain in the wound in my right thigh. Whether this was due to dampness or because I had exerted myself too much I could not tell, but I knew I should go to bed.

Returning to my room, I was surprised to find Dr. Sasada.

"What are you doing here?" I exclaimed. "I thought you had left the hospital!"

"He did leave!" Mr. Shiota broke in laughing. "Didn't you see the big black shiny car he drove off in?"

"What happened?" I asked.

My question sent Dr. Sasada and Mr. Shiota into convulsions of laughter, and between gasps for breath I got the story. Someone had engaged a car to take Dr. Sasada home in style. Near the outskirts of Hiroshima the car was stopped at a bridge by some military policemen who impounded the automobile. The car, it was discovered, belonged to the navy and the driver had appropriated it as a taxi. The driver was taken into custody and Dr. Sasada was left standing on the bridge with no alternative but to return to the hospital.

Despite the humor of the situation, I felt sorry for Dr. Sasada. I was delighted, though, to see him back. After all, he was one of the family.

The mosquitoes were not so bad tonight. Someone had found a quantity of camphor wood and set it to smolder in smudge pots around the hospital. The additional blankets I had made an effective barrier against the dampness and rain. My thigh was aching when I crawled into bed, but in a few minutes I was sound asleep.

Late in the night, I was startled from sleep by the sound of someone coming up the stairs, talking loudly and making a dreadful noise. It was Dr. Tamagawa, professor of pathology in the Hiroshima Medical School; I could recognize his voice before he came into view. He and I had been schoolmates in medical school at Okayama and close friends ever since. As a matter of fact, he had been my principal opponent in *kuchi sumō* * because we both liked to talk and were fond of an argument.

Breezing in without pausing or greeting, he addressed me abruptly: "Hachiya! Do you know I went to the Prefectural Office today and those idiots had the cheek to tell me they wouldn't allow autopsies in Hiroshima! Those great fools!"

"Tamagawa-san," I interjected quickly, "aren't you a little late?"

Without paying me the least attention Dr. Tamagawa unslung his rucksack and continued:

"What a stupid policy—not to permit autopsies! Don't you think so? Without autopsies in a situation like this, what can you learn? Come! You must agree!"

"For heaven's sakes, be quiet!" I broke in, trying to calm him. "I certainly do agree with you; and heaven be praised you are here. No one could be more welcome."

It was so late I had him sleep in my bed.

* *Kuchi sumō*—literally, mouth wrestling.

28 August 1945

CLOUDY.

The notice I posted yesterday summarizing our experience with radiation sickness had its effect because quite early several newspaper reporters came in. I tried as best I could to answer their questions about the patients, their symptoms, prognosis, and our future plans for their care.

Later, I was visited by a close friend, Mr. Yamashita, who had been employed by the Post Office Department before the *pika*. Mr. Yamashita had well-developed literary tastes and was known for his artistry and skill in the writing of *waka*,* thirty-one-syllable poems. More than once he had given friendly criticism and advice on articles I wrote for a local magazine published by the Bureau, the *Hiroshima Teiyu*, and on a clinical diary I had written, entitled *Daruma To Tora*.†

You can appreciate how happy I was to see my old literary friend and, while I prepared him a cup of *matcha*, confided that I was trying to record my experiences, personal and otherwise, as a record of what one endures after the explosion of an atom bomb.

"This is delicious," said Mr. Yamashita with a little bow. After

---

* *Waka* is a highly stylized poetic art form, dating from medieval times, written in thirty-one syllables. (A seventeen-syllable form, the *haiku*, appeared later.) In the hands of a master, it may express a great depth of feeling as well as compelling word pictures.

† *Daruma To Tora* means: The Daruma and the Tiger. Daruma, shaped like our Humpty-Dumpty, though without arms or legs, is an old god who epitomizes persistence, patience, and perseverance. His limbs withered as he sat and meditated. Upset, he always regains his equilibrium. Having once spent many days and nights in meditation, Daruma fell asleep. When he awakened, he was so chagrined he plucked out his eyelids so he would never again fall asleep. Where the eyelids fell, tea grew for the first time, and thus gave to the world a sleep-destroying beverage.

he had drunk the tea in a few swift gulps, he paused to examine the cup.

Mr. Yamashita was fond of *matcha* and more than ordinarily sensitive to the gentle courtesies appropriate to the tea ceremony. Its taste must have revived memories because he sat quiet for some minutes before resuming conversation.

"How is your account going?" he at length asked me.

"You know what difficulty I have as a writer," I answered. "I have the same trouble this time. Perhaps more, because I am out of practice and so many things distract me. Sometimes I get my notes up to date, but before I know it I find myself again several days behind. Are you doing any writing, now, Mr. Yamashita?"

"I kept a diary until the day of the *pika*," he answered, "but since then I have done nothing. Yashushi, my son, was killed; my house was destroyed; so I endure life in despair and confusion."

"Would you be kind enough to let me see your diary?" I asked. "It would be a great help, especially on points leading up to the bombing. For example, I would like to know how things were in Ushita."

"It will please me for you to see it," he replied, kindly. "I'll bring it by in the next few days."

After Mr. Yamashita left, I turned to affairs in the hospital. I no longer had the responsibility for patients I had before the group from Okayama arrived. Previously, ward rounds came first, but now I felt it was more important to see that our guests were comfortable and that they had the best conditions we could provide for effective work. I became an administrator and left the medical work for our guests.

Dr. Katsube had arranged with Dr. Yadani for the two medical students to spend their time taking histories, making physical examinations, and performing blood studies or other laboratory tests. These students proved diligent and capable. One was the son of Professor Hata, a teacher at Okayama University, and the other the son of Mr. Ogawa, a famous writer.

The Okayama nurses were cooperative and worked willingly with our nursing staff. The hospital began to look like a hospital again. The nurses and doctors from Okayama even had clean white gowns and uniforms, quite in contrast with my ragged and dirty staff.

Dr. Tamagawa was welcomed by everyone, but his coming did create a problem as to where he could work. A niche in the hospital was out of the question because we were already bursting at the seams. The only place I could think of was the rude, wooden shack the soldiers had thrown up near the outdoor latrine. With some misgivings I showed it to him and asked if it would do.

"Do?" he exclaimed. "Why, this is just fine!"

Without further ado Dr. Tamagawa set about with the help of a few workmen and converted the shack into an autopsy room and laboratory. The boards he tore out to make windows he used to make an autopsy table and work benches. In a little while, this humble structure was turned into the queerest laboratory I ever laid eyes on, but it did not bother Dr. Tamagawa. His only concern was for material to study.

I discovered after lunch that we were almost out of cigarettes and asked Mr. Shiota if he could do anything about it.

"Don't worry," was his reply. "Leave it to me. I'll get all you need."

Relieved, I divided the remaining supply among the habitual smokers, this time including Dr. Tamagawa. Surprise and delight registered on his face. He had not been able to smoke much either, what with the price and now the scarcity of cigarettes.

Before the war, a pack of Kinshi cigarettes cost eight *sen*. When war started, an additional tax of seven *sen* was imposed, boosting the price to fifteen *sen*. Later the price rose to twenty-three *sen* and before the war was over the price had soared to thirty-five *sen*. Cigarettes were now worth more than money, so I was not the only one who smoked a few puffs and then put a cigarette away to smoke again.

In the ruins of Hiroshima money was valueless and cigarettes took over as a medium of exchange. These thirty-five *sen* cigarettes will now bring three hundred to five hundred *sen* in Hiroshima.

A nice looking young student visited me and introduced himself as the brother of Dr. Morisugi, a physician on our staff missing since the *pika*. This young man, formerly a student in Tokyo, talked and looked like his older brother. Eagerly, I asked for news.

"My brother was injured in his home here in Hiroshima," he answered sadly. "On the seventeenth I received a letter dated 15 August and that night left for home. When I got here, my entire family was dead. Mother burned to death in our home and my sister died on the 15th. My brother, his wife, and our father escaped to Furuichi and there my brother died on the seventeenth and my father on the eighteenth."

"Then you are alone?" I asked.

"Yes," he replied.

Some of his brother's books and belongings were still in the hospital, so I placed them in his Boston bag and told him to keep them. Before he left, I embraced the young man and remarked: "When you have finished school, come and work in this hospital as your brother did."

Nearly two days had passed since I had made rounds, so when Dr. Morisugi's brother left I hastened to the Bureau. My notice concerning radiation sickness was posted prominently on the front entrance. Seeing it displayed so conspicuously made me a little embarrassed and I wished I could have expressed myself better.

The wards had been cleaned and rearranged.

Mr. Onomi, the patient with petechiae, stomatitis, and prolapse of his anus, was worse. His face was swollen and a small wound behind his ear, which had earlier healed, was bleeding again. Death appeared imminent.

The beautiful young girl who was so badly burned still hung on and still showed no signs of epilation or petechiae. Her neighbors did what they could for her.

Since my last visit, a few new patients had been admitted with petechiae but none were at present critically ill.

Going from the Bureau to the hospital, I concluded my rounds. The patient census had decreased sharply during the past two days although our total census was scarcely altered because of the number of families still residing in the hospital with patient relatives. Among these were the Yasui and Awatani families, whom I had known for years.

As I started to leave the ward, I discovered one situation that distressed me exceedingly. Since Dr. Chodo's death on the thirteenth from burns, his wife and baby continued to live in the hospital. Mrs. Chodo had shown no signs of injury or illness and as recently as this morning appeared to be well. I was surprised, therefore, to find her in bed.

"*Okāsan*, what is the trouble?" I asked, pausing at her bed.

In an Okinawa or Kyushu dialect, I could not tell which, she mumbled something to the effect that she had shortness of breath and palpitation.

"*Okāsan*, you will be all right," I said, trying to reassure her. "You must keep strong for the sake of your little baby."

I knew immediately I had said the wrong thing because on mentioning the word "baby," she turned to the little head sleeping on her breast and began to cry softly.

With what this poor woman had been through the sight of her crying tore at my heartstrings. What if something should happen to her; who would care for her little baby? To conceal the fear and terror in my heart I left her, trying to put up a cheerful front. But no one could conceal from her the ominous import of the dark spots that had appeared on her chest.

The chipper, easy-going Dr. Tamagawa made a bright spot in our ward and dining room. By nature cheerful and happy, he had a way of putting those around him in a good mood. Even the food tasted good to him. And he would occasionally chide us good-naturedly by saying we should not be so extravagant.

He took the lead in the idle talk after supper and told us of his difficulties after he was bombed out in Okayama. The way he belittled his hardships and made jokes about his troubles helped to restore our sense of humor. He told about funny things that happened to him in the past and pretty soon had everyone laughing. I was acquainted with many of the stories he told, but they were all new to my comrades. I made no comment although I am sure if I had begun to argue with him we would have sounded like a pair of comic dancers. My friends soon forgot that Dr. Tamagawa was a professor and took him in without restraint.

My wife was not doing well, tonight. Her temperature had gone up to 101.5° and she complained of shortness of breath. While Miss Kado was getting a stethoscope so I could listen to her chest, I tried to appear unconcerned.

"It sounds like you've caught a little cold, again. I might have guessed as much yesterday when I saw you, Toki-chan, and Miss Kado taking a nap together in the same bed."

Listening to her chest, I heard *râles* at the base of the right lung posteriorly, and I could percuss an area of dullness over the same area. To me, these signs could mean only that she had a croupous pneumonia. I made haste to find Dr. Hinoi, our chief pharmacist, to ask if he could get me any trionone, one of the sulfonamides.

Much to my relief, he informed me that we had an abundant supply.

Returning to the ward, I had Miss Kado transfer my wife to Dr. Yatani's room where she could be better protected from the wind and rain.

I should have paid more attention to her cough and sputum, but since she had complained of no pain, I overlooked those earlier symptoms of pneumonia.

Could one survive a case of pneumonia after going through the *pika*, I wondered. Why hadn't I looked after her more carefully? How could I live with myself, must less face the family, if anything happened to my wife?

Arrangements were made for Yaeko-san to receive one injection of glucose and trionone each day.

29 August 1945

CLOUDY WITH occasional clearing.

I did not sleep well during the night for worrying about my wife. Why had I not been mindful of the dampness caused by the continuing rain and the coolness of approaching autumn in the early morning? If she had not gotten chilled or wet, she would not have pneumonia.

I should have thought of the other patients, too, because they were in the same predicament, not one of them in any condition to withstand the onslaught of pneumonia. It is true we had given warm navy uniforms to the women patients and lighter khaki army clothes to the men, but that was not enough. I must get more blankets for everyone.

My thoughts went to other relief supplies. A shipment of army shoes had been given us which we distributed among the male patients. Every one seemed satisfied until the women complained because they had not been included; and their clamor continued until I promised them the next shipment of shoes. How greedy people are and how anxious for equality, whatever the basis. The women knew very well the army shoes would not fit them and when this was pointed out they countered by arguing that they wanted the shoes for their husbands and children, or as a present to take home. Such an attitude dumbfounded me because no one was charged for bed, food, or treatment, and when clothes were provided, they were distributed equally. But that was not enough. The women had to have their share of the army shoes just like the men.

This morning, as though in answer to my silent prayers, a big shipment of military goods arrived. I was delighted to find that it contained mosquito nets and blankets—and shoes, both slippers and barrack shoes. I made sure the latter were distributed among the women.

, There were not enough blankets for everyone, so I requisitioned them for the hospital and distributed them to patients.

Word came around noon that terms for unconditional surrender would be signed early in September aboard the battleship *Missouri* in Tokyo Bay.

"Will the Prime Minister and his cabinet be present?" I asked, "Or will the Emperor be there alone?"

"What if the Emperor should be captured!" someone exclaimed.

"Don't say such a terrible thing!" retorted old Mrs. Saeki. "The *tenka-sama* hasn't done anything wrong."

"It is rumored he will be taken to the Ryukyus for confinement," someone remarked.

Laying her cheek in her hand and placing a finger characteristically on her one remaining front tooth, old Mrs. Saeki murmured sadly: "They are going to take him away just like they did in the olden days."

That would be impossible, I thought, as I listened to the discussion. But was it impossible? One had only to consult history to find similar examples. Napoleon spent his last days on St. Helena, and czars and kaisers had been banished from their homes after defeat. We could only wait and see. Anything can happen to a nation in defeat.

I prayed the Emperor would be spared and not taken away on a battleship. That *would* be the end!

To free my mind of these gloomy thoughts and forget for a moment my concern for my wife I made rounds. The patients were happy over the new supplies, the women especially, because now they had shoes just like the men. A few even bowed and thanked me.

Being in no mood for their thanks, much less their happiness, I spoke curtly and with disdain: "Those things were given you by the city; thank it, not me!"

Patients on the critically ill list were increasing. They all had one sign in common—petechiae. Mr. Onomi was dead, death following profuse hemorrhage from his nose and anus.

Miss Nishii, admitted two days ago, was dead. Her last minutes were an agony of suffocation.

Rounds were almost finished when I suddenly realized I had missed Mrs. Chodo. To my horror, I learned she was dead. I could not believe it for I had seen her in the corridor this morning. What would happen to her little baby girl?

Dr. Tamagawa was already at work. I walked slowly over to the autopsy room, scarcely noticing the thousands of flies I disturbed each time I put my foot down. Dr. Tamagawa was busy at his grim task. Mr. Ogawa, the medical student from Okayama, was assisting and taking notes. I stood for a while watching Dr. Tamagawa as he worked swiftly and skillfully. Perhaps *he* could discover why our patients were dying. If he could do this, we might somehow learn to save them.

"You are skillful, Tamagawa-san," I said, finally.

"*Dō itashimashite*," he replied, without pausing from his work.

Wishing to compare autopsy findings with clinical symptoms, I returned to the hospital to study the charts of the patients now being autopsied. Miss Kobayashi had died with massive hemorrhage in her abdominal cavity and Mr. Onomi with profuse bleeding from nose and rectum. Had hemorrhage also caused the sudden death of Mrs. Chodo and the death of Miss Nishii? If so, why had it occurred?

Miss Nishii's record was summarized as follows:

Nishii, Emiko, female, aged sixteen. First seen on 28 August 1945 with complaints of general malaise, petechiae, and inability to sleep. At time of bombing patient was on the second floor of the central Telephone Bureau, a concrete building five hundred meters from the hypocenter. Immediate onset of dizziness and general weakness; vomited repeatedly. For next three days had nausea and malaise. Gradually recovered appetite but did not recover completely. Patient returned to light work despite diarrhea and slight weakness. Severe epilation appeared on 23 August 1945 and from then on malaise gradually increased. Abdominal pain and restlessness developed during night of 27 August, and for first time, petechiae were noticed.

Examination: Moderate stature. Nutrition poor. Skin extremely pale, black-brown in color, and dry. Numerous petechiae over chest and extremities. Agonized appearance on face. Inner surfaces of eyelids suggest severe anemia. Mouth cavity normal. Breath sounds over chest weak with dull percussion note over both lung fields from behind. Over pulmonary artery second heart sound accentuated. Pulse weak and rapid with rate of 130/minute, respirations 36, body temperature 104°. Constipated.

Died 29 August 1945 complaining of severe shortness of breath.

One feature was common to all the patients who had died within the last two or three days: all had been less than a thousand meters from the hypocenter when the bomb exploded. It became apparent to me, therefore, that the nearer one was to the hypocenter, the more likely he was to die.

I was so eager for autopsy reports on Mrs. Chodo, Miss Nishii, and Mr. Onomi that I returned to the autopsy room toward evening to see what Dr. Tamagawa had learned. He could tell me little, for under the best conditions it takes a minimum of several days to complete one's findings and Dr. Tamagawa was no exception. Without electric lights it would take even longer.

To make it possible for him to work at night, I combed the hospital for every available candle and asked Mr. Sera, the business manager, if he could do something to get electric lights (I had seen some begin to come on recently in the Nigitsu and Ushita areas on the other side of the river.)

Yaeko-san's general condition was unchanged. A low-hanging mosquito net had been placed over her bed and served not only as a wind break but as an adequate croup tent as well. She put up a fuss when I gave her an injection of glucose and trionone by the flickering light of a candle. Hereafter, I determined to ask Miss Kado to do this and thus spare both of us. A doctor is never good at treating his own family.

Dr. Sasada, Mr. Shiota, and I were gloomy as we sat around the table after supper. The deaths today had us all depressed, but none so much as the death of Mrs. Chodo. The memory of her figure in the corridors was vivid in our minds.

"What will happen to her little baby?" I said half to myself and half aloud.

"Haven't you heard?" asked Mr. Shiota, turning to me. "Mrs. Fujii, the dentist's wife, is going to adopt the baby."

I had forgotten about Mrs. Fujii, and Mr. Shiota's statement eased my mind a little. The adoption would be good for the baby and good for Mrs. Fujii, too, because this poor woman lost a baby, born shortly after the *pika*, and her oldest daughter had died from burns.

Late in the night, I was disturbed again by Dr. Tamagawa, noisy as ever, as he came up from his work to go to bed.

"I'll be needing more specimen bottles, Hachiya," he stated, unceremoniously. "There's been another death tonight."

I promised to do what I could.

30 August 1945

CLOUDY WITH occasional rain.

The remains of Mrs. Chodo were cremated during the night and since it looked like rain I went out early to gather her ashes and bones. Customarily, one uses an urn, but since that was out of the question, I used an empty paper box I found in the pharmacy. Choosing one bone each from the head, face, chest, and limbs, I arranged them neatly in the box, inscribed her name on the lid, and carried it to the altar in the business office.

I next tried to find some specimen jars for Dr. Tamagawa. Recalling that some old batteries had been stacked near the entrance to the Communications Bureau, I went over and appropriated ten or so. These batteries made good containers after removing the electrodes and washing out the sulphuric acid that remained. I then raided the pharmacy department and took every empty bottle the pharmacist could spare. In the meantime, Dr. Tamagawa had searched the ruins and found several broken *hibachi* big enough to hold the specimens of three or four patients.

Thinking this to be an opportune time to ask about the results of yesterdays' autopsies, I asked Dr. Tamagawa if he would let me see his notes.

"It will be better to wait until I have had a chance to study five or six cases," he answered, after deliberating for some minutes with the air of a great scholar. No amount of cajolery would cause him to relent.

My thigh had hurt for several days. The wounds on my face, shoulder, and back were healed and gave no trouble, but the thigh wound, although healing, became increasingly painful. I was convinced that the damp weather had something to do with it, but I also knew that activity made it worse. It was hurting so much this morning after my little exertion that I determined to go back to bed, but not wishing to remain idle, I sent a message to Dr. Katsube asking if I could help with the blood examinations while trying to give my thigh a rest.

Word was returned that Dr. Katsube would be grateful for my help and the messenger brought me some stained blood slides and one of the only two microscopes we had in the hospital. I placed the microscope on a table before the window and went to work.

I had thought it would be easy to sit on my bed and look through a microscope. I soon changed my mind. It had been so long since I had used a microscope that within a few minutes things began to flicker before my eyes and I found it increasingly difficult to concentrate, let alone see what I was looking at. It took three hours to examine three slides.

The slides were from patients critically ill. In the three slides together I found not more than seventy to eighty white blood cells and those I saw did not appear abnormal. The red cells appeared normal at first glance, but looking sharply, I found evidence of anisocytosis, poikilocytosis, polychromasia, and basophilic stippling.* I found no nucleated red blood cells. The low white blood count was expected, but until now, I had not been aware of changes in the red blood cells as well. I could only conclude that the entire hematopoietic system † was involved.

Each time I looked into the microscope it became more difficult to pick out the cells. My eyelids quivered, so I would gaze out the window until the quivering ceased. My attention wandered; a voice or a train whistle would distract me. Like an idle boy who hates study but is fond of play, I could not settle down to steady work. My mind repeatedly drifted towards the distractions around me. If someone passed, I made an excuse to talk with him.

Soon, I lost all patience and left the microscope sitting there on the table. What an annoyance! I could see well enough, but I could not discriminate. I tried to blame my eyes, but it was my mind that was at fault. I had been intellectually idle too long.

I tried chiding myself for keeping the microscope when someone else could be using it effectively, but that did no good. I had fallen victim again to that disorderliness of thought that had plagued me ever since the day of the *pika*. Wrapped in meditation, I began to fear my five senses had deserted me. On the day of the bombing the only pain I felt was when my wounds were sutured. Visitors to the hospital complained that the whole place smelled terrible. I was surprised, for I could smell nothing unpleasant at all. My esthetic sense was dulled because I did not mind the filth and dirt around me or even the flies and mosquitoes which ordinarily annoyed me intensely. My sense of taste had been dulled for a while but it seemed to have returned. My ears, too, had recovered for I had no difficulty understanding what was said to me and at times they seemed almost too sensitive. Perhaps it was a sixth sense that had kept me going when my others, like my powers of visual discrimination, failed me.

---

* Evidences of immaturity or abnormal growth.
† Hematopoietic system refers to these parts of the body: bone marrow, spleen, lymphoid tissue, and liver, where blood cells are formed.

Towards evening Mr. Mizoguchi came in looking harassed.

"What's the matter, Mizoguchi-san?" I asked, welcoming an opportunity to get away from the microscope and my confusing thoughts.

"It's no use, *sensei*," he replied, as he sat down wearily. "If only we could get an automobile. You know, perhaps, that we have been obliged to accommodate the homeless families who were employed by the Post Office and the Western General Bureau, and that we have tried to supply their needs with the same consideration we show for our own people.

"Well, these people are happy enough to accept our hospitality, but do you think they are willing to make my task as supply officer any easier? No! For example, you've seen the cars parked at the Bureau entrance. Most of them are official vehicles belonging to other departments and a few are private cars for hire. Time and again I have requested the use of official cars to haul supplies and each time I've had to promise them 10 per cent of each shipment even though we are giving them shelter and goods. Sometimes I even have to give them extra alcohol, gauze, and cotton goods in addition.

"Those people are blackguards, I tell you; and Mr. Sera and I would have nothing to do with them if there were any way around it. We would use the private cars if we could, but those poor fellows have such a hard time getting petrol we can't depend on them. In the meantime military goods stockpiled near the outskirts of the city are being ruined by rain or fattening the pockets of unscrupulous speculators."

What a sorry spectacle, I thought, to have such ugly behavior added to the burden of people already crushed by defeat. The ruthless and greedy were ruling the city whereas never before had there been such need for unselfishness and good breeding. Our only hope was that an incorruptible and honest leader would rise from the filth and corruption of the destroyed city.

I was reminded of an ancient Chinese proverb which stated that a large fish would not grow in clear water. We had all been small fish who lived through the clear waters of the eras of Meiji, Teisho, and Showa.* Perhaps now that the waters of our history had become muddied, a big fish would grow and in the course of time a great figure appear.

My philosophical thoughts may not have helped Mr. Mizoguchi with the hard problem of reality he faced, but they afforded me a little solace.

After supper, a flurry of excitement was stirred by a rumor that electric wires were being strung and we would have electricity in a few days. The rumor started when someone discovered two yellow wires being strung along the Hatchōbori leading to the hospital. These wires proved to be an army telephone line.

Late in the night, Dr. Tamagawa disturbed my sleep to say he found changes in every organ of the body in the cases he had autopsied.

31 August 1945

RAIN EARLY in the day. Later generally clear with occasional clouds.

My first act this morning was to go to the roof balcony and, with head bowed to the east, pray for the Emperor. I did this because of a dream that troubled my sleep during the night.

It seemed I was in a vast throng gathered to see the Emperor

---

* The Meiji era, named for the Emperor Meiji, began in 1868 with the Meiji Reform; it marked the end of feudalism, the restoration of imperial dignity, the beginning of compulsory education, and an accelerated interest in Western civilization. The Teisho era began in 1912 and continued until 1926, when the present Emperor Hirohito ascended the throne under the reign title of Showa.

go aboard the American battleship *Missouri,* anchored in Tokyo Bay. The Emperor's escort was Ambassador Grew, who conducted him to the wardroom, whereupon the crew began raising the anchor. The scene shifted, and the battleship was no longer in Tokyo Bay, but in Hiroshima on the Ōta River opposite the Asano Sentei Park. Along the steep banks of the river were thousands of atom bomb victims, and as the anchor rose they began to shout and jump in the river. Some begged for the Emperor to be left at home while others swam madly toward the ship and tried to forestall the raising of the anchor.

At this point, I awakened, terrified and drenched with sweat. My subconscious mind, grimly working while I slept, pieced together story fragments I had heard about survivors in the Asano Sentei Park and fragments of conversation I overheard about the surrender. Ambassador Grew, I had not thought of for a long time, but to many of us, he symbolized the group who tried to prevent war in the first place.

It was no less damp and gloomy today than the days recently passed, but my thigh felt better, probably because I was less active yesterday.

Going to the Out-Patient Department, I found patients lined up to get their blood examined. Dr. Hanaoka and the medical students were busy examining blood smears, and on the table I noticed a reagent bottle marked "for platelet examination." *

"You are making platelet counts," I observed.

"Yes," answered Dr. Hanaoka, "we are, but so many slides are totally devoid of platelets there is nothing to count."

"How about Dr. Katsube?" I asked.

"He's having the same trouble," Dr. Hanaoka replied. "Nearly everyone we see has no platelets or an extremely low count."

---

* In the complex mechanism controlling blood clotting the blood platelets, spherical or ovoid, light-gray bodies from 1.0 to 2.5 mu in diameter, are of vital importance. They normally number around 300,000 per cubic centimeter of blood. If the blood-forming organs are injured by radiation, the platelets decrease in number or disappear, with the result that hemorrhage occurs into the tissues.

Dr. Hanaoka's remarks recalled the autopsy cases. Failure of the blood to clot might well have been because of a decrease in blood platelets. I could hardly wait to confront Dr. Tamagawa with my suspicions.

"Is that so!" he exclaimed. "Well! That explains everything. Yes, indeed! That's why blood hasn't clotted even after seven hours!"

A cloud seemed to lift above Dr. Tamagawa and left him communicative and expansive by contrast with his brusk, non-communicative behavior earlier. It was as though my comments provided him with the key to a puzzle.

He paused to show me petechiae visible in organs he was removing from a patient and expressed the opinion that a decrease in blood platelets was responsible for the development of petechiae. His cases and the case autopsied by Dr. Katsube showed the same changes. The differences in clinical symptoms could be attributed to the degree in which different organs were affected. One did not need to look at microscopic sections of removed tissue to understand that death was caused by many internal hemorrhages secondary to a platelet decrease.

Miss Kobayashi, who died on the twenty-sixth, with abdominal pain and dyspnea, had hemorrhaged severely from petechiae in and behind the abdominal cavity. Mrs. Chodo, who died on the twenty-ninth, had a hemorrhage in the wall of her heart. It was greatest where nerve impulses originated. Mr. Sakai, who also died on the twenty-ninth, had had severe shortness of breath. On autopsy he had a large hemorrhage in the chest and abdominal cavities, again in the presence of petechiae. Mr. Onomi bled to death from hemorrhages in his nose and rectum. Mr. Sakinishi, who died on the thirtieth in delirium, had massive hemorrhage in his chest cavity. Both lungs were involved and petechiae were found in all the internal organs. Since his family insisted that we not remove his brain we could only surmise that brain hemorrhage had occurred.

Hemorrhage was the cause of death in all our cases. The extent and severity of petechiae, or surface manifestations of hemorrhage, bore no relationship to the extent of hemorrhage in the internal organs. Nor was the extent of internal hemorrhage the same in each organ. One organ might be badly involved and another spared. We could find no organ that had a greater tendency to develop hemorrhage than another, and the only organs consistently altered were the livers and spleens. In every case, they appeared smaller than normal, particularly the spleen.

Until now, we had interpreted the low white count as characteristic of the disease, but it became obvious that this was only one feature of a disease that involved platelets as well. Absence of platelets was responsible for hemorrhage and hemorrhage was the immediate cause of death.

We had overlooked the platelets because they are more difficult to evaluate than white blood cells. We now knew all the blood-forming organs were involved: white blood cells, platelets, and even the red cells because when we studied them, many abnormal forms were found. The latter changes could be incident to anemia caused by hemorrhage, so we could not be certain. Loss of hair I interpreted as a disturbance of nutrition to the hair roots. The pathologic picture of radiation sickness began to make sense.

A scolding voice at my elbow brought me back to reality. It was old Mrs. Saeki.

"*Sensei*, what happened to you?" she admonished. "Don't you know you completely forgot lunch, and here it is 4:00? You mustn't abuse yourself so. You can't live on cigarettes! You are reckless to abuse yourself this way. It's not good for your body."

"*Baba-san*," I answered softly, "we now understand some of the things which puzzled us before."

"Is that so?" she retorted. "Will you be able to cure the disease now?"

Her eyes were big and round as she busied herself with my lunch.

Afterwards, I had old Mrs. Saeki boil water and get out my tea set so I could make *matcha* for everybody in our room. They all seemed better today. Dr. Sasada and Mr. Shiota were as good as well. Mr. Kadoya's diarrhea had stopped, and Mrs. Susukida and Miss Yama were no worse. My wife no longer had fever and her general condition was improving.

Dr. Tamagawa kept us laughing far into the night with his stories.

1 September 1945

RAIN WITH heavy overcast.

Rain soaked my bed sometime during the night, but I slept so soundly I was not aware of it until I awakened this morning. In consequence, I developed symptoms of a full-blown cold.

Rain was falling in a regular downpour when I awakened. My discomfort was increased by being unable to make the usual visit to my private toilet. After waiting as long as I could, hoping the rain would let up, I was obliged to borrow an umbrella and visit the hospital toilet in the court beyond the back entrance. Since I had not used this toilet for some days I was shocked to discover how utterly filthy it was. It could hardly be called a toilet, for it consisted of loose boards thrown across a long hole dug in the ground. This hole was half full of undigested feces, scraps of paper torn from account books, medical journals, and even some pages from Krumpel's *Diagnostics*, and dirty water from surface drainage incident to the heavy rain. The utter filth of the place was made more emphatic by the presence of a little frog who sat perched under a mass of straw matting in one corner. He looked up at me and seemed to wipe his face in protest when a few drops of urine splashed on him.

The condition here could not be tolerated, and I made up my

mind to pursue the matter. Otherwise, we could expect an epidemic of dysentery. Why an outbreak had not already occurred was more than I could fathom.

After breakfast, I went to the business office, despite an increasing achiness and cough, to take the matter up with Mr. Sera and Mr. Kitao.

"Something must be done about the outdoor toilet," I stated, "or we can expect infection to break out in the hospital. We have enough to worry about without an epidemic of dysentery."

Mr. Sera sighed and, nodding his head in agreement, replied, "*Sensei*, we have been worrying about the matter and have tried to get the Bureau to do something. They keep promising to build a proper toilet and each day we hope they will get started."

"Can't you sprinkle lime around the area and pour lysol into the hole?" I asked. "Anything to disinfect the area and keep flies from multiplying."

"I wish we could, *sensei*," replied Mr. Kitao with a look of concern. "But we haven't any and haven't been able to get any."

It was obvious these poor men were doing everything they could and I was sorry I caused them the embarrassment of bringing the matter up. No one could have worked more faithfully or diligently than these conscientious members of our business office.

Not feeling very active, I pulled up a box and sat down.

"How are things going in general?" I asked.

"Very well," answered Mr. Sera. "Toki-chan (Miss Takami) and Yamamoto-san are back at work. Both were injured. You will be glad to hear we managed to get two rolls of electric wire and the electricians tell us they hope to have us some electric lights before the day is over."

That was good news. To have electric lights again would be wonderful.

We chatted for a while. Before I left a message came that Dr. Tsuzuki from the Surgery Department of Tokyo Imperial University was coming down on the third of September to discuss problems relating to radiation injury.

Our professional staff was increased this morning by two Hiroshima doctors who offered their services. One was Dr. Nagayama, who had practiced in nearby Hakoshima, and the other Dr. Itaoko who had had an office in the main part of the city. Both were in their early fifties and both had been burned and were now recovering. We welcomed their services and tried to make them feel at home.

At lunchtime, I did not feel like eating, so I went back to bed and had a cup of *matcha*. The pleasant bitterness of the tea, its warmth, and stimulating effect improved my outlook considerably.

This afternoon a medical representative of the Osaka Medical Association visited me. He introduced himself as Dr. Horie. He was staggered by the damage in Hiroshima and told me it was vastly greater than he had been given to believe from official reports released in Osaka. After expressing sorrow for the disaster, he asked if I would tell him how we handled such a tremendous medical emergency.

"You should know," I replied, "that of the 190 doctors in Hiroshima on the day of the *pika*, 72 were killed or are missing. From this, you can draw your own conclusions about medical conditions in the city. I can only speak of the situation in our hospital.

"Here, had it not been for the courageous efforts of my professional staff and the employees of the Bureau who had suffered relatively minor injury, none of us could have survived. The tremendous influx of patients they handled alone. Their work was made harder by the fire that swept the hospital and Bureau."

"What about patients in the hospital when the bomb fell?" asked Dr. Horie.

"There weren't any," I answered, "because during the first week of June we discharged or transferred all in-patients to a safer place."

"Why did you release them?" he asked.

"Because I was concerned for their safety and because I wished to have the hospital free for emergencies in case of disaster," I answered.

"Wasn't that a heroic step?" Dr. Horie asked. "What were your reasons?"

"Perhaps my reasons weren't good," I replied, "but I suspected something when the military school for young men next door to the Bureau moved to the hills, and the army began removing its stockpile of stores from warehouses in the southern part of the city. Furthermore, every time an air-raid alarm sounded the soldiers were the first to depart and the few who remained in the barracks made no preparation for action. What conclusion could one draw but that the army had decided to abandon Hiroshima in case of attack? And another thing, while our principal cities suffered severe bombing, the newspapers always reported slight damage. This deception made me worry even more about our own city.

"Furthermore, this hospital was in an extremely vulnerable position because it was so nearly surrounded by military installations. In case of attack, we might easily be mistaken for their headquarters and become the principal target. I had long since concluded there was no impregnable defense against air attack. Don't you think those were reasons enough to justify my actions? I even told the out-patients to leave the city if they could. When the bombing came, the hospital was empty except for a detachment of civilian guards who used the second floor for a dormitory."

During my discourse Dr. Horie nodded his head in agreement.

"The wound on your face?" he asked, suddenly raising his head as if to imply he was anxious to hear what had happened to me personally.

"I was in the living room of my home, resting," I replied, "because until 4:00 A.M. I had been on air-raid duty at the hospital. You can't see my home now because it was destroyed, but I was there when the bomb fell. I wasn't only wounded in the face but on my body and limbs."

As I spoke, I removed my clothing to show Dr. Horie my other wounds.

"It's a miracle you survived!" he exclaimed.

"This wound on my thigh," I continued, "was the worst. There the flesh was literally snatched from my body. These other wounds were caused by glass fragments and bits of black lacquer. The fragments came out later in the pus."

"Amazing! Perfectly amazing!" Dr. Horie replied, as he shifted his gaze to the scorched walls, the twisted window frames, and the burnt and bent iron beds.

"The only thing that saved this building was its concrete walls," he mused. "Hereafter, all our buildings must be made of reinforced concrete. Such buildings give one the only possible chance of survival."

I enjoyed my conversation with Dr. Horie. He was a quiet, intelligent man, and a sympathetic listener. His visit did me good.

Towards evening, I started ward rounds and in the corridor between the X-ray department and the janitor's room I ran into Mr. Kitao, Mr. Yamazaki, and some nurses playing with poor Mrs. Chodo's little baby daughter. I learned they were going to take the baby to a nursing home in Ujina * because Mrs. Fujii, who had adopted the baby, did not have enough milk to feed it. Mr. Yamazaki had rigged a little box on the back of his bicycle in which he was to take the baby to the nursing home.

Without being able to control myself, I burst into tears. The thoughts of this little baby, whose mother and father died in pain, had preyed on my mind ever since her mother's death, and it was a great relief to know she would be loved and cared for in a loving home.

After supper we sat around the table and whiled away the time in idle talk. Rumor about the Emperor's exile to the Ryukyus was

---

* Ujina is a precinct in southeastern Hiroshima, 4,000 meters from the hypocenter. It overlooks Hiroshima Bay and is the port area of Hiroshima. The statement has been made that most of the troops who fought in the southwestern Pacific embarked at Ujina. Farewell instructions were given in a large auditorium, near the quay, which bears the name "Gaisenkan" or "hall of triumphal return."

the principal topic of conversation until one after another my companions excused themselves and went to bed, leaving me alone in the mess room.

With no one to talk to I soon went to bed, but I could not go to sleep because the bed was still damp. Besides, I could not get the thoughts of Mrs. Chodo's baby out of my mind. Thinking of her called to mind other orphans left by the bombing. There was an eight-year-old girl whose only home now was the hospital because her only relative, her grandmother, had died. There was a thirteen-year-old boy and his eight-year-old sister who had come to the hospital looking for their parents. They found their mother and an older brother but they both died, leaving these children alone in the world. Mr. Mizoguchi more or less adopted them. These children, attractive, well-mannered, and intelligent, became favorites of everyone in the hospital. My thoughts wandered to my son and to my mother who was taking care of him. I felt lonely and sad.

It was late in the night before I got to sleep.

2 September 1945

DRIZZLING rain.

The hospital was quiet this morning and I lay for a long time in bed and gazed absently from the broken windows at the patterns made by the drizzling rain. It was old Mrs. Saeki who finally came in and broke my trance:

"*Sensei*, what is the matter with you? Breakfast is ready, and here you are lolling about in bed!"

Yawning and stretching, I got up and followed old Mrs. Saeki into the dining room. I tried to eat, but nothing tasted good. I made a cup of *matcha*, but that did not taste good either. Nothing tasted good, and what I tried to eat seemed to upset my stomach. I took some stomach medicine and with an effort went back to my room and sat down. My nose was stopped up and my head felt heavy. My cold was now certainly full blown, but even with my cold I was too restless to sit still and so decided to go over to the Bureau. Everything there was as quiet as it was in the hospital and on asking why everything was so quiet I learned it was Sunday. Until now, the days had meant nothing. This was the first day since the *pika* that the day of the week was impressed on my consciousness. From now on, however, Sunday was to be a day of rest for our staff, but I was not sure I liked it. Accustomed as I was to the noise and confusion, this sudden quiet depressed me.

Mr. Ushio, the chief of general affairs, was sitting alone in his room. He had become old and haggard in contrast to his appearance a month ago. It was the same with his office. Before the *pika* it had been a cheerful, attractive, cozy room, but now it was scorched and scarred, the walls covered with soot like a kitchen in a tenement house—an old burnt-out man in an old burnt-out room.

Trying to put on a cheerful front in spite of my thoughts, I complimented Mr. Ushio by saying how much better he was looking and how fortunate it was that his office had not been as badly damaged as some of the other rooms in the Bureau.

"I am fortunate," he replied. "I can at least enjoy a dry bed because, as you see, with it placed against the opposite wall the rain doesn't reach me. Why don't you move in with me? I would be delighted to have you."

I thanked him and replied I might accept his offer if the rain did not stop pretty soon. We talked for a while and I returned to the hospital. On the way, I met a little boy scolding a small girl, presumably his sister, for dropping his toy pistol in a muddy puddle.

"You fool!" he scolded. "You stupid fool! Get my pistol for me!"

"Don't fight," I admonished. The boy looked up at me and scratched his head.

"She dropped my gun!" he said defensively, as if to justify his rude behavior. The little boy ducked off around the building, and the little girl followed. In a moment, the boy reappeared, picked up his gun, and pretended to shoot me. He then aimed at his sister and pretended to shoot her. Since this frightened her, he kept it up until she fled in alarm.

In the dining room, I found Dr. Tamagawa working over some notes. He looked at me over his eyeglasses and remarked: "Tomorrow's my birthday and also the day for Dr. Tsuzuki's lecture."

Without further comment he returned to his notes as if to imply that two such important statements required no further comment. Not wishing to disturb Dr. Tamagawa, I returned to my room. Dr. Sasada and Mr. Shiota were talking about the weather. Mr. Mizoguchi had found a boarding house in Seno for Dr. Sasada and he was planning to leave again as soon as the rain let up. Mr. Shiota was also making preparations to go. I began to wish I was going, too, but since my place was at the hospital, I dismissed the thought.

3 September 1945

DRIZZLING rain.

The rain showed no signs of letting up. Because of it, a pall of gloom hung over the hospital. The unceasing downpour made everything damp and we were chilled to the bone. Drops of water glistened on the walls, our clothing and bedding were moldy, and everything had a musty odor. Yesterday, Mr. Imachi and

Mr. Yamazaki built a bath near the kitchen entrance for the hospital staff. Built from an old iron tub, rocks, and strips of zinc, it was not much, but if we could get enough dry wood to fire it, a hot bath would add immeasurably to our comfort and morale. Many of our people had not bathed since the *pika*. If we could get clean, and look forward to the pleasant warmth of a bath each day, the rain would not seem so bad.

Returning from the toilet this morning, I stopped under the marquee and looked out over the rain-soaked ground. I saw a thin, woebegone dog making his way between the Bureau and the hospital fence. He had something in his mouth and when he got nearer, I discovered it was a bit of vegetable. He must have found it on the garbage dump near the kitchen. What a pitiful sight, I thought, to see a dog reduced to eating vegetable scraps. By nature a flesh eater, this poor dog now had to eat vegetables to live. Most of his hair was gone, so I guessed he suffered radiation injury, too. Somehow, this dog was symbolic. What a dismal view, standing there in the hospital entrance. The straw-matted toilet under the willow tree; a dull, weeping sky; the destroyed barracks and storage houses; and the shabby figure of a dog trudging along with his hips bent, tail down, and hair gone.

Although it was a little early for breakfast, I went up to the dining room and managed to get in old Mrs. Saeki's way.

"*Baba-san*, everything you have is burnt or scorched," I observed, as I watched her preparing breakfast. "Can you cut with that knife?"

"*Sensei-san*, this is a butcher knife," she explained, giving me a smile. "With the handle burnt off you may not recognize it, but it's a butcher knife all right and it can cut."

"You can make anything do, *baba-san*," I replied with sincere respect. I admired the charcoal cooking brazier she had made by cutting a draft hole near the bottom of an old bucket and lining the inside with clay.

"Oh this!" she exclaimed in a tone of modest pride. "This sort of thing is easy to make. All you have to do is to mold some clay, cut a hole in the bucket and then line the inside with the clay and you have a *konro*. *Sensei-san*, when you build a home again, I'll just make one for you. One like this won't break and I'm sure *okāsan* will like it too."

Old Mrs. Saeki's optimism and cheerful good nature were like a tonic. One could not remain unhappy or gloomy in her presence.

Since Professor Tsuzuki was going to speak on radiation sickness this afternoon, I went to the wards after breakfast and spent most of the morning reviewing our records, questioning patients, and making notes, so I might be prepared to comment if the occasion arose. Some new patients had been admitted. They had petechiae but differed from earlier patients in that they insisted they were well after the bombing and had not become ill until three or four days ago. Some were beginning to lose hair.

After lunch, I walked with the students and doctors over to the ruins of the Geibi Bank in Yamaguchi where Professor Tsuzuki was to give his lecture. It had been some time since I was out of the hospital and it impressed me to see makeshift houses beginning to rise from the ruins. A typical example was a small shack in the ruins of Kyōbashi-dori made of four wooden uprights with strips of sheet metal crudely joined to make a roof and four walls. Such an iron-plated, wooden building would not be difficult to build, I thought.

In a little while we reached the scorched, concrete ruins of the Geibi Bank on the streetcar line near the Inari-bashi. The talk was to be given in a room on the second floor. From a window one could look out across the ruins to Hiroshima Bay and see the island of Ninoshima as clearly as if it were right in front of you. To the south could be seen the districts of Ujina and Eba and they, too, seemed to be within hailing distance. Again, I was impressed at how small Hiroshima looked with its buildings and houses destroyed. It was like a small fishing village rather than the once proud city on the banks of Hiroshima Bay.

I was surprised to find a small audience. A few had undoubtedly been prevented from coming because of rain, but the poor attendance was really because there were not enough doctors left in Hiroshima to make a showing.

Some old friends came in by twos and threes and we congratulated each other on being alive.

Chief Kitajima came in with Professor Tsuzuki. They were followed by Professor Miyake, a pathologist, and a few others whose names I did not know. After a brief introduction, Professor Tsuzuki * took the platform. He made an impressive figure as he faced us, erect and precise, attired in a neat khaki uniform and leggings. The scorched, blackened walls made an appropriate background for his discourse on the atom bomb. He began by discussing the theory behind the development of the bomb and then proceeded to talk about its power and the kind of casualties its detonation would produce. He spoke of the blast effects, the injuries due to heat, and the effects of radiation. Finally, he discussed radiation absorptivity.

After Dr. Tsuzuki finished speaking, Dr. Miyake was introduced and he told us of the autopsy findings observed in patients who died with radiation sickness. What he had to say was almost precisely what we had discovered in our hospital and it disturbed me for a while to think he had managed to be first in the matter of reporting his findings. When he began to speak of some of the troubles he went through trying to arrive at his conclusions, I felt more kindly disposed toward him because we had had the same difficulties. I was especially interested in his account of the blood dyscrasia produced by radiation because there were many points that still bothered us, particularly from the clinical point of view. All in all, I thoroughly enjoyed both lectures and was pleased to find our findings confirmed by others.

* Dr. Masao Tsuzuki was professor of surgery at the Tokyo Imperial University and during the war an admiral in the Japanese Navy. While a graduate student at the University of Pennsylvania in the early nineteen-twenties, he studied the effect of total body radiation in rabbits and reported his findings before the twenty-seventh session of the American Roentgen Ray Society in May, 1926. (Masao Tsuzuki, "Experimental Studies on the Biological Action of Hard Roentgen Rays." *Am. J. Roentgenology and Radium Therapy,* 16:134-150, 1926.) With this background, after the atom bomb was dropped, there was probably no one better qualified to discuss the subject than Dr. Tsuzuki.

The importance of summarizing and presenting our findings became all the more apparent to me as we walked back to the hospital. Dr. Tamagawa was getting along with his pathologic studies and I made up my mind not to let him down from the clinical side. Returning to my room, I got out all my notes and tried to get them in order. The harder I tried, the more difficult it became, and I finally gave up in despair. Perhaps I would do better to try a statistical analysis and summarize our conclusions rather than try to organize my scattered and confused notes.

After supper, I related to Dr. Sasada and Mr. Shiota what we heard this afternoon.

Dr. Sasada was impatient to leave the hospital and annoyed that the continuing rain prevented his going.

"When you leave next time, Dr. Sasada," I remarked jokingly, "be sure you don't run into any more military policemen."

My wife was better this evening and it pleased me to catch her joking with some of the other patients. I told Miss Kado she could stop the injections of trionone but to keep an eye on her for a few days.

4 September 1945

RAIN WITH heavy overcast.

Most of the morning I spent trying to arrange papers and collect the statistical data necessary to report our findings. Again, I got confused. Impatient to see the work finished, I neglected the work itself. I was convinced our observations would make a more detailed report than any others collected in Hiroshima. Outside investigators only stayed a short while and thus could never acquire the intimate knowledge of the situation permitted those who were here all the time. Still, I could not get started. I sat and kept drinking tea and smoking cigarettes.

I was back at my desk worrying over my papers after lunch when I had an unexpected but welcome visitor, Mr. Hashimoto. He had helped us as a civilian volunteer for several days after the *pika*. He had been the first to give me first aid when I was brought to the hospital, and he later helped Dr. Katsube operate on me.

When the bomb exploded, Mr. Hashimoto was in a suburban electric car which had just left Itsukaichi * station for Hiroshima. Since electric power was disrupted the instant the bomb exploded, he walked to Koi and from there reached Hakushima by following the railway tracks. He barely reached the hospital before the entire city was engulfed in flames. One of his first assignments was to help Dr. Katsube and the nurses clean out the operating room. His next was to gather firewood so they would have boiling water to sterilize the instruments.

"I owe you a great deal, Mr. Hashimoto," I said warmly, after we exchanged greetings. "Without your help, there are many of us who wouldn't have survived."

He accepted my comments modestly and tried to minimize the value of his assistance. He told me no one expected me to live, and the only way he could account for my survival was the care doctors and nurses had lavished on me. My comments had caused Mr. Hashimoto some embarrassment, so to change the subject, I asked, "Won't you tell me about yourself and what you experienced when the bomb fell?"

"It was an awful experience," he replied and paused a moment. "The electric car had just left the Itsukaichi station and was almost parallel to the Miyake surgical hospital when I heard a tremendous '*don*.' Simultaneous with the sound the electric car came to a halt and everyone began to jump off and run toward the station. Thinking danger would lie in that direction, I ran

---

* Itsukaichi is a village on the road to Miyajima about 4 miles southwest of Hiroshima. The railway line passes through Koi at the western border of the city and then curves north through Yokogawa and east to pass through Hakushima, the precinct where the Communications Hospital is situated.

towards the highway. Just then I saw a huge cloud rise angrily over Hiroshima, and on both sides of the main cloud beautiful smaller clouds spread out like a golden screen. I have never seen anything so magnificent in my life!"

"When did you reach Hiroshima?" I asked.

"It was about 10:00 A.M., I think, when I reached Koi," Mr. Hashimoto replied, "and I got to Yokogawa around noon. By then everything was completely burnt down right up to the Yokogawa station. Big drops of rain began to fall and I remember going behind the station to take shelter under the eaves of a house that had not yet been reached by the fire. I encountered an old lady who was apparently looking for someone because she kept saying: 'Kimi-san, Kimi-san, why haven't you returned?' She must have had a daughter working on one of the labor gangs.

"When I reached the Misasa railway bridge, some of the cross-ties were on fire. There, at the first guard station, I encountered a dead man. I saw many others in the water tanks fighting for breath. The sight was horrible."

"Let me see," Mr. Hashimoto continued, trying to collect his thoughts. "I think it was around 4:00 in the afternoon when I reached the Bureau. Do you know, my shoes were ruined by the sticky asphalt, and later, when they were giving out army shoes, I asked for a pair because mine had been ruined, but they wouldn't give me any.

"Where was I? Oh, yes. This sounds like nonsense now, but when the bomb exploded—I don't know how many bombs were really dropped—I clearly saw two parachutes coming down. There were some twenty or thirty soldiers watching, too, and they were clapping their hands in glee because they thought the B-29 had been shot down and the pilots were trying to escape."

"Were the soldiers on the same electric car?" I asked.

"Yes," he replied, gesticulating. "That beautiful cloud! It was neither red nor yellow. Its beauty defies description."

"Was the cloud clear-cut?" I asked.

"Yes, it was. It was as clear-cut as if a straight line had been made in the clear blue sky. Other straight lines spread out one after the other."

Changing the subject, Mr. Hashimoto went on: "I arrived at the hospital around 4:00. Dr. Fujii was standing at the reception desk near the entrance trying to handle the rush of patients. Dr. Koyama and Dr. Fujii asked me to take charge of the reception desk, which I did for a few minutes. It soon occurred to me I could do something more important than record the names and addresses of patients, so I quit and began helping the doctors. At first, I was given the task of painting wounds with iodine, but all I got from patients was a scolding and cries of '*Itai! Itai!*' That was my first failure. I then changed to mercurochrome and began painting the wounds of a girl dressed in *monpe* who was sitting near the entrance. To my surprise, I found I knew the girl. Her wounds were mostly on her buttocks and these I found hard to bandage, for when she stood up the bandage slipped off. I bandaged her over and over and each time she stood up she would lose the bandage. She really gave me a hard time. Finally, I gave up and in desperation pulled down her *monpe,* and after repainting her wounds, pulled up her *monpe* and put the bandages on right over them."

I couldn't help but laugh at his account and Mr. Hashimoto laughed, too.

"*Sensei*, you may not believe this," he continued, "but I wasn't the only one out of my element. It sounds funny now. You probably know that Mr. Ishimaru, who was head of the accounting department, took over as the acting chief of the Bureau. Well, he was in charge and taking his authority rather seriously when Mr. Okui, an employee, was brought in with his carotid artery severed. He was dead almost by the time he reached the entrance. About 12:00 in the night Mr. Okui's family came to claim the body, but Mr. Ishimaru would not let them have it because from somewhere he had gotten the idea nobody could be removed until an autopsy had been performed. Nothing we could say would change him.

"The family was naturally upset and threatened to make trouble unless the body was released to them at once. Mr. Ishimaru's position was made all the more ridiculous by the fact that even if an autopsy had been permitted, there was no one to do it. In desperation, I went to his office and told him a bold-faced lie to the effect that Mr. Okui was still alive and the family anxious to get him home before he died. This proposal, Mr. Ishimaru could accept without loss of prestige, so he gave his consent. Mr. Ishimaru and about ten of us lined up when the body was removed and saluted at attention.

"That was the first time any of us had had to deal with a corpse and we didn't know how to go about it. It wasn't Mr. Ishimaru's fault because there was a rule which stated a body couldn't be released until certain papers had been filed. But where were the papers, or the people to see them properly executed? I was told that in the east drillfield people were having a difficult time disposing of their own relatives for that very reason. Hundreds of people were desperate in their efforts to get the dead cremated and not being permitted to do so for lack of some stupid form. After a couple of days, there were so many bodies stacked up no one knew who was who, and decomposition was so extensive the smell was unbearable. During those days, wherever you went, there were so many dead lying around it was impossible to walk without encountering them—swollen, discolored bodies with froth oozing from their noses and mouths."

After Mr. Hashimoto had gone, I tried to picture in my mind the beautiful sky with the golden screen he described. While he was admiring the sky, we were trying to escape our ruined homes or were wandering through the darkened town. There was a vast difference between what those inside and outside the town had to say about the *pika*. Within the city the sky looked as though it had been painted with light *sumi*, and the people had seen only a sharp, blinding flash of light; while outside the city, the sky was a beautiful, golden yellow and there had been a deafening roar of sound. Between Hiroshima and Itsukaichi there had been that much difference.

Mr. Hashimoto impressed me as a keen observer. Many people

had described a big, puffy cloud, rising like a mushroom, or an angry, puffy cloud which went up and assumed the form of a mushroom with black smoke covering the sky, but until I talked with Mr. Hashimoto I had no idea what the sky around the cloud was like. I had, of course, heard people say the sky was beautiful, especially those who were as far away as Fuchu and Furuichi,* but it was now, for the first time, that I could picture the cloud sharply defined against a clear blue August sky. It was at the moment of the birth of this cloud, with its ever-changing color, that Hiroshima was wiped out. It was at this moment that Hiroshima city, the culmination of many years work, disappeared with her good citizens into the beautiful sky.

5 September 1945

CLOUDY; LATER clearing.

The 210th day, which marks the beginning of the typhoon season, passed uneventfully. Possibly because of the rain there was no storm, but great cloud masses flew through the sky and the wind blew hard enough to make things rattle. My sleep was interrupted by the rattling and I dreamed something was chasing me, but in the morning I had a vacant head and no memory of what the dream was about.

I had breakfast and reinforced it with a strong cup of *matcha*.

Hearing that some newspapers had come in, I went to the Bureau to see if there was any news about the surrender. To my disappointment I learned there were no newspapers, and even Mr. Ushio had heard nothing but that unconditional surrender had

---

* Fuchu is a village east of Hiroshima, 5,000 meters from the hypocenter, partially shielded by hills. Furuichi is a town 3 miles north of Hiroshima.

been accepted by the general staff and the foreign minister. I did learn that our activities since the *pika* had been reported to the Communications Ministry. I was glad to hear this and hoped the ministry would commend my staff since this was the only reward I could expect for their devoted work.

Returning to my room, I worked for the rest of the morning on my notes. When Mr. Matsumoto of the *Sangyō Keizai* * newspaper stopped in to chat, I could report that I might have some news for him in a couple of days.

In the afternoon, I arranged our clinical findings in the same categories Professor Tsuzuki enumerated during his talk yesterday, namely: blast injury, flash burns, and radiation illness. I was still handicapped for information on our earlier patients because then we had no records and the ones I was really concerned about had all died. We had over two hundred records on the later cases and these I set about correlating with regard to symptoms, signs, and blood studies, and the relation they bore to distance from the hypocenter. The reports of Dr. Tsuzuki and Dr. Miyake were proving extremely valuable because the destruction of our libraries and complete loss of contact with the outside world had denied us details of a technical and scientific nature so necessary for an intelligent appraisal of our findings. I worked all the afternoon, putting my tabulations on large sheets of cardboard obtained from the Bureau, stopping only long enough to say good-bye to Dr. Sasada and have a bite to eat. Before evening was over, I began to pay the penalty for too much concentration and too much smoking. My throat became sore and I began having stomach pains. By gargling and drinking some bicarbonate of soda my throat felt better and after a few good belches my stomach quit hurting and I went to sleep.

* *Sangyō Keizai,* the newspaper of industry and finance.

6 September 1945

CLEAR! Occasional clouds.

Today, for the first time in weeks the sun was out in all its brilliance; the sky blue, the air clear. Once again we could see and worship the sun. Everything moldy and damp was put out in the sun: bedding, clothing, and even the colored flags from the Engineering Battalion were included which gave a splash of color, almost a note of gaiety.

Mr. Shiota took advantage of the bright day and prepared to leave. Dr. Sasada's leaving yesterday and Mr. Shiota's plans to go today made me sad although I knew they would be better off away from the hospital.

Mr. Shiota left in the afternoon and with him his faithful wife and Miss Miazaki. Their going left a gap in our little community we could never refill. Shortly after their departure, the hospital received an unexpected gift of army sugar in bags that easily weighed from 100 to 150 kilograms. This gift was a real treat, hungry as we were for sweets. We wished Dr. Sasada and Mr. Shiota could have shared it with us.

Towards evening, I got down to work again on my papers. Using a map of the city, I made circles of 500, 1000, 1500, and 2000 meters with the Hiroshimo post office as the center of explosion. I then tried to locate the precise position of each patient for whom we had records. This proved more difficult than I had thought, for our information regarding position was sketchy and the map was so badly marked that some places were impossible to identify. As I worked, new ideas kept popping into my head to prevent my concentrating on one thing at a time. I gave up in despair, took a sleeping powder, and went to bed.

My wife was better today, almost well in fact, and Miss Yama and Mrs. Susukida were improved. As I drifted off to sleep my tranquility was disturbed only by the thought that Dr. Sasada and Mr. Shiota had left us.

7 September 1945

CLOUDY.

I awakened with a cool, light head, refreshed from a sound, dreamless sleep. For the first time since the *pika* I felt like concentrating and before breakfast had abstracted ten cases.

After breakfast, I completed twenty more cases before my work was interrupted by visitors. It was hard to control my impatience until they left and I was able to resume work. Before noon, I had completed half the cases.

I returned to my work after lunch with vigor and enthusiasm. Now I was well under way, the study became pleasant and interesting. By revising my distance tabulations to read: 500 meters or less, 500-1000, 1000-2000, and 2000 or more, I found it easier to bracket the location of patients at the time of exposure. When they called me to supper I had gone through 170 records.

It became apparent that the white blood cell count decreased in direct relation to nearness to the hypocenter. I made this tabulation first because it was the easiest. Next, I compared symptoms with distance, dividing cases into two groups: severe and mild.

I took advantage of the quiet and cool of the night, worked until 3:00 A.M., had a sleeping powder, and went to bed.

8 September 1945

CLOUDY WITH occasional rain.

I awakened around 8:00, refreshed and ready for work.

In general, I found those closest to the hypocenter to have the severest symptoms, and the greater the distance, the fewer and milder the symptoms. There were, however, a few exceptions. Some patients quite near the hypocenter had minimal symptoms and a nearly normal white count. By studying these cases individually, I found the reason. These patients had been shielded by reinforced concrete buildings, large trees, or other barriers.

Today, I received several newspapers, all of which contained articles on radiation injury. One had been written by Dr. Tsuzuki. I was torn between a desire to read these articles and the urge to go on with my work. The latter won and I laid the papers aside for later perusal.

I tried after lunch to summarize my findings in a short paper, but this I discovered to be far more difficult than the accumulation of data. Try as I would, I could not express my thoughts. Evening came, and still I worked. Finally, late in the night, my mind grew sharper and my pen stronger. Writing became easy and I worked on and on, charmed by the clarity of my thoughts and the ease with which I could put them on paper. The night was half gone when I finished.

I thought surely I would sleep well tonight, but my mind was so active I had to take some more barbital to calm my nerves.

9 September 1945

Cloudy with clearing skies.

I got up at 8:00 and looked over my paper until breakfast time. What had appeared so good last night when I was in the high heat of my writing ordeal now seemed poor, indeed. I had gone up like a rocket and come down like a stick. Or like the old proverb: "The head is like a dragon and the tail like a snake." Worrying over it this morning, I shaved its head and pulled its tail up and down but still my paper was not good. I patched legs, wings, and fins on it until it finally assumed a shape, but the shape was something funny.

When Mr. Matsumoto, the newspaper man, returned shortly after lunch to get the manuscript, I asked him if I could not have at least one more day to work on it. He laughed and said he would rather look at the manuscript first. After reading it he reassured me somewhat by remarking:

"*Sensei*, this manuscript is excellent! I'll take good care of it and return it as soon as it is published."

Before he left, he took my picture holding the manuscript.

What I had written was as follows:

Atom Bomb and A-Bomb Disease

What was the power of the atom bomb that blasted the city and the citizens of Hiroshima, scorched the hills, and killed the fishes in the rivers? It was a momentary white flash which possessed the most astounding destructive power. I am a survivor who barely reached the hospital. I was covered with blood from wounds that were caused by bits of flying glass, and I was pinned under my house. My home was about 1700-1800 meters from the hypocenter and the hospital about 1500-1600 meters. After my injuries, I thought I would die and decided if I were to die, I wanted to be in my hospital. The fires had not started by the time I reached the hospital and on arriving my first words were: "Anybody killed?"—and from there on I was completely demoralized. I was placed on a stretcher where I became a burden to my staff and nurses and was carried hither and thither by them as flames from approaching fires spread around us. Fortunately, nobody was killed for the hospital was some distance from the hypocenter and the building itself strongly constructed. All the staff were wounded, but despite their wounds, they fought courageously. Through the excitement and commotion of the day they were the epitome of brotherly love. Even though enured to death and disaster I was amazed at their calmness and coolness and from my heart wish to express gratitude. During the critical period I only wished I could have shown the same calm the nurses expressed. From that day to the present I have been living in a well-ventilated hospital. I have been able to experience the feelings of a patient as well as those of a doctor and have tried to study the changes occurring day by day in our patients.

The explosion was a momentary happening but it profoundly changed the lives of the Hiroshima citizens. Those who were close to the hypocenter are dead. Those who were somewhat removed have recovered. A month has passed and we have treated and studied some 5,000 patients and our work continues. I would like to summarize the results of our study and present the following conclusions:

1. Those who were exposed within 500 meters out of doors were killed instantly or died within four or five days.

2. Some who were within 500 meters were protected by buildings and hence not burned. Within a period of two to fifteen days many of these people developed the so-called "radiation sickness" and died. This sickness was manifested by anorexia, vomiting, hematemesis, and hemoptysis.*

3. Those exposed in the 500-1000 meter zone have shown symptoms similar to those who were exposed within 500 meters, but the onset of symptoms was late and insidious. The death rate in this group has been high.

4. I have studied the location of the in-patients and a great number of the out-patients and found most of them were exposed between 1000 and 3000 meters. Those in this group who were closest to the center became critically ill and some have died, but the majority are in stable condition or well.

* Hematemesis means "bloody vomitus" and hemoptysis "bloody sputum."

5. A great number of patients have complained of falling hair that began as late as two weeks following the explosion. Some of these patients have had an uneventful course while others have had a bad one.

6. The most serious clinical sign of radiation sickness is a decrease in the white blood cells, and pathologically, great changes were found in the hematopoietic system, especially in the bone marrow. Those who received fatal injuries have died within the past month. Patients with low white blood counts who survived this period are now stable or convalescing. Within the past week the hospital has become very cheerful.

Recently, we were told the effects of the bomb were announced through American newspapers or radios, but we had no way of knowing this for there were no radios or newspapers in Hiroshima. Earlier, public feeling was agitated by the rumor that a place baptized by this bomb would be uninhabitable for seventy-five years. Because of this rumor people living in the outskirts of the city, not to mention those in other places, were reluctant to come into Hiroshima, so our hospital and the Communications Bureau were isolated and very nearly paralyzed for lack of outside assistance. In an effort to combat this rumor we began doing physical examinations near the end of August on the few who had come into the city from the suburbs and surrounding areas after the bombing. None of these people showed any abnormalities. Their white blood counts were within the normal range of 5,000–7,000. We even examined some persons who were very near the hypocenter, for example: persons who were in the heavily shielded basement of the Telephone Bureau, persons thoroughly protected in nearby air-raid shelters, and a few persons near the hypocenter who were otherwise shielded by heavy pieces of machinery or other objects, and all of these showed normal white counts and a normal physical examination. These findings convinced us there was no poison abroad in Hiroshima subsequent to the detonation of the bomb itself.

The results of this study were announced to everyone working in the Communications Bureau and they were urged to continue work without fear of suffering any consequences, providing they had not been exposed near the center of the explosion. Almost simultaneously, Professor Tsuzuki and a group from Tokyo visited Hiroshima and after a similar study expressed an opinion similar to ours and likewise denied the rumors that Hiroshima would be uninhabitable for seventy-five years.

Almost without exception the staff of the Communications Hospital was exposed and has remained in Hiroshima and lived in the hospital, which is not far from the hypocenter, for over thirty days already. The fact that we have not suffered any ill effects is further evidence that the rumor is untrue.

One cannot but marvel at the power of a bomb which can devastate the city of Hiroshima and leave 500,000 dead or injured people. We were defeated in a scientific war, not by one of quantity. If one thinks of the past and future, he will find matters for reconsideration.

By way of treatment, the hematopoietic system should be stimulated and what is lacking should be supplemented. Professor Tsuzuki of the Tokyo Imperial University has recommended vitamin C injections or foods rich in vitamin C, liver preparations or cooked liver, blood transfusions, auto-transfusion, heterogeneous protein therapy, and moxibustion.* We are using all the recommendations made by Professor Tsuzuki. On ten patients I have followed the old Chinese proverb which says that patients with an appetite will not die. To these patients we gave ample food without injections or transfusions and saw to it, of course, that their burns or wounds received the greatest care. This group of ten patients had a smoother course and showed more rapid improvement than patients given ordinary food, injections, and transfusions. Those who were in Hiroshima at the time of the bombing should receive a careful physical examination at once, and if the white blood count is low or any other symptoms of radiation sickness are present, they should remain quiet and eat plenty of good food. Even those who show no evidence of trouble should eat more than usual, and those who are sick should try to eat as much as possible. In view of the serious shortage of doctors and medical supplies it is our belief that adherence to this simple form of home remedy will provide the best insurance toward recovery.

I prayed in my heart that Mr. Matsumoto would fashion my paper into a good report by cutting off the dragon's legs without

---

* Moxibustion is the practice of burning small cones of dried herbs on specified areas of the body for purposes of counterirritation. It was probably introduced into ancient China from Egypt and thence into Japan by Buddhist priests.

changing the meaning. Why had I not insisted that he give me one more day to improve it? It was too late now, so all I could do was wonder when it would be published and what the reaction would be.

10 September 1945

CLOUDY WITH occasional rain.

I slept well last night because the tension I had worked under while writing the paper had disappeared. Morning passed pleasantly, for I loafed about the room, drank tea, and joked with old Mrs. Saeki and others who came in.

In the afternoon, I made rounds, but there was little to do since all the patients except Bureau employees and dependents were under the expert care of Dr. Nagayama and Dr. Itaoka. On a bench in front of the janitor's room I found one of our nurses, Miss Futakami, staring blankly into space. She was a healthy, quiet, hard-working girl attached to the dental department, and she had been working night and day without rest since the *pika*. She looked tired and worn and had lost weight. When she became aware that I was gazing at her, being shy, she blushed and fled. It was girls like this and others in the hospital, working inconspicuously, who had held things together. Their devotion should not go unrecognized, and I went to find Mr. Sera, the business manager, to see if there were some way they could be rewarded. He felt just as I did and I was pleased to find he had kept a careful record of the hours each employee had put in, which he intended to present to the Communications Ministry.

Upstairs, I ran into Mr. Oyokota, one of the city councilmen, who had dropped in to visit some of the patients. When he visited us last month, he had several severe wounds on his legs and looked ill, but today he seemed restored to health. We chatted about conditions in the city, and I told him how things were with us in the hospital.

"There's a big difference here in the hospital between day and night," I said. "During the day we have only patients to contend with, but at night their families, who have been out working in the daytime, return and the whole place takes on the appearance of a free hotel or a slum settlement house. I know these people have no homes to go to, but we can't continue like this forever. If I could have some big army tents and set them up in the ruins of the southern barracks, it would make a nice home for these people and free us of the burden of feeding and housing them. What do you think of it, old man?"

Mr. Oyokota gave me a big nod and said: "*Sensei*, let's see what we can do. I agree with you, and I'll go to the city office and see what can be done."

Returning to the mess room, I found fifteen or so letters lying on the table, six or seven of which were addressed to me. They were all from old friends of mine in Okayama who wrote to tell me how glad they were to learn I was alive and in good health. I was not only pleased to hear from these friends but pleased to know my report had already been published and read by people as far away as Okayama.

"Did you see the letters?" exclaimed old Mrs. Saeki excitedly, as she came into the room. "*Sensei*, lots of letters came today and most of them for you! And do you know what? We're going to have electric lights from tonight on. Look at that bulb over there." She took my hand and dragged me over to the corridor. "It's going to be bright from tonight on!" She looked up at the light with a happy look on her old face.

The delivery of letters and now—electricity! Just think of it! From now on we could relax and sit back. The letters came just in time for I was feeling homesick and wishing for Dr. Sasada and Mr. Shiota.

When night came, the light in the corridor was switched on

and even though the bulb was small the light appeared very bright. Never had the value of electricity impressed me so strongly. As soon as possible we must get light bulbs for the entire hospital.

Since Mr. Mizoguchi had gone to Seno and Dr. Tamagawa was nowhere to be found, old Mrs. Saeki and I sat alone under the dim glare of the light and talked late into the night.

11 September 1945

CLOUDY WITH occasional rain.

Early this morning Mr. Shiota came in, and I asked how he had found things at home. I neglected to mention that when he left the hospital to visit his home, it was the first time since the bombing.

"Sensei, my home was badly damaged," he informed me. "Some of the 250 soldiers who had been sent down from Tokyo to help clean up the city were quartered in my house and during one week of occupation they put the finishing touches on what had already been done. The ceiling, furniture, roof tiles, everything that was damaged they threw out and left my home as empty as a cave. You can see the sky through the roof and when it rains the water comes in through the holes. The tatami and mattings are rotted. Everything is a miserable sight. Worst of all, they destroyed the gaku * of Kaioku Nukina which you left at my house for safe-keeping."

When Mr. Shiota told me about the destruction of my gaku, I felt depressed and miserable. The gaku of Kaioku was a rare piece of old art, written on abaca-cloth, handed down from my

* Gaku as here used refers to a philosophic homily written in Chinese, matted and framed for hanging like a scroll or picture.

forefathers. Signed Ho, at Okayama, in semi-cursive writing, it expressed the following injunction: "Be thrifty, honor simplicity; be a man of strong fortitude, and follow the steps of the old." From earliest childhood I could remember my parents reading it to me, and at times they referred to it when they scolded me for doing something unmanly. When I grew up I took great pleasure in looking up at the *gaku* of Kaioku, but when I was a child it was at times painful to look at it. Then, those verses represented lectures on moral culture. Even as I write this diary, I can see the *gaku* of Kaioku plainly before me and can write exactly each *kanji* and point out to you the little damage marks of age and the fly specks. It was gone now and there was nothing I could do about it.

Another *gaku*, the work of Bokudo Inukai, I had left for safe-keeping at the house of a friend, Mr. Ieshima, who lived a short distance beyond Mr. Shiota, and I began to wonder if it had been spared or lost like my other one. This latter *gaku* I had also prized highly. It used to hang in my reading room. The homily it expressed I remember vividly: "Ganshi * who did not cease in his study of virtue was so poor that he had only one gourd † and nothing else, but his poverty did damage to no one. One who is haughty without virtue is not good even though he be King Keriko ‡ with a thousand retainers in attendance on horseback."

I suddenly realized how precious things like this were. When I was filled with faith in the certainty of victory and when I was working with thoughts only for the Emperor, nothing was precious. I had felt this way when my home in Okayama was destroyed early in July. Many of our family treasures I had sent there from Hiroshima for safe-keeping because I thought Okayama would be safer than Hiroshima. When everything was lost, I did not fret for a moment. I believed I had been relieved of a heavy burden. The loss of the family Buddhist altar failed to stir any sense of remorse. Its loss left me free to go wherever I wished

* Ganshi was a pupil of Confucius.
† Gourds were carried as containers for wine or water.
‡ Keriko was an ancient king of China.

and each new place I might wish to visit could be my home. This attitude was engendered by the feeling that one should sacrifice everything for his country out of patriotism. Surely, our ancestors and our grandchildren would excuse us for such an attitude.

Now things had changed. Since the *pika* we had all become desperate and our fight was the fight of defeat even if we had to fight on stones. Our homes and our precious family possessions were no longer meaningless, but now they were gone. Mr. Shiota remarked that even though his home was half ruined, a home was still a home. I felt lonesome and alone because I no longer had even a home.

Conditions on the wards were gradually changing. An occasional patient died, a few went home, and some new ones were admitted. The beautiful girl in the puddle of pus was improving and this afternoon she took pride in telling me she was able to go to the toilet. The fact she was improving suggested her burns had been caused by fire rather than the *pika*. Among thirty or so new patients, I found four or five whose clinical course was different from those we had seen earlier. These patients had seemed well until the end of August when they developed general malaise, anorexia, petechiae, epilation, and mild stomatitis. Their symptoms, though, were milder than the earlier cases. All these patients had been over a thousand meters from the hypocenter and one as far away as 1700 meters. 1700 meters!—I thought. Why my home was only about 1500-1600 meters. This disclosure frightened me and I went back to my room with a feeling of uneasiness around my heart for fear I might come down with a chronic or delayed form of radiation sickness. I began to worry about my wife for fear she might develop symptoms, and I was relieved to find her sitting up in bed happy that she could now go to the toilet by herself.

In the evening, some friends came and we talked late.

12 September 1945

CLOUDY WITH occasional rain.

For a day or two it looked as though we might have some fair weather, but rain set in again and left us as uncomfortable as ever. Nearly every morning, I would awaken with my blankets wet, and each day, old Mrs. Saeki would hang them out in the corridor to dry. This morning, when she came in to get them, she said:

"It doesn't do any good to keep trying to dry out your blankets because as soon as I put them back on the bed the wind blows the rain in again. Today, I'm going to ask Mr. Mizoguchi to put boards across the windows. It's bad for your health the way it is now."

After breakfast, *baba-san* had a cup of *matcha* with me. I had hoped Dr. Tamagawa would join us but he was too busy. There were still enough patients dying so he was obliged to spend all of his time in the autopsy room. It was as though he were being chased by the dead. Dr. Miyasho, who had just been demobilized from the army, was assisting him as well as the medical student, Mr. Ogawa, but even the three of them were unable to keep up with the work and showed signs of the strain. To their growing fatigue was added the discomfort of the rain. Every day, they looked more and more like wet rats.

In the afternoon, Mr. Matsumoto brought me the newspaper in which my article appeared. I had been given an entire page and my picture was published with the article. The headlines read: "The Atom Bomb and Radiation Sickness." The leadlines stated it was possible for one to live right under the hypocenter and that radiation illness could be cured with nourishing food. In speaking of me and my work, I was described as badly wounded and obliged to conduct my studies under handicap and in isolation, denied the benefits of previous reports. The article itself was published almost verbatim and appended to it I was surprised to find the notice about radiation sickness I had posted in the hospital and Bureau. All in all, the newspaper had dealt with my article generously, much more generously, in fact, than the work merited.

I was pleased, but at the same time, chagrined. The article was hardly out of my hands before I realized I forgot to mention the decrease in blood platelets, and in the second paragraph I had used the term "without complaining symptoms" where I should have used the term "asymptomatic course." Moreover, it now seemed I had spoken a little too confidently; two hundred cases were hardly enough to permit sweeping conclusions. I did not doubt I had been a little too bold.

I made up my mind to bathe today. I had endured my dirty, clammy, sticky skin, and my repulsive body odor as long as I could, and if my thigh wound was not completely healed, I was not going to let it stand in the way any longer. Around 9:00 in the evening the rain let up a little, and I went down to the kitchen and took off my clothes. The air was cold to my skin and cold rain drops splattered over me as I walked barefooted across the courtyard from the kitchen to the bath. Finding the water a little too hot, I poured in two or three buckets of cold water and then eased myself down in the tub, adhesive tape and all. The walls of the tub were hot, so I had to sit carefully to keep from being burned. I quickly discovered this outdoor bath tub was hardly a luxury. Each time the wind blew, cold drops of water fell on me from the oak tree overhead. Smoke came up around the tub, and since the wind was constantly changing, I almost suffocated. Smoke got in my eyes and made tears run down my cheeks. Notwithstanding these annoyances, this bath, the first I had had since the *pika*, was wonderful. When the wind was not blowing too hard, I could be fairly comfortable and enjoy the sparkling drops of water as they caught the reflection of the fire. Beyond the foliage of a low-growing hedge I could admire the black silhouette of the Futaba hills in the distance. Behind me was the Bureau.

From time to time, lights appeared in the windows and I could hear people talking. Gradually, I got used to the hot water and began to relax. Deeper and deeper I allowed my body to submerge in the delicious warmth of the hot water until only my head showed above the surface.* Before I knew it I caused the tub to overflow and there was a hiss of steam as water splashed on the fire under the tub. At once, I was in complete darkness and from then on enjoyed my bath in privacy.

Warmed and relaxed by the bath I returned to my room and fell asleep instantly. Nor was my sleep interrupted by the rain because the window by my bed was now shielded with a cloth screen.

13 September 1945

CLOUDY WITH occasional rain.

I awakened to find my blankets wet as usual. Sometime during the night rain must have got in under the screen. Looking closely, though, I found the screen undisturbed, so water could not have come in through the window. To solve the mystery of the wet bed I began a systematic search of the room. After looking carefully, I found the reason. The walls and ceiling glistened with moisture, to such an extent that one could write his name in the droplets. In the early morning hours when the walls cooled,

---

* The bath figures prominently in the Japanese daily routine. A generous-sized tub, big enough for one to almost completely submerge, is set in the floor of the bathroom in such a way that it can be fired from outside the house. The bather dips up a bucket of water, and soaps and washes himself thoroughly because it is bad manners to dirty the tub with one's washings. Once clean, the bather eases himself into the tub to steam and soak. Not only is this method of bathing pleasant and relaxing, but during the winter it will keep one warm for several hours in a cold house.

moisture in the air condensed on their surfaces and then dripped on objects below. One could not see this during the day when the temperature increased. The condensation only occurred in the early morning and since my bed happened to be under a low place in the ceiling where the drops of water could come together, I got more of the rain indirectly than I would have otherwise. Another source of dampness, I concluded, was from my own breath. The whole building had absorbed so much water as a result of the continuous wind-driven rain we might as well have been living in a water-soaked jug. There was no use trying to close one or two windows. It was bad for our health, but there was nothing one could do. At breakfast, I told old Mrs. Saeki about my discovery.

"Is that so!" she exclaimed, nodding her head. "It isn't sanitary, but nothing can be done."

A young doctor visited me this morning, bringing a microscope, and asked if he might have permission to study some of our cases. I was delighted and only wished we might have had help of this kind earlier. Our problem would not have been so difficult if some of the famous doctors who visited Hiroshima had stopped in to help during the early days when we were struggling with lack of knowledge and lack of equipment. The problem was now somewhat clearer, and I had doubts that he could uncover much more. I could not help sympathizing with this young doctor. When I told him he could make all the studies he wanted, he looked as happy as if he were to go on a treasure hunt.

Rumor reached us today that the allied forces were to land in Japan. As a result, many people in Hiroshima became alarmed. The same alarm gripped our hospital and caused some patients to flee. When I made rounds in the afternoon, the wards were almost deserted. Even Mrs. Susukida whose burns were not healed left without permission. In general, the women were more frightened than the men because some one spread the rumor they might come to harm. Why this fear had sprung up I could not understand because Americans and Englishmen had been observed walking in the ruins of Hiroshima since the beginning of September.

I felt we had nothing to worry about because westerners were a cultured people, not given to pilfering and marauding. The best I could do would be to write signs in English, post them near the entrances, and raise a Red Cross flag on the balcony. When they saw this was a hospital, they would understand our responsibility for our patients and not make trouble.

Despite my objectivity regarding the hospital and patients, I became an ordinary husband when I thought of my wife. My one desire was to get her out of Hiroshima as soon as possible, preferably to her home where our son was. I sympathized with and envied Mrs. Susukida, who left the hospital quietly, and Miss Yama who left alone. Certainly, no one would have harmed either of these women, burned as they were. Even the most hardhearted soldier would have taken pity. But how about the healthy young girls in the hospital? Would they go unharmed? I had to confess there were doubts in my mind. As for my wife, she took it all quite nonchalantly.

The more I thought, the more I worried, and I ended by smoking a lot of cigarettes.

A visitor interrupted my meditation. He was an employee in the General Affairs section of the Bureau who had had the grave responsibility of protecting the Emperor's picture in case of emergency. He was on a streetcar which had just reached Hakushima when the bomb exploded. Making his way through the darkened streets and around fallen houses, he managed to reach the Bureau ahead of the fires. His first act on arriving was to run to the fourth floor where the Emperor's picture hung and pry open an iron door behind which it was kept. With the assistance of Messrs. Awaya, Oishi, and Kagehira, he carried it to the chief's office and discussed with Mr. Ushio what should be done with it. After much discussion it was decided the safest place would be the Hiroshima Castle, where less smoke appeared to be rising than elsewhere. Thereupon, the picture was placed on Mr. Yasuda's back and with Mr. Kagehira in the lead, Mr. Ushio guarding the rear, and Mr. Awaya and Mr. Oishi covering the flanks, they made their way to the inner garden of the Bureau and announced they

were going to take the Emperor's picture to a safer place. Two
or three times they repeated: "The Emperor's picture will be
transferred to the West Drill Field by the Chief of General
Affairs!" Those among staff and patients who heard this announcement bowed low and the procession went out through the back
gate. Suddenly, it was realized they had forgotten the Communications Bureau flag, a part of the ritual necessary when the Emperor's picture was moved from one place to another, so Mr.
Awaya was chosen to go back for it. Before he could return with
the flag the party was threatened by fire and went on without him.
At the castle entrance they explained to a soldier the purpose of
their mission and asked the nearest way to the drillfield. The
soldier told them the field was threatened by fire, so they changed
course and went in the direction of the Asano Sentei Park.
Reaching the dikes of the Ōta River skirting the park Chief Ushio
got the picture across to a safer place.

During its flight, the party encountered many dead and
wounded, as well as soldiers near the barracks, the number increasing as they neared the dikes. Along the streetcar line circling
the western border of the park they found so many dead and
wounded they could hardly walk. At one point it became impossible, so great were the masses of people around them. The
party shouted: "The Emperor's picture! The Emperor's picture!"
Those who could, soldiers and citizens, stood and saluted or
bowed. Those who could not stand offered a prayer with hands
clasped. Miraculously, the crowd opened and the picture was
borne triumphantly to the river's edge!

"Oh, it was magnificent!" Mr. Yasuda exclaimed. "When I gave
the Emperor's picture to Chief Ushio and when the chief got in
a boat someone unaccountably provided, I was desolate. An officer
drew his sword and gave orders in a loud voice for the crossing
and in response all the officers and soldiers lining the river bank
stood at attention and saluted. Civilians stood in line and bowed.
I can't explain how I felt, but I prayed that nothing would happen
to the Emperor's picture."

Taking a breath, Mr. Yasudo continued, his voice awed and

subdued: "Well, the river was calm and I can still picture Mr. Ushio holding the Emperor's picture amongst the wounded soldiers."

I had thought the Emperor's picture destroyed by fire, but after hearing Mr. Yasuda's story, I felt a warm glow around my heart.

"You have done a noble thing," I said. "You are the *tehon* of the Japanese people. When the Telephone Bureau was on fire Mr. Hirohata, its chief business officer, felt the same way you did about the Emperor's picture. Holding it close to his chest, he carried it through the fire to a safe place. Both you and Mr. Hirohata deserve recognition, for you are both *ichiban*. At present, we are a defeated nation and under the rule of occupying powers, so for the present your noble acts will go unrewarded, but in some way and at some time you will be rewarded."

Mr. Yasuda became red in the face and eplied modestly he did not think he deserved recognition since we lost the war.

"What you did was done during wartime," I objected. "If you had been a soldier, you would have received the medal of the Golden Eagle, the highest award a soldier can get. Don't worry; you will be rewarded!"

I might conclude Mr. Yasuda's story by saying that shortly after Mr. Ushio got the Emperor's picture safely across the river, the entire Futaba-no-Sato became a sea of fire. Whirlwinds and rain came. The river became turbulent and treacherous, its surface churned into great waves. Balls of fire flew over the river from the Futaba-no-Sato area and set fire to pine trees in Asano Sentei Park. As these great trees burned, swayed, and toppled, the heat became unbearable. Houses were consumed and people crowding the river banks in an effort to escape the inferno, jumped in the river. Thousands were drowned. Mr. Yasuda and Mr. Oishi clung to a rock and escaped death.

While we were at supper the smell of burning flesh was wafted in through the open windows. Miss Takata had died and she was being cremated in front of the hospital beside the bath. The smell, not unlike burning sardines, recalled days immediately after the *pika.* We ate supper undisturbed, so readily do we become accustomed to the most dismal environment. The smell of death could not affect our appetites.

After supper, I related Mr. Yasuda's story to Mr. Mizoguchi, old Mrs. Saeki, my wife, and Miss Kado.

14 September 1945

OVERCAST SKIES with recurring rain.

Dr. Tamagawa was visiting in Okayama when Miss Takata died, so no autopsy was done. Until she died, we had had no deaths in several days. The history of Miss Takata's illness was recorded in detail and is interesting enough to justify presentation:

Takata, female, aged 28.
Date of examination: 28 August 1945
Chief Complaint: General malaise.
Past History: Not remarkable.
Present History: Exposed at The Food Distribution Company, Hatchōbori, about 0.7 kilos from the hypocenter. Shortly afterwards, developed weakness, nausea and vomiting, general malaise, and diarrhea, which continued for two days. Gradually recovered strength with return of appetite. Able to look after herself and do light work, but sense of taste did not recover, and she was easily fatigued with slight malaise always present. Even though sense of taste was absent, she ate a great deal. Noticed falling hair three days after exposure. From the 25th of August noticed a large amount of falling hair, so on the 28th visited the hospital for physical examination.

Date of Admission: 28 August 1945.
Present Status: Moderately well-developed, nutrition poor, severe weakness. Epilation of head—about two-thirds. Pulse normal. Respiration: regular. Face: apathetic. Conjunctivae: Anemic. Mouth: normal.

No abnormal findings in chest or abdomen. Nothing remarkable in urine. Severe decrease in white blood cells.

1 September 1945: Petechiae over chest. Complains of severe general malaise.

5 September 1945: Petechiae larger and greater in number. Many as big as tip of little finger. Temperature: 101.5°. Pulse slightly weak. Complains of weakness; no appetite. Stool three times a day.

9 September: Pulse small and weak. Petechiae increased in number and from needle-head size now big as tip of thumb. Color: Purple-brown to red.

13 September 1945: Died.

This patient's history and course were typical for patients dying with radiation sickness.

After breakfast, I went to the Bureau to try to find Mr. Oishi. He was back at work and I wished to hear his account of saving the Emperor's picture. During a fruitless search, I ran into several storeroom workmen who were injured by the *pika*. They seemed tired and despondent, and one man told me it was getting increasingly difficult to purchase food for the staff and patients and their families, now numbering about three hundred in all. The difficult articles to procure, he told me, were fresh fish and vegetables— because of rising prices. This disturbed me, and when I found I could learn little more from this man, I thanked him and went to find Mr. Imachi, chief supply officer in the Hiroshima Communications Bureau. I found him under the willow tree between the Bureau and the hospital and we went to our mess room in the hospital where he told me the following story:

"After the *pika*," related Mr. Imachi, who habitually spoke of himself by his last name, "Imachi went to the ruins of the branch office, but Imachi found everything destroyed by fire, so Imachi cried and cried. Imachi thought the safe would be all right, so Imachi pried it open but found all the bank notes amounting to between 2,000 and 3,000 yen were burned with only one yen and 65 sen in coin remaining. Seeing this, Imachi cried out loud and tears rolled down Imachi's cheeks.

"To the present, Imachi has been able to get along somehow in spite of rising prices, but now it is impossible. Following the *pika*, the city's food distribution center was set up in the University. We had a small wagon in which to carry things, but the wheels broke down and we were without a wagon until we managed to get one wheel from the Bureau and another someone picked up at Yokogawa. We were given rice and some post offices in the country sent mail bags filled with rice and wheat, so we didn't have to worry about our main food. Imachi is having a hard time getting vegetables. At present, we have to go to Yagi and Hesaka * to buy vegetables, for we can't get them here. As you know, there is no vegetable ration, and, of course, we can't buy vegetables or fish with money. Whenever we go out to buy things from people we know, we take a little present, but still they won't give us what we want. This is a tiresome job, for we have to pray and worship the farmers and merchants.

"We will get along somehow, for everybody treats Imachi well; so, *sensei*, please be relieved. Never will you feel hungry. The prices of things don't make sense, anyway. After all, price is determined by what the buyer has to pay with. It is hard to get cucumbers and tomatoes. Imachi went out yesterday to buy food, and look at this!"

Mr. Imachi gave me the notebook he used to record purchases and the amounts paid and pointed to the entries. This was my first encounter with inflation and what it could mean to the citizens of a war-torn city. As Mr. Imachi said, money was worthless. Under such conditions, how he managed to get what he did was remarkable.

Along this same line, I learned a new term. People had come to refer to "the mines of the town," by which was meant articles of value buried in the ruins. Some made a regular business of digging in "the mines of the town." At first, I felt this sort of thing was beneath one's dignity, but the more I thought, the more interested I became.

* Yagi is a village near the northern edge of Hiroshima and Hesaka is on the Geibi Railway Line about 4 miles northeast of the city.

In the afternoon, giving way to impulse, I decided to have a treasure hunt myself. Going to the ruins of the barracks south of us I found a couple of people digging away. Stopping to see what they had uncovered, I found they had picked up some iron cooking utensils and a few rusty tools. I dug around a bit and found a few odds and ends, but nothing intact or worth saving. An old axe head I found under a roof tile I lugged around a while and discarded. Coming to a dirt enclosure that had evidently been a shooting range I kicked around the ashes and uncovered some gun barrels with burnt out stocks. Seeing these reminded me of a skeleton after the flesh has disappeared. Near the rifle barrels were some shell cases, but instead of brass they had been poured from some gray, inferior-looking metal, the like of which I had never seen. Looking farther, I found some bamboo bullets and broken bamboo spears. Farther on were various axes, hatchets, and saws. This is what happens to a nation that loses a war, I thought. Substitutes for brass, wooden bullets, bamboo spears. Soldiers had been trained to use the bamboo spears in one heroic attempt to kill an enemy. I now realized why the army had allowed its soldiers to go home on a brief holiday last spring. They were told to return with every bit of metal they could find, around their homes or in their villages. This junk had been stacked near the barracks to be turned into tools of war. Suffice it to say, I found nothing worth keeping.

Late in the night, Professor Tamagawa returned from Okayama and brought me a can of *matcha*. He had bought the tea from an old friend named Nakamura. My friend and his family were burned out and had reopened a small store at Higashi-yama. Dr. Tamagawa said the Okayama people were really suffering more than those in Hiroshima, and by comparison, our hospital was like a heaven. Dr. Tamagawa had not smoked a decent cigarette for two days, so I gave him some of our still bountiful supply.

"Cigarettes are extravagant, Hachiya; you are taking life a little too easy!" he scolded, at the same time smoking furiously on one of our cigarettes.

15 September 1945

CLOUDY WITH occasional rain.

After breakfast, some of the Kure Post Office staff came to visit and I learned for the first time that occupation forces had landed. Even the term *shinchu-gun*, which in general means an occupation force, was as strange and foreign to me as the forces themselves. It saddened me to think of the great naval port of Kure being occupied by the Allied forces. Since childhood, I had known of Kure as the last and the greatest stronghold of the Imperial Navy. Now, it was in foreign hands and no one could say whether it would be an open port or a restricted area.

My friends informed me that the port of Hiroshima in Ujina would soon be occupied. In anticipation, people were building fences around their houses and putting locks on doors and windows because they had heard that the Allied soldiers would not break locks or windows or tear down fences. The Allied soldiers, they told me, were exceedingly fond of women and very kind to them.

Before long occupation forces would appear at our hospital. Already, they were seen more and more frequently around Hiroshima station.

Mail had been coming since the first of September, so I was surprised today to receive twenty-four or twenty-five letters. I read each letter carefully and examined the envelopes. Some, dating from September the twelfth, came from friends who read my article in the *Sangyo Keizai*. They praised the article and congratulated me on being alive. Other letters, dated around the tenth of August, were from friends inquiring for my safety. Wondering why I should receive letters with so widely different post dates, I went to the Bureau and asked the reason. A post office employee informed me that the Hiroshima Post Office was completely destroyed and unable to resume function until the first of September. With the opening of temporary offices in the Postal Saving Bureau, Hiroshima station, and a railway post office near the Bureau, mail distribution was resumed. Until these branches were opened all the mail bags marked Hiroshima were stored at various post offices along the Hiroshima train route. The earlier letters being at the bottom of the pile and the later ones on top accounted for their being delivered together.

The hospital census was steadily decreasing. Only those too sick to move remained; the others fled as their fears of the occupation mounted. Many of our occupants were orphaned children and they continued to live with us since they had no fear of the occupation.

I encountered a group playing happily on the hospital steps. The toys were anything they could find: bits of grass, pieces of wood, and odd-shaped stones. One group had a picture of the Emperor Meiji over which they had plastered a large mud pie.

"Where did you get this picture?" I asked the children. "Do you know it is a picture of the Emperor Meiji?"

"*Sensei*, there are lots of them at the old general headquarters!" they exclaimed, innocent of having committed any indignity.

"You must be respectful of the Emperor's picture," I remonstrated. "Otherwise you may be punished. Perhaps you had better let me take it."

The children gave me the picture and their faces registered surprise and hurt pride for having unwittingly done something wrong. I knew they had no intention of misbehaving and by the time I got back to my room I was ashamed of the way I had handled the situation.

After lunch, I was told that occupation forces could be seen if one went to the station, so in spite of the rain I went down to have a look. On the way I experienced a strange feeling when I encountered some young boys with long hair and bare heads, walking around proudly. Nearer the station I encountered more boys with long hair and was told this was the latest style. Lose the war and win long hair, I thought to myself. During my student days, if our school lost a game with another school, we paid the additional forfeit of having our heads shaved. Short hair was in vogue during the war, but now, no one wished to be mistaken for a demobilized soldier for fear of occupation reprisal.

The station, or what was left of it, was packed with people milling about in confusion, but I saw no soldiers. On the streets around the station were little booths or stalls no larger than a *tatami*, often smaller, and so closely jammed together one could hardly get around. In these tiny places of business people were selling all kinds of things. Small shacks had sprung up and bore the dubious titles of eating places. One would specialize in *sōmen*, a form of small noodle-like vermicelli served with seaweed; another in *kantoni*, bits of meat, fish, or fishcake spitted with vegetables on thin strips of bamboo and charcoal broiled over a *shichirin*; and another in *yomogi*, a form of rice cake. These little eating places looked dirty, but business was good.

Most of the men I saw wore army uniforms, and I saw a few girls wearing them too. I saw very few in navy uniforms. Those who wore the brown aviator's uniform with the short boots looked the smartest. To tell the truth, I wished I had an aviator's uniform. One poor woman I saw startled me because she was wearing her wedding kimono and carried a sack of sweet potatoes across her back. She had probably lost all of her everyday kimonos and was reduced to wearing the one kimono she had treasured enough to evacuate before the bombing.

An improvised ticket window had been constructed in the gutted station and there was a small area that had been roofed over where people could sit while waiting for trains. I stopped here to watch the people coming and going. Demobilized soldiers with big bags on their backs mingled with the civilian war victims. I saw a little child, naked except for dirty pants, begging food from those who crouched eating their *bentō*, and he would not move until someone gave him a scrap of food. The sight of this little child was pitifully sad and reminded me of children I had seen in war-torn, defeated Manchuria and Korea seventeen or eighteen years ago. They, too, had begged for scraps from our *bentō*. Nothing could more graphically symbolize defeat than these poor waifs of humanity.

Unable to endure any longer the wretched sights I witnessed around the station I returned to the hospital. On the way back I detoured through the Western Command and Cavalry Corps headquarters. In the quiet of these ruins, with no sound but the falling rain, I became sentimental and thought of the officers who had once been the objects of our admiration. What future did they have now? They were still part of the nation. I learned a lot by looking at the situation in front of the station. There was an old officer with long, matted hair, squatting in a corner with waifs around him begging for food. A panorama spread before me: tired war victims, demobilized soldiers, old people leaning against the burnt pillars, people walking aimlessly, heedless of all around them, and beggars. They were the *real* conquerors!

After supper, my thoughts again reverted to scenes at the Hiroshima station. How selfishly everyone acted. What an unhappy society was coming to life. While some wandered around poverty-stricken, others appeared to come to life, as though suddenly they had come into their own. People with evil faces and foul tongues were wearing the best clothes. Those who wore the aviator uniforms looked like gangsters or cheap politicians. These fellows would enter the little shacks near the station, boldly and obscenely fondle the uncouth girls, and otherwise behave outrageously. The country was in the clutches of the mean and unintelligent. I felt hate in my heart for them and gritted my teeth to think they had come to power. How conditions had changed. What did the future hold for the old officer?

16 September 1945

RAIN WITH low hanging clouds.

Early this morning I was visited by Dr. Akiyama. It was unusual for him to be abroad so early. Something must have upset him although he was always easily disturbed and ready to jump to conclusions or give life to the vaguest rumor.

"Let me compliment you for coming to work so early," I said. "Or has something happened?"

Usually ready to make a joke, Dr. Akiyama ignored my remark. His pale face had a serious, worried expression and he looked around cautiously. Something was wrong.

"*Anonē!* Why so formal?" I asked.

"*Sensei*, let's escape!" he blurted out. "Conditions here are very bad! Your wife is in danger, and if ever we are to escape, now is the time! After the Allied Forces land, we'll all be lost. This is the truth; I know what I'm saying."

"Is that so?" I replied, raising my eyebrows.

"Of course it is, *sensei*," he answered, annoyed at my attitude. "They will stop at nothing. Please let me get you out. If you won't go, at least let me take your wife. I know what I am talking about, for once!"

Dr. Akiyama was so thoroughly disturbed and so sincere, I was touched. Dr. Akiyama, who had been in China, was afraid the same thing would happen to us that he had seen happen in North China.

"Dr. Akiyama, I appreciate your concern for us," I stated. "I may ask you to help us, and I'll tell my wife of your good offer, but please let me think it over a bit. What you say has swept me off my feet."

While I talked to Dr. Akiyama, my nephew, Masao, from

Okayama, appeared at the door and stood respectfully until we had finished our conversation. Masao was sixteen, a quiet and modest lad who had grown up since I last saw him. He brought a little box of muscat grapes from Okayama and set them on the floor beside me. After exchanging greetings, he told me about Okayama. This boy had had an unhappy childhood, and it told in his face and body. To look at him recalled my sister, who was the boy's mother, and his father. His father had been sent on official business to Java before the war, and when fighting started he was inducted without being permitted to come home. It had now been over two years since the family had received any word of him. Their home in Okayama was destroyed, and since June they had lived at Yokoi, my home village. I asked how his two sisters were and if things were well with his mother and the other members of the family. All were well, apparently. It did me good to hear from home. I tried to cheer Masao about his father.

I picked up two new rumors when I made rounds today. One was to the effect that people coming to Hiroshima after the *pika* were now developing radiation sickness. The other rumor claimed that those who stayed in Hiroshima would become bald and die in a year. The patient census was still decreasing, but those who remained were stable or improving.

My wife and old Mrs. Saeki were laughing and talking in excited whispers when I returned to the room. Our Aunt Shima had brought a *haori* and she was showing it off. I, too, received the unexpected gift of a uniform and overcoat from the Western General Bureau. Now, my wife and I could be warm for winter.

"You've got something good there," exclaimed Mr. Mizoguchi, who came in while we were admiring our presents. "It fits you, too. It must have been a non-commissioned officer's coat because the others are usually small and tight."

Seeing my new clothes made Mr. Mizoguchi wonder if a new shipment had come in and, not being one to miss any chances, he rushed over to headquarters to see if he could get some things for the hospital. Towards evening, he returned and gave me the following report:

"There were great stores of things, many of them piled in the open. I had no trouble with the authorities. They told me to set aside what we wanted, and they would look after them until tomorrow. Bright and early we'll be there with our cart. You don't need to worry, *sensei;* there is enough for the patients with some left over for the staff."

After supper, the unconditional surrender came up again for discussion. There was no question about the army and navy being disbanded and their arms and ammunition confiscated. Rumor had it that the Chinese National Army would occupy Shikoku, and the military stores, including uniforms, would be appropriated by the occupying Chinese. That may have explained why so much military goods was becoming available and why efforts were being made to get so much stuff moved into the mountains. Goods were stored in open fields, storehouses, and even private homes. Much of it was being moved by railway into small villages and hamlets in the mountains for distribution among war victims and demobilized soldiers. The railways out of Hiroshima—the Kure-Mihara Line, the Sanyō Line, and the Geibi Line—were all busy. Many people were appropriating military goods on the excuse that they were making withdrawals against the tremendous taxes they had been charged during the war; others made no bones about deliberately stealing. Some said the goods rightfully belonged to them since, with the army demobilized, no one had a better claim than the taxpayers.

The city was infested with burglars. A few had a touch of chivalry in their behavior because what they stole they gave to the poor and needy. Most, however, sold their loot, and overnight became rich. A scarcity of sentries made looting easy. During the war no one would have thought of stealing, and goods would lie in open fields without even the need for a guard, but now nothing was safe that was not locked up.

It made us giddy to recall how our incomes had been taxed up to 80 per cent during the war to provide the military services with these supplies. Now that the war was over, perhaps taxes would not be so high. None of us thought about the matter of reconstruction. The longer we talked the more philosophic and optimistic we became. Late at night, we stopped with the happy thought that we could look forward to a better life in a peaceful country, with easier taxes, and no hard military police to lord it over us.

17 September 1945

RAIN. LATER, a violent storm.

It was raining when I got up. After breakfast, I got my mail and found a letter from Dr. Moriya with some pictures enclosed. These were pictures he had taken during his visit. Studying the pictures, I was surprised at how poorly our scars showed up. I had at least 150 scars and Dr. Sasada's face was burned, my wife had fifteen scars, though small; and Dr. Koyama was wounded about the head. In the pictures, though, the scars could not even be seen. I stroked the scars on my face and wished they would disappear as in the picture. If they did not, I would look like Yosa, the legendary figure who was always getting cut and scarred in fights so his face came to look more like a gangster's than a simple rascal's. I could not imagine that Dr. Sasada would ever again have his childish face or my wife a face that was not pocked and scarred. We had wondered how we could face the public again. The pictures did show some bandages and I could recognize the scorched, twisted beds, the piles of fallen wall plaster, and the dangling electric wires. The pictures would be valuable records, and I was so pleased to receive them I wrote to thank Dr. Moriya for his thoughtfulness.

Since others would enjoy seeing the pictures, I made the rounds of the hospital and Bureau. During my tour I ran into Mr. Oishi, whom I had been trying to find ever since Mr. Yasuda related to me the rescue of the Emperor's picture. I asked if he would come to my room and tell me his account of the deed.

"*Inchō*, you look better than you did when I last saw you," Mr. Oishi told me. "You looked as if you were dying then. Did you know how worried we were?"

"I've been told," I answered. "But enough of that. Tell me about yourself."

"When they brought you in," Mr. Oishi repeated, "I was sure you wouldn't pull through. I was helping clean out the operating room when Dr. Katsube and Mr. Sera came in and told me to work as quietly as I could because you were in the next room, critically injured. Well, we tried to be quiet, but that was impossible. How can you clean quietly if you have a roomful of debris, broken glass, and instruments? We tried, though, but ended up as noisy as we started. I'm glad to see you so well because we thought you would die."

"Please let's not talk about me anymore," I begged Mr. Oishi. "Let's hear about yourself. Mr. Yasuda said you had a hard time but did a wonderful job."

Mr. Oishi bowed and his face registered a look of pride. "I saw a white flash and surmised we had been bombed. To protect myself I ducked to the floor and covered by eyes and ears, and at the same instant something struck me. Later, I sat up, and to my surprise, could find no injuries. My first thought was the planes had missed their target. Not until I stood up did I discover I had been thrown some distance from where I was originally, and it was then I saw the damage to the room. Seeing this, I guessed we had been hit after all. As far as I could see there was nothing but a smoking, destroyed city. Something *really* serious had happened, and I rushed downstairs shouting at the top of my voice that we must do something. I mustered several people who were standing around dazed and uncertain and had them help me move wounded into the hospital. In no time the rooms and corridors were full so we began lining patients up beside the fence. I carried about five patients myself and found it a strenuous job. Later, I went to the

Bureau and looked between and under the desks and in the closets to see if anyone was trapped. Fortunately I found no one. I next went up to the room where we kept the Emperor's picture and found Kagehira, Yasuda, and Awaya. They were furiously beating on the door with an axe. They finally got the picture, and with Mr. Ushio, we carried it outside. Taking a circuitous course around the barracks, we reached the river near the Asano Sentei Park. Mr. Ushio carried the picture across the river to a point slightly north of the Hakushima streetcar terminal."

Mr. Oishi lowered his voice out of reverence to the Emperor. After a pause, he continued: "While they were carrying the picture across, the Industrial Research Laboratory near the Tokiwa Bridge caught fire and was a raging inferno in a few minutes. Those near the building had to jump into the river when it collapsed and many were drowned. The next day there were thousands of bodies floating and bobbing in the water. As we stood watching the people burn or drown like rats, a boat floated past. A man with his head injured lay in the bottom of the boat, while a woman sculled. I shouted for her to bring the boat to the bank, and she did so, though in the most absent-minded fashion. I carried a number of people across the river, going back and forth a number of times, but since the chain of injured seemed endless, I turned the boat over to someone else as soon as I could and took off."

Changing the subject, Mr. Oishi continued: "Those fellows in the army were shrewd. I met one on a bicycle the next day who said he was going to Hesaka to spend the night. He had two chickens tied over the rear basket of the bicycle. I asked him where he had gotten the chickens and he said he'd picked them up at the drill field. I asked about the bicycle and he replied nonchalantly: 'Oh! You can find them anywhere around here,' as though picking up bicycles was the easiest thing in the world."

The way Mr. Oishi said this and chuckled to himself set me laughing. I could not tell whether he was praising or criticizing the army. I asked him about rations and he went on:

"Oh! that was easy. Those fellows in the Prefectural and City

Offices have no sense; they don't understand a thing. Police and officials who look smart and important don't know a thing. How could they? None of them belong here. If you talked big and looked important, you could get anything and it was fun fooling them. I didn't have any trouble getting three hundred bottles of *sake*, but I did have trouble getting them from Kusatsu back to the hospital.* I don't know where they went because I didn't get a chance to drink a mouthful."

We tried to get him to say more because quite a crowd had gathered, but Mr. Oishi thought he had said enough. He excused himself and left.

My stomach was hurting when lunch time came, so instead of eating, I had a cup of *matcha*. While I was drinking the tea and thinking about Nakamura's tea shop in Okayama, the wind picked up. Pretty soon it was blowing strong and the wind was warm. Fearing more rain, I went back to the room and tried to secure the window covering. I also helped move our beds as far as possible from the windows, so if we did have a hard rain we would not be so likely to get wet. I told my wife about Dr. Akiyama's offer to get us out of the city, but she only laughed and went about her business in a completely calm fashion.

After supper, the wind picked up and the rain came in torrents. This was no ordinary storm but a typhoon. Every little while the rain swept right through the room like waves in the open sea. The sheet I had secured to the window was torn to shreds and the mosquito nets waved like flags. We might as well have been out of doors, so hard did it rain. After a particularly heavy gust of wind, the lights went out. From left and right, winds swept whirling into the room as we crouched hugging the walls in an effort to avoid the rain. By 9:00 the rain became a deluge. People outside flocked to the hospital and Bureau. Some barely escaped their little shacks before they were demolished. The water rose until we feared there would be a flood. Everyone was drenched to the skin and before midnight everything in the hospital was as

* Kusatsu is easily 5 miles from the hospital. It *is* a wonder how he got 300 quart bottles of *sake* all the way across town.

thoroughly soaked as though it had been in the open. The wind died shortly after midnight and the rains stopped, but no one could sleep because we were miserably wet and too excited to relax. Toward morning we dozed a bit.

18 September 1945

CLOUDY, LATER clearing.

I awakened to find the storm passed, and it was unbelievable the morning could be so quiet. I had tried to sleep huddled on the concrete floor and now my shoulder and hip ached and my nose was stopped up. Going up to the balcony, I saw a great lake of water in front of the hospital, and the small shacks that had sprung up on all sides were blown down or their zinc roofs torn away. Letters and postcards were scattered between the Communications Building and the hospital. I went down and picked up all I could. Most of them were registered letters. Going to the office in the Bureau, I related what had happened and in no time everyone was out picking up mail. Picking up these letters recalled a story I had heard of papers from Hiroshima being blown as far off as Minochi, Hongi, and Suzuhari, some fifteen to twenty miles distant, on the day of the *pika*.

I went to the business office to inquire from Mr. Sera and Mr. Kitao how much damage we suffered in the typhoon. They answered that nothing was lost but some blankets. It seems the people from outside who sought refuge from the storm managed to make away with the blankets we loaned them. Having seen what happened to their shacks, I could not object to their taking the blankets. They needed them more than we did.

Going through the hospital and Bureau, I found water puddled everywhere, and there was not a *tatami* or other piece of bedding that was not thoroughly soaked. Patients complained they had caught cold, but I found none who had suffered too much. The beautiful girl who lay so long in pus and filth was now able to get about without help.

Morning passed without incident except that my nephew, Masao, returned, and a messenger came with a note from Professor Hata, a friend, asking if I would go to Miyajima to examine a director of the Hiroshima Bank of Japan. My answer was that for the present I did not feel strong enough to make the trip.

Masao, I urged to go to my Uncle Shima's home in Saijo where he could be better received than here in the hospital. I thought he had already gone home, but he apparently wanted to see the ruins and so stayed over last night.

The weather had improved so much by afternoon that I decided to take a walk. After all the rain, it was wonderful to see the sun again. I meandered about until I reached the moat surrounding Hiroshima Castle. An old man was fishing for frogs. Using a bit of bait on a bent nail, I saw him catch six or seven big frogs in a few minutes. Everytime he pulled one up a small crowd who had collected to watch would shout: "Fifty *yen!* One hundred *yen!*" Imagine frogs bringing such a price, yet, to my amazement, he was selling them—one hundred *yen* for the big ones and fifty *yen* for the small ones!

After supper, I told my companions about the frog fishing and they, too, were impressed how times had changed. Tired after our past nearly sleepless night, I went to bed early. Sometime during the night I was awakened by shouts of "Robber! Robber!" and discovered it was Dr. Tamagawa. He had apparently had a nightmare and apologized for disturbing us.

19 September 1945

CLEAR.

The morning was clear and beautiful, the sun bright and warm. I had slept so well and felt so rested and refreshed that I thought it might be a good day to go to Miyajima to see the bank director Professor Hata had asked me about yesterday. Then, I had not thought I could feel so well so soon.

In the dining room, everyone was in good spirits and joking with Dr. Tamagawa about his nightmare. I announced my intention to go to Miyajima and asked old Mrs. Saeki if she would make me a *bentō*.

Starting out by way of Koi, I took the road Mr. Yasuda travelled every day on his way to work. As I crossed the Misasa Bridge, I met a man pushing a cart loaded with beef. It had been so long since I had seen any meat I became hungry and my mouth watered. In past times, I was finicky about the sight of raw meat and seldom, if ever, went to a meat shop. "How much you have changed," I said to myself. Going on, I passed the destroyed Yokogawa station and a little farther a street on one side of which the houses had all burned. Farther still, I saw houses only partly destroyed. At Koi, the houses around the station had been turned into little shops which seemed to be doing more business than the ones around Hiroshima station. The atmosphere, though, was the same. It was 12:00 by the time I reached Koi station and found a place on the crowded Miyajima Guchi electric car. Between Koi and Takasu, I saw houses whose roof tiles were blown off, their windows broken, and their walls damaged. They looked as though an earthquake had hit them. Beyond Kusatsu * roof tiles did not seem to be damaged, but windows were blown in. These

* Kusatsu was 5,000 meters from the hypocenter.

signs of damage I noticed as far as Itsukaichi. It was not until I reached Hatsukaichi that the houses appeared intact. A short way past Jigozen I could see Miyajima rising from the sea. To the right I feasted my eyes on the beautiful *bessō* wealthy people maintained for summer homes.

I was surprised, on reaching Miyajima Guchi, to find some houses at this distance from Hiroshima with their windows blown out. I stopped at the Goneido pottery works and ate lunch. Old Tosai, master of the pottery works, had been my pottery teacher and he seemed happy to see me. He kept saying over and over he felt as if his son had come back and, from time to time, wiped tears from his eyes. Even his young son and his wife seemed happy to see me. The son told me he had been standing in the town square just outside the entrance to the pottery works when bomb exploded, and the blast had knocked him off his feet.

Since Tosai-san's pottery works were just to the right of the ferry terminal, I talked with my friends until the bell rang, announcing the ferry departure. Bidding them good-bye, I ran down the pier, just managing to make the boat as it began to move away. The voyage to Miyajima requires between twenty and thirty minutes, and from the decks, one gets an excellent view. To the west and north one can see the mountains rising from the sea that guard those approaches to Hiroshima and in the hazy distance the shoreline of Hiroshima City itself. Miyajima is never more beautiful than when viewed from the decks of an approaching boat. Even from a considerable distance one can see the great *torii* of Itsukushima Shrine rising majestically out of the sea, and in the background the pagoda and the old Buddhist temple with its hall of a thousand mats. In the foreground, along the shoreline one can see the shops, restaurants, and hotels that cater to the thousands of visitors who come each year on pilgrimage to this sacred island. The crowds are largest in the spring when the cherry trees are in bloom and in the fall when the red maples tint the forests with their beautiful, iridescent colors of scarlet and gold.

The ferry docked at the lower end of Miyajima's principal

street. I debarked and walked back toward the shrine until I came abreast of the Miyajima Kan, a quiet little inn, run by some old friends. I thought it would be a good idea to stop for a few minutes before going on to the Bairinso, the exclusive inn where the bank director was staying. Madame Korenage came out when I called and for a moment stood speechless, so surprised was she to see me alive. Sumi-san, the head waitress, accompanied her, and she, too, expressed surprise and pleasure I was alive. My scars shocked them for a moment, but they recovered and begged me to come in for a rest and something to eat.

I thanked them and explained I was on my way to examine the director of the Hiroshima Branch of the Bank of Japan, and I had stopped only to pay respects and see how they were. I agreed to stop on my way back, and this mollified them. Since I did not know where the Bairinso was, Sumi-san offered to show me the way. I thanked her, and we set out.

The Bairinso was located on the top of a small hill with old homes on either side. It commanded a magnificent view of the town, the Inland Sea, and the distant mountains. On being announced, I was shown into a Western-style drawing room next to the entrance. Through a broad open window that looked down over the town I could see the Shrine of Itsukushima, the majestic old *torii* rising from the sea beyond the shrine, and the dense pine forests on either side. The foreground of this beautiful view was framed by a stately old pine and an exquisite little garden. In the far distance was the misty shore line of Hiroshima Bay, and I could barely discern a train passing along its edge. The smoke from the engine made a trail of white paint against the dark outline of the mountains. What a beautiful room and how magnificent the view! How pleasant it would be, I thought, if I could remain here and rest for a few days. My thoughts were interrupted by the appearance of a tall, elegantly attired woman who brought me some tea. She, I learned, was the director's wife, and after exchanging greetings, she related the story of her husband's illness. He was in the bank when the bomb exploded but fortunately received no major injuries. Since the bank was between four hundred and five hundred meters from the hypocenter, my first thought was that he must have been severely exposed, but his wife said that his only complaints were weakness and loss of appetite.

After I had some tea, the director's wife led me to a large, well-ventilated room where her husband was reclining on a Japanese bed. He was a fat man in his early fifties with an edematous face. Despite his subjective complaint of weakness, the physical examination showed no disturbing signs. Following the *pika*, it was some time before he could be evacuated but, once removed, apparently he was all right. Dr. Matsuo, director of the Central Hospital in Hiroshima, had also been evacuated to the Bairinso, but two days ago was removed to the Red Cross Hospital at Ono because he was in need of treatment. When the typhoon struck, Dr. Matsuo was tragically killed with many other patients when their part of the hospital washed into the sea. The bank director told me this to point out how lucky he was because he, too, had thought of transferring to the hospital at Ono and by mere chance missed going with Dr. Matsuo.

We talked for a while after my examination was complete. I assured the bank director his chances of complete recovery were excellent.

"Although your bank was a short distance from the hypocenter," I stated, "it is so solidly built you were protected, not only from the blast, but from radiation injury. You may be interested to know your bank is now an information center. Its walls are covered with bulletins inquiring about and giving information concerning the lost, the missing, and the dead. If you will eat heartily, you need not worry about getting well. A patient with a good appetite isn't likely to die. Remember! Rest and nourishment are the best medicines you can take."

Bidding the director and his wife good-bye, I returned to the Miyajima Kan, where my friends were expecting me. I told them all I could of Hiroshima, and in return, Madame Korenage told me about Miyajima. The storm of the seventeenth washed away the annex of the Iwaso Hotel which sat at the edge of the Momiji Dani, and many of the guests were killed. The Itsukushima

Shrine was damaged, and since it stands in water at high tide, much of its base was buried in sand. They had had the same experience with survivors in Miyajima that other communities had experienced. Thousands of wounded and ill fled to the island after the *pika*, and many died with vomiting, diarrhea, and the other symptoms we had learned to recognize with fearful respect.

My friends gave me a good dinner and, after a refreshing rest, I bade them goodbye, but not before they heaped all kinds of presents on me.

I got back to Miyajima Guchi around 4:00, and, as I passed the Goneido Pottery Works, old Tosai called out to me: "Please come to our home! Please come with your wife!"

I promised we would and stood and talked until the bell at the station announced the approach of a car.

In the crowded car to Hiroshima I overheard some snatches of conversation between two young fellows near me.

"That girl is unsafe," one of them stated. "She was not even shy in public. How could she ever do such a thing! That's why I threw her in the sea!"

Apparently, one of them had become angry when he saw his girl walking with a soldier of the occupation forces. The attitude this young man expressed was typical of many who had been taught to hate the enemy. He still had a feeling of hostility. I could not exactly condone his treatment of the girl, but I thought to myself that had I been in his position and my girl acted as this one had, I might have reacted the same way. The best solution, I thought, was for girls to get out of the city so neither they nor the soldiers would be tempted.

Shortly after we left the Itsukaichi station the electric car came to a sudden stop. Looking out to see what had happened, I saw three drunks behaving outrageously. They had forced the car to stop by stepping into its path, and now they pushed the conductor aside and climbed aboard. Belligerently, they bullied the conductor, roughed up the motorman, and stalked back and forth through the car, making threatening gestures to any one who got in their way. They tried to sing the Ariran, a Korean love song, and every now and then stopped to shout: "*Banzai.*" Before the car reached Koi, they forced the motorman to stop again so they could get out. Not one of them paid his fare. There was no one to make them.

The behavior of these drunks distressed me. How long could the old wartime maxim—"Strength is justice; and justice, strength" —go on. People like this seemed to dominate the picture since the surrender.

I was so tired when I got to the hospital and so upset at what I had seen and heard on the trolley car from Miyajima Guchi that I hardly felt like telling my friends about the trip. I took a bath, massaged my leg, and went to bed without supper.

20 September 1945

CLEAR, GENERALLY, with passing clouds.

The trip to Miyajima had been almost too much. I was so tired last night, in fact, I slept poorly, and when I awakened this morning my legs were aching so I hardly felt like getting up for breakfast. I returned to bed after breakfast and was resting when an old friend, the proprietor of a former Hiroshima store called the Eriben, came to see me. He was terribly upset and broke down in tears.

"*Sensei*, Oyone is dead!" he blurted out. "I don't even know where she was when she died, but my poor wife left home that morning * to work on a labor gang and that was the end. My daughter and I haven't heard from her since."

* The day of the bombing quickly became the basis for recording events in popular speech. "That day" would mean the day of the bombing; "the next day," the day after; and so on.

"How is Masao?" I asked, concerning his daughter.

"She broke her arm," he sobbed, "when the typhoon destroyed our house."

My old friend's words were hardly intelligible through his sobs and I could get only a smattering of what he tried to say. He had been hurt, too, and his head was still bandaged with a dirty old piece of cloth. I never saw a person more woebegone and miserable. At first, I tried to soothe him, but before I knew it I was crying, too. It was thus old Mrs. Saeki found us. Her glance went from one to the other and then she went up and put her arm around his shoulder.

"Old master of Eriben, please don't cry," she said, in a soft voice. "We are your friends and we'll take care of you."

My wife broke in to comfort the forlorn old man. "*Ojiisan*, let us help you," she said softly. "Make your home here at the hospital. We'll take care of you."

I think we eased his loneliness a little because when he left he seemed to know we were sincere in our desire to take him and Masao in with us.

After lunch, I was dozing on a bed near the window when Mr. Sera hastened in, out of breath, and whispered excitedly, "*Sensei*, there's an American officer outside!"

Startled by his words, I was speechless for a moment, and felt fear and anger surge through me. Feelings of hostility got the upper hand and before I had collected my wits I exclaimed in a curt voice, "Sera-san, ignore him!"

"*Sensei*, don't say such things!" he rebuked me and went on excitedly. "He's at the entrance, now. Please see him!"

Gradually, my feelings of hostility gave way to fear and I knew I had no alternative but to see the officer. I was dressed in dirty pants and shirt and, with my mind in the state it was, hardly felt up to confronting the foreigner.

The next moment, I heard steps on the stairs and in walked a dignified, stately officer accompanied by a dark-complexioned guard wearing a pistol at his side who assumed the role of interpreter. I informed the pair I was the director of the Hiroshima

Communications Hospital, and after acknowledging each with my eyes I offered to show them around the wards. The officer was more interested in the typhoon than the A-bomb casualties. He knew what had happened at Miyajima during the storm and kept asking me how we had fared. The interpreter, I discovered, knew little Japanese, so what we had to communicate to each other was poorly relayed. After we had looked around and were making our way to the entrance, we ran into my wife. The officer asked if she had been injured and I told him she was anemic and had received some wounds. I rolled up her sleeves and showed some scars. He nodded slightly and left.

After he had gone my heart pounded violently and my legs began to ache. I had forgotten to go down to the entrance with him, I was so disturbed.

With the sudden appearance of the American officer, the quiet atmosphere of the hospital changed. Patients and employees were agitated. My wife, who until now had been quite nonchalant, showed signs of uneasiness; and Miss Yama, with escape in her mind, began to pack her things. I, too, felt uneasy.

If only I could have communicated with the American officer, I might have explained our fears, and he might have been able to reassure me. If only I had a dictionary, perhaps I could converse with him. I knew how to read and write English, but I could not speak it, and I could not understand when it was spoken to me. I made up my mind from now on, when the Americans came, I would show them to the drawing room and speak by writing. After supper, we had a conference and I explained our difficulties and questioned everyone carefully to find if anyone could speak English. No one could. It was finally decided we should do everything possible to get a Japanese-English dictionary, and even though I knew for certain mine had been destroyed in the fire, I suggested we search for it.

After all, what if another officer should come to see us without an interpreter? We were under occupation and understood clearly that the Japanese Islands had become a prison camp. We must be able to convey our thoughts in English. I thought of the proprietor of Eriben, miserable and destitute, who looked like a beggar, with the dirty bandage around his head. Before the *pika* he had lived in a mansion and never lacked for anything, but now he was indeed a beggar, at the mercy of the conquerors. He seemed to symbolize the past and present of Japan.

21 September 1945

CLOUDY. LATER, light rain.

This morning, I learned that after the twenty-fifth of September navigation in Hiroshima Bay would not be permitted. This news came from Mr. Sumitani, the Godo newspaper reporter, who had lost his wife. He had returned to Hiroshima to be present on the forty-ninth day, a Buddhist fast day in memory of the dead, which this year was to fall on the twenty-third of September. His visit reminded me that I should observe the fast day and pay respect to my dead friends in Hiroshima.

My wife finally decided to go to my family home near Okayama, and plans were made for her to depart on the twenty-fourth. Miss Yama was to leave today as soon as her sister could come for her. At first, I was reluctant to see the patients leave the hospital, especially those seriously ill, but since the arrival of the occupation made everyone so fearful, I was glad to see them go. The fewer patients we had the less responsibility, especially since we did not know what the occupation policies would be.

The patients in the temporary wards of the Bureau actually appeared less disturbed today than the ones in the hospital. Miss Niimi still had a high fever and dyspnea. I had developed a real affection for her and frequently sat by her bed. Her hair was still falling, but her petechiae had disappeared. This gave cause for optimism although we were still fearful she might succumb to her pulmonary tuberculosis. I tried to tell her the chest symptoms were due to a cold she caught during the typhoon, but I think she did not believe me.

The wards on the second floor were practically empty. One patient remained, a Miss Fukuji, who was exposed near the Hijiyama Bridge while working in a labor battalion. She had sustained major burns of her face, arms, and hands and since admission had been subject to attacks of epilepsy with the result that her body was covered with bruises and scars. I tried to tell her about the American officer's visit and reassure her. I avoided joking because her face was so badly burned any movement provoked by laughing or smiling would be painful. She was deteriorating, and I expected she would die. Old Mr. Oki, a seventy-six-year-old man who developed pneumonia after the typhoon, was at death's door. Pneumonia was an unwelcome complication and, since the storm, threatened to increase our death toll.

Part of the afternoon I spent filing my correspondence. One letter, in particular, is worthy of mention because it had been ingeniously contrived on *gasenshi*, a special Chinese drawing paper, by an artist friend, Mr. Shuka Takahashi, from Tokyo. He and I grew up in Okayama, and fame came to him after he executed some magnificent murals in the Meiji Shrine. He had written to me with the imagination and the skill of an artist. The *gasenshi* on which his letter was written had the elongated scroll form of a *kakemono*. At the top of the scroll he depicted the god of wind releasing air from a great bag, and at the bottom was a scene depicting Hiroshima after the *pika* with telephone poles and houses blown to pieces and consumed by fire. The text of his letter is as follows:

To: Dr. Michihiko Hachiya
From: Shuka (Takahashi)
I am sorry I have neglected you so long, and I would like to apologize for not having enquired earlier after your condition. I am stunned by a fact which no one expected, namely: that war came to an end and left Hiroshima in ruins. Since, I have been worrying about

your family and would like to ask how they are. I wondered how I could get in touch with you, until I read in the papers the other day that you were investigating radiation sickness. It relieved me to know you are alive. I wish you luck. For the time being, may I send you wishes for happiness.

Yours respectfully,
Signed _____
13 September 1945

The envelope for the letter in *kakemono* form had two stamps: one for seven *sen*, with Admiral Tojo's picture; and the other for three *sen*, with General Nogi's picture. This rare and thoughtful souvenir, I put away in my drawer.

For supper tonight, we had frog legs, a rare delicacy which set our mouths to watering when we smelled them cooking. It made me think of the old man fishing for them near Hiroshima Castle. The shouts of "fifty *yen*" or "one hundred *yen*," depending on the size, I could all but hear. If the old man did not hook the frog just right, it would fall off. He rarely lost one, though, because when a frog wriggled free, he would drop his pole and pounce on it like a player stealing bases. Sometimes, the frog was the quicker, and by the time the fisherman was down with both hands it would be far away. The faster he chased the frog, the faster it jumped. If the frog were dazed by his fall off the hook, the old fisherman could catch it, but he had to be quick.

Before I knew it, I was imitating the old fisherman, and we all had a good laugh as well as a good supper.

22 September 1945

RAIN WITH thunder and lightning.

This morning, I awakened earlier than usual. Old Mrs. Saeki was already up, busy getting our breakfast in the kitchen. Mr. Mizoguchi was still asleep on his bed in the corner of the mess room. Stealing out quietly, lest I wake him, I stopped in the corridor and looked at Miss Yama's empty bed. I wondered if she could get the treatment she needed at home. I thought of the time shortly before the war ended, when we moved to the upstairs room. My eyes went from one empty bed to another and my heart filled with longing for those who were no longer here. All we had now was a hotel for Dr. Tamagawa, our medical staff and nurses, and the students who were here to help us. Memories of this room suddenly became dear, something I would not have thought possible a few weeks ago.

After breakfast, I asked old Mrs. Saeki to clean the room we had used for a ward, so we could use it as a drawing room in case foreign soldiers returned to visit us. We removed the military swords and old arms we had picked up in the ruins and pushed the beds to one side and arranged the chairs and tables near the center. Our guest sofa was a board with four legs, but we made things as presentable as possible with room to seat four or five guests.

With the census diminished and little to do but sit and wait, I fell to brooding. For the first time in days I was undisturbed, so I could view the past with some objectivity. I was worried about the evil influences that had descended on Hiroshima. The drunken, rampaging soldiers I saw when I returned from Miyajima typified the present. The old proverbs: "Justice is strength" and "Better is character than birth" were no longer applicable. At least they were not adhered to. It seemed to me the discipline of education was effective only during peace time when there was law and order. Character cannot be improved by education. It reveals itself when there are no police to maintain order. Education is a veneer, a plating. Educated or not a man exposes his true character in times of stress, and the strong win. The proverbs invert and strength becomes justice, and birth more important than character. Force then rules the country.

23 September 1945

CLOUDY, LATER clearing.

Today was the forty-ninth day. I awakened pondering how I could hold a Buddhist Mass for my friends killed by the *pika*.

After breakfast, old Mrs. Saeki departed to pray for her three sons. I was preparing to go too and was changing my clothes, when two visitors appeared. They were Mrs. Kaneko and her son's wife. The moment she saw me, she began crying and informed me her son had been killed.

"You are lucky," she said between sobs. "At our home, Yoshi-hide was killed."

When she looked at her son's wife, she cried all the harder. Tears came as I tried to comfort her. She quieted down at last and I learned that her husband was in good health. I had known this old couple for a long, long time and was especially sympathetic because Mr. Kaneko reminded me of a favorite teacher, Professor Inada. Mrs. Kaneko recounted her experiences:

"The next day my husband, my son's wife, and I returned to the city and dug in the ruins of our home. I dug while my husband went around examining each corpse he found. In one dug-out near the drill field, he found a dead man standing up. I dug, and dug desperately, but found nothing."

"How did *ojiisan* take this?" I asked.

"It demoralized him," she replied.

"*Obāsan,* did you find your son's bones?"

"Well, I found some bones still steaming, but I began to wonder, and so returned the next day and looked again. This time, I found his bones. I knew they were his because I recognized his belt buckle."

"What did you do with the other bones?"

"I made an arbitrary gift of three hundred *yen* and had a mass held for them," she informed me. "Please come and visit us at Fukawa. My husband is there and nothing would do him more good than seeing you. I was on my way to the temple when we decided to stop and see how you were. Please come to see us. *Sayōnara.*"

"*Sayōnara,*" I answered, returning her valediction. With a smile and a bow, old Mrs. Kaneko and her daughter-in-law departed.

I went out to worship, beginning in the neighborhood. I stopped first at the gate of the Sasaki home and prayed for the repose of Mrs. Sasaki's soul. Closing my eyes, I could almost see her standing here with a smile on her face.

"Hachiya-san, where are Shuchan and Yaeko-san?" She seemed to ask for my son and wife. I opened my eyes and she was no longer there. I closed them again and she reappeared. It seemed I could see her although we were living in different worlds. I had been fond of Mrs. Sasaki, and I closed my eyes and talked with her for some time. I then prayed for two neighbors who were killed in their offices near the center of town and returned to the hospital.

Borrowing a bicycle, I began a round of the town to pray for other friends. I crossed the Misasa Bridge and the Yokogawa Bridge and pedaled slowly along the banks of the Ōta River. Thinking of friends, I passed through Teramachi and pushed on until I reached Sorazaya-cho. When I reached the place Dr. and

Mrs. Morisugi had been killed, I got off the bicycle and prayed for their souls.

I approached the hypocenter where I found the smell of incense strong. People were praying for their loved ones. I crossed the Aioi Bridge and passed through the hypocenter. The ruins of the Museum of Science and Industry were on one side and a little farther along, I passed the ruins of the Hiroshima Post Office. In front of the post office was a tombstone with the following inscription: "The entire staff died in honor." After praying for my friends who had died here, I wandered about burdened with grief for their loss. Farther on, I passed the ruins of Dr. Shima's hospital where all his staff, patients, and family had been killed. Dr. Shima was out of the city when the bomb fell, so he was spared. I thought of Dr. Kurakawa and Dr. Tenaka who were killed. They had been friends and had cared for me as well.

I thought of the four boys who died near Tenjim-machi and turned in that direction to pray for them. I passed through the main street and stopped in front of the Kaneko home to pray for Hoshihide-san. I could see a house leaning crazily out over the street. A sign indicated it had been the Shimomura watch store. It was only because this building had been made of reinforced concrete that it stood at all.

After more wandering, I visited other places where friends had been. Late in the day, tired and depressed, I returned to the hospital.

I found a *sukiyaki* supper waiting, which Mr. Mizoguchi had prepared as a send-off treat for my wife. Miss Kado, old Mrs. Saeki, Mr. Mizoguchi, and the two or three of us who had eaten rice from the same *hitsu* ever since the *pika* gathered at the table and after the meal talked for a long while. It was my wife's last supper in the hospital. With her were the friends who had experienced and shared so much since the *pika*. She would leave tomorrow, and now that her heart was set on going, she was happy as a child.

24 September 1945

CLEAR GENERALLY with occasional clouds and thundershowers.

My wife was to leave at 6:00, and the car was at the entrance before we had finished breakfast. Mr. Iguchi was to chauffeur her in an old Buick which belonged to the Bureau, and this was the first time the car had been used since the *pika*. It looked like an old covered wagon. My wife's departure was attended by a great clatter and a following trail of gray smoke. She was fortunate to be treated so kindly.

I slept for a while and awakened with an inclination to have a bowel movement. Going to the toilet, I had a soft stool and before I could get back to bed a feeling of profound weakness overcame me. Perhaps the meat in the *sukiyaki* last night had not been good; perhaps I had overeaten. At any rate, I did not feel well and it was all I could do to get back to bed. In a few minutes, I felt inclined to go again and somehow made my way back to the toilet. This time, it was watery and large. I strained until I was exhausted. Back in bed, I tried to eat but had no appetite. Shortly my bowels moved again. I must have developed acute colitis.

The third time I returned to my room, I drank a cup of tea and sent word I did not care for lunch. I asked old Mrs. Saeki to get me an astringent from the pharmacy, and when Dr. Hinoi heard about my gastro-intestinal upset he came rushing up to give me some sulfaguanidine with some kind of stomach medicine. The medicine he dispensed with a lecture on how I should take better care of myself, emphasizing that many patients died with diarrhea after the *pika* who did not follow a strict dietary regime.

I wondered if I *had* inhaled the "bad gas" people spoke about, during my wanderings in the ruins yesterday?

The next time the amount was less, but mucous was present and tenesmus greater. Pain appeared in the lower part of my abdomen. Fever developed, my heart beat madly, and weakness increased to the point of prostration. The least effort made me so short of breath, I could no longer visit the toilet.

Old Mrs. Saeki found a bed pan somewhere and placed it under me. The medicine did not seem to help because the abdominal pain increased and I became distended. Soon, mucous and blood were passing in equal amounts. It was now obvious I had dysentery. Weak, sweating and confused, I could hardly stay on the bed pan. My whole consciousness seemed to center on my rectum. When old Mrs. Saeki came back, I asked her to get me a bag of hot sand to put on my abdomen. In a little while she returned with a clean bed pan and a cider bottle filled with hot water. Dr. Koyama and Dr. Katsube came in but neither had much to say. The hot cider bottle placed between my buttocks made me feel a little more comfortable. A couple of visitors appeared at the entrance, but old Mrs. Saeki shooed them away and hung a curtain to give me some privacy. Between bouts of tenesmus, the pain gradually lessened until I was able to rest.

By evening I felt an overpowering thirst. I wanted nothing so much as great quantities of cool water, but fearing even water might upset my digestive track, I resisted my thirst. Later, old Mrs. Saeki brought in a bag of hot sand and laid it on my abdomen. She lay down on the bed next to me.

"*Sensei-san*, you are fortunate," she said, in a soothing voice. "Yes, you are. You have many friends and they are interested in you. They really are. You don't know how much you mean to us."

Old Mrs. Saeki continued her soothing words until she fell asleep. Each time I had to use the bed pan, I tried to move without disturbing her, but she would hear me and get up to help me.

I slept very little, if any, all night.

25 September 1945

CLEAR.

I had a drink of tea with salt in it and asked if we had any plum vinegar because I wanted something sour. Later, I asked if I might have some *omoyu* or rice gruel. Tenesmus continued with the passage of bits of blood and mucous. Never had I felt so empty or so weak and helpless.

At lunch, I gulped a bowl of rice gruel sprinkled with salt and took my medicine. The dose of sulfaguanidine was increased. By evening I was passing pus as well as blood and mucous.

I drank another bowl of rice gruel at supper and controlled my thirst by taking small sips of tea.

I was weak.

26 September 1945

CLEAR. LATER, cloudy with rain.

I remained much the same today as yesterday with continued tenesmus, diarrhea, aching, and profound weakness. Codeine was added to my other medicine and all day I ate nothing but three bowls of rice gruel. Altogether, I had a miserable day.

Toward evening, the codeine seemed to take effect, tenesmus became less, and I felt better. During the night, I had only a few movements and slept quietly between times.

27 September 1945

RAIN. LATER cloudy.

I awakened with a dry throat. Old Mrs. Saeki was boiling water for tea and it seemed like hours before it was ready. This morning, a cup of hot sugar water was added to the rice gruel, which I now detested. The sugar water was delicious and I decided to drink hot sugar water instead of tea. During the entire morning, I had only two inclinations and with much less tenesmus. My improvement I attributed to the codeine, so I took a little more and at more frequent intervals. I washed the medicine down with hot sugar water and thought what an extravagant patient I had become.

For lunch, they tried to get me to drink two bowls of rice gruel, but I could barely get the first bowl down and only half the second. By evening I was better and slept soundly through the night without having to get up once.

28 September 1945

ALTERNATING cloudy and clear.

My appetite was better and at breakfast I managed to swallow two bowls of gruel in addition to a cup of hot sugar water. Old Mrs. Saeki praised me and remarked:

"Everything will be all right, now. Just you rest. Pretty soon

Mr. Mizoguchi ought to be back with news of your wife's journey."

During these four or five days I had forgotten completely about my wife and son. Now that I was improving I began to think of my old mother in the country and how happy she and my son would be when my wife came. I did not let my thoughts dwell on the family. I felt I had to concentrate on getting well, so I could look after them.

For lunch, I consumed two bowls of rice gruel, and it did not taste so bad. In the afternoon, Mr. Yamashita was allowed to come in and he had the diary I asked to see some days ago. He stayed only a few minutes, and after he left, it was pleasantly diverting to examine what he had written.

An excerpt from Mr. Yamashita's diary:

I heard the sound of enemy planes. Turning to my wife, who had Kunio strapped to her back, I asked:

"Isn't that the sound of a "B" (B-29)?"

I looked to the north just in time to see a yellow flash and hear a big sound and was blown away. I looked toward the southern window and saw fire eat up the paper in the *shōji*. I yelled out:

"We have been struck!"

I hugged a column, but the house did not collapse. From behind I heard a shriek, and my wife came running and embraced me.

From then on we moved frantically.

"The Murata home is burning!" my wife exclaimed.

I dressed and we escaped from the house. The straw-roofed house about sixty feet away was already burned down.

Another excerpt from Mr. Yamashita's diary:

Our desperate action continued until the morning of the ninth. This was the biggest disaster of the Second World War.

It was the last bitter fight of the Empire of Japan—and victory could not be seen. I believe the last step will be taken against this bombing. I have absolute faith in this. Every scientific weapon that has been produced by the brains of man has appeared on the stage. Fear is not known in this war. I believe not one Japanese will remain. May all the rivers and mountains be burnt and destroyed—that is the penalty

of war. I am yet alive and I have offered a son, but I will not cry.
I will hear from my child's mouth his "*banzaï*" for the Emperor. His
name is Yasushi. Though not enshrined at the Yasukuni Shrine, his
name "Shi" will definitely be engraved in *rekishi*.*

Myōhō-shitchoku-dōshi is the Buddhist name for Yasushi, son of
Nichiren, a priest who offered his life for the country. So it is customary to use his name when one dies for his country, and the
Myōhōrengekyō, the Sutra of the Lotus, will be chanted by the forefathers. He was *my* son, who was born to die for the country. Just
before he died, he found for himself a quiet philosophy. He was in his
thirteenth year. In the confusion I hear my son's voice. Oh! I hear the
voice of God.

> Yasushi, my son, who has forsaken life
>   for the land of the Gods
> Is now the son of Nichiren—his name
>   Shitchoku-dōshi
> I am grateful for this cigarette
>   For in this darkness the faint light
>   Brightens reality.
>   (Written during the night of the 9th)

I think I stated earlier that Mr. Yamashita had been living in
the foothills of Ushita, about 2,500 meters from the hypocenter.
His house was spared, but he lost his son. Being a man of letters,
he wrote his diary in an effort to express the feelings of a parent
for a lost child. This, I think, he did surpassingly well, and his
belief in absolute victory was unmistakable.

As I laid aside his diary, I wondered if there were any precedent
of a nation suffering defeat while its people believed so firmly in
victory and were willing to endure any hardship?

My stomach was better and my weakness so much less that I
got up and went to the mess room for a pencil and paper. I
wished to bring my diary up to date, for, after perusing Mr.
Yamashita's writings, I hoped I could avoid that confusion of

---

* *Rekishi* means "history." There is a play of words, word symbols, and
meaning, here.

thought in prose or poetry that comes from letting one's thoughts go too long unrecorded.

Supper came, and I had two bowls of rice gruel. My appetite was so much better I even asked for some *omajiri*, a thin rice soup. The codeine had relieved my tenesmus and the sulfaguanidine had destroyed the infection.

Despite my improvement, I was still a long way from well. The little exertion attending my looking at Mr. Yamashita's diary and the walk to the mess room was enough to upset my nerves. I slept poorly and had unpleasant thoughts during the night. Before day, I wondered if my foot were not still in the grave, and the rumor about people who died after wandering in the ruins kept crossing my mind.

29 September 1945

CLEAR WITH occasional clouds.

This morning I stayed in bed. I had little appetite for breakfast but succeeded in downing two bowls of gruel. I visited my outdoor toilet after breakfast; and the warm, bright sunshine seemed to make me feel better. I passed a plug of mucous about ten centimeters long and cylindrical in shape, with surface markings like a casting of intestinal mucosa. I was not a little startled to see this, and on examining it closely was convinced I had had a mucous enteritis rather than radiation sickness. I went back to bed a good deal relieved and with a new resolve to keep up the dietary treatment.

For lunch, I ate one bowl of rice gruel.

Two young officers of the Occupation Force visited me this afternoon. Even though I did not feel well, I thought I should be nice to them. I wrapped a knitted scarf around my abdomen to keep it warm and conducted them on a tour of the hospital. Neither of us could understand what the other was saying although I sensed a note of friendliness and warmth in the voices of these young officers. Screwing up my courage, I said to them in English: "How are you?"

In answer, one of the officers offered me a cigarette. Timidly, I accepted it, and he lit it for me before lighting one for himself. The cigarette had a pleasing smell and the big red circle on his cigarette pack impressed me.

We toured the hospital and I tried to show them everything I could, despite my weakness. After we had finished looking around and returned to the entrance of the hospital, they shook hands with me and, by way of a parting, said in Japanese "*konnichi wa*" instead of "*sayōnara.*"

Those who were standing around burst out laughing because "*konnichi wa*" is a Japanese greeting similar to "good afternoon" in English. I laughed, too, and the young officers laughed with me. They got in their truck with big smiles on their faces and waved until they were out of sight.

"Everything will be all right," someone said, and there was hearty agreement. Everyone was much relieved.

We were impressed with the appearance of the American soldiers, the smart uniforms they wore, how light-hearted they seemed. The smell of the American cigarette did not leave my nose. It was different from the ones the Japanese officers smoked. There was nothing arbitrary or fussy about the young officers; they, too, were different from the Japanese. These men impressed me as citizens of a great country.

I drank a bowl of rice gruel for supper, and, being hungry, was about to take a second helping when a little voice told me to be careful. I drank a little and set the bowl away. Even old Mrs. Saeki could not persuade me to finish it.

It had become a great joke around the hospital that the American officers had said "*konnichi wa*" instead of "*sayōnara.*" Laughing aloud, old Mrs. Saeki said: "Amerika-san is kind. I think they are very nice. They are different, but they are gentlemen—and they are trying to learn Japanese. Don't you think they are nice, *sensei?*"

I laughed and said nothing. I had just remembered that when the Americans came today I greeted them with a "good-bye" instead of the "how are you" I sprung on them later. The joke was on me!

Tonight, a son was born to Mrs. Hiyama, a woman who had lived with us since the bomb destroyed her home in Kako-machi. She had been in labor since last night, and I was delighted and relieved that the baby was normal in every way and baby and mother were doing well. Hers was the first birth in our hospital since the *pika*.

I went to bed early and was soon asleep.

30 September 1945

HEAVY RAIN clouds throughout the day with repeated showers.

I awakened shortly before dawn, feeling better. My stomach was so much easier, in fact, that I was impatient for day to come. How nice it would be, I thought, if more Americans like the ones we saw yesterday would come today. I looked over at old Mrs. Saeki. She was asleep, her mouth open, a finger touching her solitary front tooth. I lay there thinking of her. This poor old woman had worked unceasingly since the day of the *pika* and, despite her age, seemed never to tire. Her high spirits and ever present sense of humor had sustained us all. The only time she had shown any emotion was when word came that three of her children were dead, but after that she never again mentioned her sorrow. Here was a noble woman, a real lady. There was nothing harsh or mean in her character. Simple and plain, she possessed a solid sincerity that gave comfort and strength to all of us. Occasionally, she would lecture the young people, and if I happened to be around some of her comments would be turned on me, for she would say:

"*Sensei-san*, it's the same with you."

The way she talked you would have thought I was one of the young people. I felt as though she was my own mother.

Baba-san stretched and began to stir, so I closed my eyes, pretending I was asleep. She got up slowly, stole out of her bed, and made her way to the kitchen to see about breakfast.

I went to my toilet to urinate and was pleased to discover the urge to defecate which heretofore accompanied urination was no longer present. This, I thought, was a good sign.

For breakfast I had two bowls of rice gruel, and though *baba-san* tried to get me to eat more, I shook my head and had some tea. I was not going to do anything to risk a flare-up. Mr. Mizoguchi returned while we were at breakfast, and I was happy to learn that my wife had reached home safely.

They left Ujina by boat at 7:00 A.M. that morning and sailed up across Hiroshima Bay through the Inland Sea. They passed the big naval base of Kure, where the wrecks of battleships were lying in confusion, some slanting crazily in the water and others upside down. Towards evening, they reached Onomichi and spent the night. Early the next morning, they took a train and reached Bitchu-Kawamo-mura a little after noon. From there, they would have a walk of about seven miles through the mountains before they reached my family home at Uji. They stopped for lunch with the Nakata's at Tai, and since they were able to telephone, my son, Shuichi, and the entire family were waiting when they reached the mountains. Mr. Mizoguchi described to me their various reactions. My son looked at his mother with great, big, brown eyes and was speechless with happiness. My wife's mother was afraid to look at first because she had pictured her severely burned. My mother looked at Yaeko-san right off and was relieved to see she was not so badly burned as everyone thought. After that, they stayed up nearly all night talking.

Mr. Mizoguchi told me of my ten-year-old son's reaction when his grandmother informed him Japan had surrendered.

"It's ridiculous!" he exclaimed. "You shouldn't say such things; if you do, the Military Police will take you away. If it is true, we will become slaves of America. If that happens, I'm going to escape when they come to get me. I have already dug a hole in the mountains to hide myself. I'm not going to be a slave."

When Mr. Mizoguchi left, my son told him to tell me I should escape at once. I laughed when I received this message and told Mr. Mizoguchi the Occupation Forces were not bad at all.

"They were kind and quite amusing," I added. "Only yesterday, we were visited by two officers who said 'konnichi wa' when they left."

Mr. Mizoguchi laughed and appeared relieved.

In the afternoon, we were visited by two groups of soldiers. The first group I took on a tour of the hospital. They made a minute examination of everything I called to their attention. One of this group had apparently been a schoolteacher because each time I tried to speak to him in broken English he would take pains to correct my pronunciation and usage. The second group had a Japanese-American interpreter whose family had come from Tanna. With this group, I stayed in our improvised drawing room and talked through the interpreter. One of the men stood at the window, looking out over the ruins and, at length, said through the interpreter:

"There must be dead still in the ruins, and I have the feeling that if the ruins aren't removed and the bodies disposed of, ill will between both countries will be prolonged. What is your opinion?"

"I agree with you," I answered. "I hear you are using a useful machine in Kure to clean up the ruins, a 'bulldozer,' I think it is called. Couldn't you have one sent to help us clean up the city? Otherwise, I am sure those who were injured and those who lost relatives and friends will be continually reminded of the day they were bombed and hate you when they come back to Hiroshima."

"It's out of the question," the officer replied. "America can't afford to send such equipment in here now. What are your thoughts regarding the bombing?"

"I am a Buddhist," I replied, "and since childhood have been taught to be resigned in the face of adversity. I have lost my home and my wealth, and I was wounded, but disregarding this, I consider it fortunate my wife and I are alive. I am grateful for this even though there was someone to die in every home in my neighborhood."

"I can't share your feelings," the officer replied, sternly. "If I were you, I'd sue the country."

The officer stood a while longer and gazed out the window. Finally, he and his party departed. After he had gone, I told my friends what he said.

"Sue the country! Sue the country!" I repeated, over and over, to myself. But no matter how many times I repeated it, and however hard I thought, the statement was altogether incomprehensible.

Postscript

I wrote whenever I could find time after August 8, 1945. The result, I have incorporated in this diary. The case histories depicting radiation sickness I chose from patients whose symptoms and clinical courses were typical. I have studiously tried to avoid duplicating stories people told me of their experiences and observations. I am sure there are things I have missed, but I do not believe I have exaggerated. The whole account is a statement of fact.

During the period covered in the diary, I lived in the hospital amidst the ruins of the city, and during this time was unmindful of the outside world. In contrast with conditions around me, my lot was not a bad one. We all lived in poverty, and it is said that one must be content with honest poverty. I think I was not only content, but even grateful, because of the kindnesses everyone showed me. I do not believe there was anyone in Hiroshima who was treated with such kindness by the staff in the hospital and by friends. I had nothing—not even money—but I did have the sympathy and kindness of my friends. The well of sympathy from which I could draw saved my life.

This diary covers the worst period any of us had to endure. Towards the end of September, we had many American soldiers visit us. Because of my illness I was unable to work for two or three weeks. When my health and strength had somewhat returned, toward the middle of October, I was visited by Professor Sasa of Tokyo University, who brought an investigating committee of Americans. This group remained in Hiroshima for about a month, studying radiation sickness. The doctors who remain particularly in my memory are: Dr. J. Philip Loge, Dr. Calvin O. Koch, and Dr. Averill A. Liebow.

Dr. Loge was a young medical officer who came to my hospital every day and spent all his spare time examining patients. Though we could not speak the same tongue, we understood each other's feelings. He was a gentleman, and all my staff and patients became fond of him. There is no boundary where sympathy and understanding are present. Working together, the month passed happily, and all too quickly. Dr. Koch was a young medical officer, like Dr. Loge, but he came to the hospital only occasionally. They both, however, left bright impressions of the Americans. Dr. Liebow was a little older than the other two, and I met him only once or twice. If I remember, he was not a clinician but a pathologist.

After these three doctors left, I was visited frequently by Colonel John R. Hall, Jr., whose headquarters were in Kure. I think he was the chief surgeon. He was a tall, stout officer, without question the biggest Westerner I had ever seen. He visited our hospital often and brought with him high officials from various countries. He introduced patients with radiation sickness to General Patterson and other officials. I was included among the patients. Colonel Hall gave us great help, materially and spiritually, in the reconstruction of our hospital. Other officers and soldiers from the Allied Forces visited us from time to time, but no one came to understand us so well as Dr. Loge and Colonel Hall. They could look at the picture with a broad view, much broader than mine, and these two doctors removed fear and hostility from our hearts and left us with a bright new hope. The harsh winter that followed the autumn was less harsh for their having come.

When I think of the kindness of these people, I think one can overlook thoughts of revenge; and even at this moment, I feel something warm in my heart when I recall those days and those friends.

(Written at night, 10 April 1952)

Glossary

ahano—a local slang expression of understanding and agreement.

ah sō—an expression of agreement.

anonē—well, listen, look.

atsui ne—It sure is hot.

ayu—a fresh-water trout.

baba-san—an old lady.

banzai—cheers, hurrah.

bentō—boxed lunch.

bessō—a villa or country house.

chan—an affectionate, diminutive suffix.

daimyō—a feudal lord.

dō itashimashīte—"don't mention it" or "think nothing about it."
A modest way of acknowledging a gift, favor, or compliment.

eraiyo—the pain is unbearable.

fundoshi—a breech clout.

gaku—a philosophic homily, in Chinese, often displayed as a
hanging scroll.

gasenshi—Chinese drawing paper.

gembaku—a place of suffering.

geni—really? indeed?

genshi bakudan—atom bomb.

haiku—17-syllable poem.

hanare—see hanareya

hanareya—the semidetached part of a Japanese house where one may retreat for rest or contemplation.

haori—the outer coat worn over the kimono. It is generally made of silk and for winter wear is quilted or padded. The quality, cut, and color are governed by sex, age, and affluence of the wearer.

hashi—Japanese equivalent of chopsticks which vary in design and balance from the Chinese version.

hibachi—a wooden, metal, or earthenware container, partly filled with ashes, usually from straw, supporting a charcoal fire.

hitsu—a wooden rice tub for keeping rice hot at the table.

ichiban—number one, the best, first.

inchō—head physician or hospital director.

itai—painful; "it hurts."

Jintan—a confectionated medicament with a strong odor and taste between menthol and peppermint.

kakemono—a hanging scroll.

kamaboko-goten—fishcake castle.

kanji—a Chinese character or ideograph.

kantoni—bits of meat or fish spitted with vegetables on thin strips of bamboo and broiled over a charcoal fire.

ken—about six feet (1.99 yards)

Kinshi—a brand of cigarettes. Literally, "golden kite."

konnichi wa—"good afternoon."

konro—a bucket-shaped cooking pot, made usually of clay, with a small grate and damper.

kuchi sumō—mouth wrestling.

kurushii—unbearably painful; even mortal agony.

mā—dear me! oh, my!

makoto-ni—really? indeed?

matcha—a finely powdered green tea, usually reserved for the tea ceremony.

matsutake—a delicious mushroom gathered from the pine groves in the early fall (Aremellaria edoles).

momo—a peach.

monpe—baggy pantaloons worn by women at work.

mō sukoshi—a little more.

Myōhōrengekyō—the Saddharma Pundarika Sutra, the Sutra of the Lotus.

niisan—brother, frequently used to address a relative or friend.

obasan—aunt.

obāsan—grandmother, old woman.

obi—a long, wide sash worn around the waist.

oishii—delicious.

ojiisan—grandfather, old man.

ojisan—uncle.

okāsan—mother. *Okusan* means "Mrs." and is used to address a married woman. *Kanai* refers to one's own wife specifically.

omajiri—a thin rice soup.

omoyu—a thin rice gruel.

o-tōsan—father.

pikadon—*pika*—a glitter, sparkle, or bright light, like a flash of lightning; *don*—a boom! or loud sound. Hence: flash-boom came to mean the atom bomb.

rekishi—history.

rōka—a narrow outside hall which skirts the south and west sides of a Japanese house.

rōnin—a samurai without a master.

ryū to hebi—dragon and snake.

sake—rice wine.

samurai—a warrior.

sanin-dō—the road of shadow and cold, the Great Japan Sea highway of Tokugawa times.

sanyō-dō—road of sunshine and warmth, the Great Inland Sea highway of Tokugawa times.

sayōnara—"farewell," "adieu," or "good-bye," in the sense that you are bidding God speed to a friend and look forward to seeing him again.

sensei—a teacher, an instructor, a master. Here it means doctor or professor.

shichirin—a small, portable, charcoal stove.

shinchu-gun—occupation forces.

shōji—sliding doors made of translucent rice paper.

sōmen—small noodle-like vermicelli.

sukiyaki—an excellent dish prepared at the table by first rendering a piece of beef fat in a large iron pan over a charcoal fire. Thinly-sliced pieces of prime rib of beef are then added and cooked until they are well braised. Vegetables are now added but not mixed with the beef or with each other. Young onions, bamboo shoots, lotus root, burdock, spinach, bean sprouts, and fresh mushrooms (*matsutake*) are especially good. Glass noodles, bean curd, and bread sticks (*fu*) are gently added. Seasoning is with sugar, *shōyu*, and *sake*. As the dish simmers down, guests are served from one side while the hostess or young women of the house add more ingredients to the other side. The patient, last-eaters are rewarded with the blend of flavors and rich juices extracted from the ingredients. A raw egg sauce enhances this superb dish, if that is possible; and a plentiful supply of hot *sake* stimulates the appetite and creates a pleasant, happy mood without depressing or intoxicating. Rice is eaten at the end of the feast with a sour or wine-cured pickle. Fruit and tea come last.

sukoburu genki—very well.

sumi—black ink or charcoal.

sushi—boiled rice and other foods flavored with vinegar.

tatami—a rectangular mat approximately 6′ x 3′, woven from a marsh grass called *i*, placed over a straw cushion of the same dimension to provide the floor covering of a Japanese room.

tehon—example.

tenka-sama—the lord paramount.

torii—the sacred archway approaching a Shinto shrine. Literally, a bird roost.

tsubo—a unit of land measure 3.95 or roughly 4 square yards.

waka—a 31-syllable poem.

yarareta—"We've had it."

yomogi—a form of rice cake.

zashiki—living room.